POWER SECRETS
OF
MANAGING PEOPLE

CRAIG RICE

Prentice-Hall, Inc.
Englewood Cliffs, New Jersey

Prentice-Hall International, Inc., *London*
Prentice-Hall of Australia, Pty. Ltd., *Sydney*
Prentice-Hall of Canada, Ltd., *Toronto*
Prentice-Hall of India Private Ltd., *New Delhi*
Prentice-Hall of Japan, Inc., *Tokyo*
Prentice-Hall of Southeast Asia Pte. Ltd., *Singapore*
Whitehall Books, Ltd., *Wellington, New Zealand*

Third Printing . . . . . September, 1981

© 1980, by

PRENTICE-HALL, INC.
Englewood Cliffs, N.J.

Library of Congress Cataloging in Publication Data

Rice, Craig S
    Power secrets of managing people.

    Includes index.
    1. Supervision of employees. 2. Personnel
management. I. Title.
HF5549.R4866   658.3'02   79-21649
ISBN 0-13-686931-9

Printed in the United States of America

Dedication

This book is dedicated to the reader, today's manager, who is seeking help and, with an open mind, is willing to consider solutions found by scores of others as we all look for both employment and enjoyment in our careers.

This book is also dedicated to my good partner and wife for helping to put it all together . . . and to our four fine children in college and graduate school who, with their spouses, have made suggestions and have already gained from this project in more ways than one.

Other books by the author:

How to Plan and Execute the Marketing Campaign
(Dartnell Publishing Company)

ACKNOWLEDGMENTS . . . to YOU

You, the modern manager, executive and supervisor are the one who really initiated this book. You and your problems focused on the need for better ways to manage people. You struggled with this effort, you asked questions and you wanted answers. You, in a group and as an individual made your contributions. You developed answers or at least workable solutions to some of these problems. You offered these to be shared in scores of meetings over past years. Your ideas are collected, organized and refined here.

Those of you who have spent many years studying all or just one part of the motivation system also made great contributions. YOu, in general, include fine authors for *The Harvard Business Review, Nation's Business* magazine, *The University of Chicago Graduate School of Business Journal* and over thirty of our nation's largest corporations.

I am specifically indebted to the following authors:

Bob Katz, "Skills of an Effective Administrator" *(Harvard Business Review)*

Peter Drucker's "How to Be an Effective Executive" *(Nation's Business)*

Doug McGregor, "An Uneasy Look at Performance Appraisals" *(Harvard Business Review)*

Henry Golightly, "How to Keep on Target" *(Nation's Business)*

Bob Schaffer, "Demand Better Results" *(Harvard Business Review)*

John R. Smith, "Managers with Motivation" *(University of Chicago Graduate School of Business Journal)*

Royal Bank of Canada, "Improving Managerial Skills" *(Monthly Newsletter,* July 1978)

You deserve a sincere thank you and acknowledgment from all of us who try to solve daily problems. You have, together, helped many people lead happier, more productive, enjoyable and fulfilling professional lives.

How This Book Can
Give You the Power Secrets to
Manage and Motivate People

"I just don't seem to have the power, the clout, to influence or control people, to direct and motivate them in order to get the job done. Frankly, I feel downright weak and powerless. This is our biggest problem, and it bugs us."

Does this sound familiar? Have you ever felt that way? Sure you have. Join the club. Most managers face that problem, all too often.

But increased power can be yours, when you know a few secrets about how to manage, motivate and build enthusiastic co-operation among employees, who are mostly just common ordinary people with everyday wants and needs.

Your "power" may not necessarily be the arm-wrenching, conniving or manipulating kind. The word "power" is used here to mean simply the ability, the capacity, to get things done through people, as the dictionary says, "to influence people," to do constructive things for the good of all concerned, including oneself.

For example, key figures in business, medicine, religion, sports and other fields have found secrets that gave them power. These are people such as Armour, Bassett, Bernstein, Burnett, Carnegie, Christ, Chrysler, Churchill, Drucker, Eisenhower, Ford, Hunt, Hutchins, Kennedy, Lincoln, Mellon, Parker, Penney, Pfizer, Rockefeller, Reynolds and Stevens. They and many others found power to bring out the best potential and best action from individuals . . . action that helped those same people to later become winners and leaders in those very fields. These individuals were motivated and stimulated by authority figures who knew the secrets of constructive power.

These power "secrets" are not necessarily mystic, esoteric, hidden or totally unknown. The "secrets" used by successful people are usually just techniques or methods that, while somewhat familiar, are only rarely remembered, recognized, recalled or realized as being effective. Webster calls secrets "things known by only a few." Some people know of ways to encourage others, but don't often *think of these things at the right time*, or appreciate their power, or know how to use these steps, or join them with other effective systems and programs. So, when we use the word "secrets" in this book this really refers to little-used and seldom-appreciated or understood steps that you can adopt and apply directly toward building your own power, just as a handful of key business leaders are doing right now.

Why not just use more money to create power? For two simple reasons: First, you and I face budget constraints. These simply mean that more money is usually not readily available. We do not have unlimited funds. We can't wave extra green at people every day and we can't give them an increase every week or month. And second, we all know that money alone won't do everything. Even after people are given an increase (and sometimes *especially* after an increase), people are often unresponsive. So money and more money is rarely the answer because it has very limited availability and very limited effectiveness.

So, the key idea in this book is: "power secrets that really work . . . without using more money." These methods provide you with some A-B-C's of social pressures, devices, simple psychology and proven systems that you can use right now, without the need for extra cash.

Good managers are always looking for ways to work more effectively with people. Many supervisors even collect their own secret "tool kit" of techniques for motivating others to perform at their optimum, with their best talent, skill and ability.

This book for managers will provide you with dozens of powerful techniques, devices and methods for getting people to do what you want them to do—and to do it willingly, even enthusiastically, without the need for added effort or resources on your part.

How does this benefit you? It gives you a way to light their fire so they actually want to take the constructive action that you need done. The employee becomes *self-motivated* toward your goal. He becomes his own blow torch on his own tail feathers. This saves you a lot of work and time, and it takes a lot less of your effort.

When you use these techniques, you can motivate people, more people, more ways, with more inner enthusiasm than ever before. You might well double your motivation results, your personal power and constructive influence. Why? Because now you will know what buttons to push and what methods to use.

These techniques can be fairly simple. Just read a few pages about one method, give it a couple practice tries, and you have a tool you can use for the rest of your life! This book describes many such tools. Soon you will have a whole kit—just as most successful executives do. If you watch them closely for a few days, you will see them use these very same techniques.

But with this book you have one big advantage; it took those major executives years of trial and effort, re-trial and revision. But you have these techniques all worked out, assembled, pre-tested, streamlined, described and held right in your hand.

This book is unique, different and innovative for at least four reasons: First, it is *strictly practical,* pragmatic and nitty gritty. No complex theories are presented, just things you can use right now, today or tomorrow. Second, it is designed for *today's attitudes* and today's people—for the different way people now look at things, a way that has become far more personal and humanistic and less hard-hearted or purely economic than was the case only a few years ago. Third, every technique suggested here has *been tested*, not just once but many times. The methods that did not do well were dropped. The good, productive systems have been retained, expanded and sometimes even improved. Fourth, these techniques each have at least one and usually several *true case histories*, described here, to illustrate how you might apply the systems and to show what you might expect to gain for yourself.

This material parts company with many ancient myths, half-truths, old wives' tales and out-dated ideas which at their best worked poorly and at their worst caused disaster to morale, careers, organizations and managers. Instead, here we talk about the real world in line with the "new" feelings, beliefs and life styles, where money is still important but not as much as it once was. Young and middle aged men and women march to a different drummer than they did just ten or 20 years ago. Surprisingly, this is even so with many older people who, contrary to popular belief, really have seen many changes and do know how to adapt to new circumstances. The concept is growing that money is not everything—that quality of life is more important—and so motivation techniques that are above and beyond financial return fit increasingly into today's attitudes. Those managers who know how to use these methods will have greater power and effectiveness.

This book and almost all of the ideas in it are based on the S-O-S formula. This stands for "Situation-Objective-System." It can be of substantial help to you, as a manager, in at least three ways: *First*, it will help you understand and seek the practical advantages of this book. *Second*, you can use this "Situation-Objective-System" technique when you apply your motivation program to people in your real life. *And third*, you can use the S-O-S methods in almost any other program beside motivation, just as many executives do every day.

S-O-S explained a bit further simply means: Situation: the facts, problems, opportunities, trends, conditions, resources and circumstances facing you. Objectives: goals or targets you wish to achieve. And Systems: methods, plans or procedures needed to reach your goals. In short, where you are now, where you want to go and how you can get there. This book follows that pattern closely. It has a situation chapter, an objectives chapter and, most importantly, many systems chapters.

Chapter 1 is the first secret in your S-O-S power plan: **situation**. It looks at the tough, practical problems, challenges and opportunities you face in today's employee attitude Situation. We see the "Great Motivation Gap" of *more* employee independence and *less* employer freedom. The chapter brings you some powerful but often unrecognized solutions and methods for dramatic motivation, the LLAD formula of "Look, Listen, Ask and Discuss" that provides you with insight plus many other direct advantages for increasing your power.

Then you get a second secret step in the S-O-S pattern: your best power **objectives** *or goal opportunities are discussed in Chapter 2. This is based on one of the most powerful new management* ideas now taking nearly all industries by storm: M.B.O. or Management By Objectives. Under this system, every resource is aimed toward your goal, so effort and energy are not wasted. Clearly, these objectives of yours will greatly influence the system or steps you decide to take. If your goal is to snuff out a mosquito, you don't need a cannon. For example: one company's managers set reachable goals for the fresh milk sales force. These resulted in some new, practical promotions, enthusiasm and motivation that helped the group far exceed their goals. A similar thing happened with managers at another company. Their selection of a good motivation goal ("We want to be leaders") again resulted in the team achieving far more than expected. You will see that *objectives* not only motivate others, but become a strong personal servant for you, that will help you all the rest of your life.

Chapter 3 is your third secret step in the S-O-S plan: strategy or power systems. The chapter reviews one of the most powerful (and misused) motivational devices, fear. You will learn where this can be applied effectively, but also where it can cause you more trouble and expense than it is worth, while a dozen other methods are more efficient.

Then we look at a giant power secret: respect. In chapter 4 you will see some surprisingly effective, easy, low cost, yet dramatic results you can obtain, since the timing is especially ideal for this approach today, if you do it right. We will look at ways you can even create a self-fulfilling prophesy, among employees, with your respect for their good work.

Chapter 5 shows how practical meetings can motivate people in powerful ways, when you use secret or rarely recognized techniques. And we look at these systems step by step. Actual case examples show how meetings motivated programs that started at ground zero, yet resulted in many millions of dollars in extra sales.

How to use personal power plans plus seldom understood time management is reviewed in Chapter 6. You will see how you can take simple steps to gain personal employee participation, get employees to "hyp" themselves up, make best use of time and get highly constructive action.

Meaningful work, when presented properly, can be a secret and surprisingly powerful motivator, as illustrated by Chapter 7. And we list suggestions for how you can put this concept into harness to serve you.

Secrets to powering up "both heart and mind", or emotions and intellect, are reviewed in Chapter 8. You will be given a number of well proven methods for stimulating and encouraging creativity and "brainstorming" ideas. You will see how to use the AIDA formula (Attention, Interest, Desire, Action) to generate positive, helpful results for both employer and employee.

Chapter 9 demonstrates powerful secrets for delegation of tasks to other people. These are dynamic motivators when applied properly. They are tools that not only take no extra effort on your part, but actually reduce your work, by employing other people's wants and drives to help you reach mutual objectives. You'll discover a handy "pride formula" that can serve you from now on to get you dramatically successful results.

Coaching guidance: A Powerful but Overlooked Motivator (Chapter 10) and *Secrets for Creating Dynamic Communication* (Chapter 11) together give you a sort of one-two punch capability. You can double your personal, informal coaching effect by using the "Ex-Dem-Pra" formula of Explanation, Demonstration and Practical work. You will see how to triple the impact of your more formal communications with the FOWD/PA formula of Frequency, Oral, Written, Done carefully, Played back and Adjusted plus the O-S-P system or One Strong Point. Examples of this include how an ad agency's use of "Green Sheets" improved guidance communication to motivate award-winning, creative action.

Secrets for Using Power Directions, Plus "Butt-Out" to Motivate More is Chapter 12. It shows you a few fine, rarely remembered points of *not* working too hard. It shows you how to get others started right and then let them do it themselves—do their "own thing" to develop dramatic progress for you and for them.

Chapter 13 demonstrates seldom understood but powerful emotional awards at a very low cost. If these are done properly, using any of a dozen proven methods, they can get you remarkably effective results.

A Surprising Secret: How Candor and Leveling Build Your Power, is covered in Chapter 14. This is a refreshing concept of openness that most of us like because we were all born honest and so are inclined that way. Used properly, this method strikes deep, normal, natural human vibes. Leveling is also a concept that can be closely used with all the other motivation methods just mentioned above. It gets action that is pleasant for both the employer and employee.

Chapter 15, "The Lonely Crowd" a Secret Power for Motivating, is a new departure even from recent methods for influencing people. You are given a secret but dynamic three-point formula for motivation based on David Riesman's book. Here we have a chance to look at our own "roots" or ancestor's attitudes, and use these as ways to excite, delight and motivate people to enthusiastic mutual goals.

Power Secrets for Motivating Small Units (Chapter 16) is comprised of special notes to three special folks: the small business, the small department and the service group. Selected motivation systems are tailored for each of these three organization types. Cases are given as examples including a small retailer, bakery, a department store chain, a N.Y. deli, a drug company, an appliance maker and the White House in Washington.

The World's Greatest "Power Deflators" and How to Avoid Them (Chapter 17) takes some strong cuts at old-fashioned and dangerous ideas that some people still use. It shows you how you can avoid these super demotivators and so double your motivational effectiveness.

"I'll Work for Nothing!" (Chapter 18) proves the dynamic effectiveness of all these power secrets. It outlines the growth of an almost unbelievable concept that has recently been popping up among millions of what we thought were greedy or money hungry people. We will look at how to use this and will see it applied by scores of groups as examples. This includes the Harvard business graduate who, as sales manager for a string of forty bottling plants, made the chapter's title statement, which eventually brought a dramatic doubling and re-doubling (a fourfold) sales increase.

I hope you enjoy reading this book and letting it serve you—as much as I enjoyed preparing it and putting it to work for me for the last six years.

Craig Rice

Contents

**How This Book Can Give You the Power Secrets
to Manage and Motivate People** 7

**1 New Challenges and Opportunities in Managing
and Motivating People** 23

An Obvious but Ignored Secret • The Power Motivation Gap •
Eight Power Advantages You Can Gain • How Awareness of
Others' "Hot Buttons" Can Be Your Secret Power • LLAD:
Secret Formula for Learning Employee's "Attitude" Situa-
tion • Three Secrets You Can Use • Four Secrets for Boosting
Power Once You Know "Attitudes" • Three Advanced Oppor-
tunities for You to Increase Your Power • Case: Money Is
"Zero Motivator" for a Tyrant • Giant Power Opportunity! •
How to Look for Hopes and Dreams • How to Use Your
Secret S-O-S Formula • How This S-O-S System Can Work in
Four Powerful Ways

**2 Power Secrets of Using Goals
and Objectives to Get Action** 35

Objectives Are a Key Power Secret • Secrets for Using
M.B.O., or Management by Objectives • How to Set "Motivation or Power Goal" • Four Ways Power Objectives Are Useful to You • Another Goal Setting Secret • How to Apply
These Three Steps

15

3   Fear: How to Use It and How Not to Use It **43**

How an Advertising Agency Increased Motivation by Decreasing the Fear Factor • The Fear of Humiliation • The Fear of Being Fired • Case: How a Department Head Paralyzed People with Fear • Power Secrets for Eliminating the "Fear" Atmosphere • Five Ways to Increase Your Power by Setting Rules of the Game • Case: Manager of Bottling Plant Fired a Whole Department

4   Easy Ways to Make Respect Work for You **56**

How You Can Use "Respect for Others" to Build Your Own Power • Case: How a Manager's Respect Motivated Progress • Why Everyone Secretly Wants Your Approval and Respect • The "Respect Gap" • A Three-Step Formula for Showing Respect • Secrets for Displaying Your Respect to Build Your Power • How Showing Respect Builds Power • More Secrets You Can Use to Gain Power Through Respect • Three Extra Secrets Why This Increases Your Power • How Your Respect Becomes a Self-Fulfilling Prophecy • How Bassett Furniture Used Respect to Become America's Largest • Summary: How Respect, a Power Secret, Builds Your Influence

**5   Practical Secrets for Using Meetings
    As Powerful Motivators** **66**

Case History: A Soap Manufacturer Plans a $20 Million Brand • Secrets for Using Meetings to Build Powerful Action • Seven General Power Secrets for Meetings • Seven "Mechanical" Secrets for Building Power with Meetings • Another Power Secret: Label Your Problem as "the Situation" • Secret Ways You Can Focus Attention on "Their Goals" • Power Secrets for Using Programs and Plans in Meetings • The Schedule Secret—How It Builds Motivation Power • A Final Power Secret to Meetings: the Re-Cap • Case History: How Meetings Produced $30 Million • A Summary of Power Secrets Using Meetings to Motivate

**6   How to Use Planning and Time Management
    As Key Managerial Tools** **81**

Case History: Respect and Priorities Get a New Soap Package and Sharp Sales Jump • Power Secret: "To Solve Our Problem, Let's Make a Plan!" • There's Secret Power in Prob-

6 How to Use Planning and Time Management As Key Managerial Tools (Cont.)

lem Review • Your Respect Secretly Magnifies Your Power • Case History: A Cleaner's Unique Package Generated $20 Million • A Secret for Setting More Potent Group Participation • A Secret and Powerful Application of Your S-O-S Method • The Power Secret to Saying "Look at That! You Made a Plan!" • Case: How a Major Soap Group's Plan and Time Management Solved a Tough Problem • A Secret Inquiry That Nearly Always Gets Action • The Powerful Secret of Using "You" • The Power Secret of Using Time Control for Management by Objectives • Twenty-Seven Time Management Tips • How Personal Planning and Time Management Motivate • Case: Pharmaceutical Manager Used Flip Chart Plan for $100 Million Program • Case History: How a Consultant Motivated with a Plan • Summary: The Secret Power of Plans and Time Use Can Motivate Major Action

7 Secrets of Using "Work" As a Powerful Motivator 97

Case: Fire at the Government Office; People Donate Labor • Here Is the Secret to "Meaningful Work" • Surprise! It's Often Your Best Power Tool • "Are You Kidding? People Hate Work!" • Work Has Most Power When You Use These Three Secrets • How Difficult Jobs Attract People • How the Man Who "Died and Went to Hell" Left You a Power Secret • "Pavlov's Dogs Loved Work," Says Peter Drucker • Gaining Power from People's Secret Dislike of "the Dole" • Three Secrets for Challenging People with Work • Ian's Multimillion Challenge • Case of the Warehouse Production Clerk Inventory Chart • Summary: Work Can Be Your Best Power Secret

8 How to Get Through to the "Heart and Mind" of People 109

What Is the Secret Power in "Heart and Mind"? • How Do Heart and Mind Generate Secret Power? • Here's How You Can Secretly Stimulate Powerful Ideas • "Brainstorming": A Powerful Secret to Serve You • Challenging Secretly Builds Your Power • How to Put the Five W's Toward Building Your Power • Case: How a Steak Chain "Challenged" and Five W's Stimulated Employees and Sales • Employing Others' "Heart and Mind" Techniques to Increase Your Power • Your Secret

**8 How to Get Through to the "Heart and Mind"
of People (Cont.)**

Objective • Secret for Using the A.I.D.A. Formula for Power
• Secrets for Building a Powerful "Gung-Ho" Team • Case:
Heart, Mind and A.I.D.A. Build Gung-Ho Team • Summary:
"Heart and Mind" Generate Secret Power

9 Power Secrets for Using Delegation Effectively 121

1. The "What"—Four Secrets to Powerful, Modern Delega-
tion • 2. The "Who"—Secrets of Selecting Your Designate • 3.
The "When"—Three Secrets to Power in Timing of Delega-
tion • 4. "Where" to Delegate for Maximum Power • 5. Power
Secrets of "Why" You Should Delegate • How Delegation
Secretly Helps Build Power • Power Secrets for HOW to
Delegate • The "Honor" Secret • The "Assistance" Secret •
The "Assignment" Secret • How a Hamburger Chain Man-
ager Used Delegation to Solve Problems • The Three Power
Steps • Power Secret: Help a Person BE Somebody • "I Am
the Head Knocker!" or the Pride Formula • Using the "Ter-
ritorial Imperative" • Ten Power Secrets • Case History: How
SCORE Used Delegation to Help Build the World's Largest
Consulting Group • Case History: How Production Team
Delegation Solved a Sales Crisis • Summary: Delegation Can
Be a Great Power Secret for You

**10 Coaching and Guidance: a Powerful
and Overlooked Management Tool 138**

Coaching: Its Power and How It Secretly Motivates • A Se-
cret Formula That Always Improves Your Power: "Ex-
Dem-Pra" • Here's Proof That "Ex-Dem-Pra" Coaching Has
Secret Power • Case: A Car Dealership Coaching Motivation
Ex-Dem-Pra Cured "Big-Effort/Little-Results" Pattern • The
Coaches' Power Secret • Four Power Secrets for Handling
"Coach's Surprise" • How to Coach When He's Doing Pretty
Well • Case History: How a Division of an Aluminum Com-
pany Used Coaching Secrets to Build Powerful Motivation

11 How You Can Triple Your Communications Impact . .150

Communication Can Be Your Easiest Power Secret • What
Communication Power Means and How It Helps You • Three
Power Secrets • Management's Major Failing • Secrets for

11 How You Can Triple Your Communications Impact (Cont.)

Avoiding Typical Modern Extremes • Secrets for Getting the Powerful FOWD/PA Formula to Serve You • How an Advertising Agency Executive Used "Green Sheets" and FOWD/PA to Motivate • Ten Power Secrets for Using the New Mechanics of Communication • $1 Million Spent by a Giant Publisher and Agency Provides You with 40 Communication Power Secrets • Using the "O-S-P" Formula: One Strong Point • How to Plan This Week's Secret Power: Communication • Summary: Communication Is a Powerful Secret to Serve You

12 How and When to Let People Be Their Own Bosses ..164

How a Government Branch Manager Used "Sliding Scale" of Power • Power Secrets Using the "Sliding Scale" • Six Power Secrets for Firmness: When and How to Be Tough • Five Power Secrets for Permissiveness • Four Power Secrets for Using the "Movable Spot" to Motivate • Three Power Secrets for Being Autocratic Yet Democratic • How to Employ "Independent" Group Feelings and "Butt Out" • New Products Group with Independence Generates Millions • Why People Have a Secret Desire for Power • How to Use "Extended Independence" • Four Power Secrets for Handling Errors • How a Government Clerk Was Allowed to "Mess Up," Yet Output Doubled • Summary: Proper Directions and Butting Out Are Great Power Secrets

**13 Powerful Reward Techniques That Move
People to Action 176**

The Power of Compliments and Awards • Four Power Secrets for Using Compliments • Three Power Secrets for Using Honesty to Turn Folks On • Five "Extra Techniques" for More Effectiveness • Power Secrets for Using Comparison Charts • How a Utility Soap Company's Comparison Charts Motivated Action • Five Power Secrets for Using Trophy Awards for Best Results • Don't Let Trophies "Make One Person Happy but 50 Sad" • Gas Station Owner Weeps • Four Common Award Errors to Avoid • How a Company's Awards Generate Extra Effort • Summary: Compliments and Awards Are Major Secrets for Building Power

**14 A Surprising Secret: How Honesty and Candor
Can Build Your Managerial Power** 188

How Openness Can Be a Remarkable Secret Power • What
"Leveling" Means As a Secret Power Source • Four Power
Secrets of Why Leveling Works • Power Secrets for Using
Leveling to Stimulate Motivation • How to Get People's
"Monkey" Involved in Self-Motivation • Three Power Secrets
for Applying a "Leveling" System This Week • Power Secrets
for Using a Group Plan and Involvement • How Salesmen Set
Their Own Motivators and Tripled Sales • Examples of Can-
dor as a Power Secret in 14 Major Motivators • The "Go-
Getters" Club • Summary: Surprising as It Seems, Candor Is
a Key Power Secret

15 A Three-Point Formula for Management Power 199

The "Three Point Formula" of Secret Power • How to Use
"Tradition Direction" to Motivate • Five Power Secrets for
Using "Inner Direction" to Motivate • Case History: How a
Company Motivated with "Inner Direction" • How to Use
"Other Direction" to Motivate • How to Adapt to Today's
Changing World • Power Secrets for Using All Three Points
of "Lonely Crowd" Formula • How a Leading Furniture
Maker Applies the "Lonely Crowd" Formula • Summary: The
Lonely Crowd, a Dramatic New Power Secret

16 How to Get Action from Small Groups of People 209

How Ten Million Small Businesses Struggle to Motivate •
Power Secrets for Using Attitudes, Action and Motivation to
Win the Game • The Pivotal Power Secret: Motivating Just a
Few • How Departments Can Be Motivated • Fourteen Power
Secrets for Small Departments • How Millions of Small SER-
VICE Unit Managers Can Motivate Effectively • The Solu-
tion: Ten Ways to Better Service Unit Motivation • Summary

**17 The Biggest "Power Deflators"
and How to Avoid Them** 221

Power Deflator #1 • Power Deflator #2 • Power Deflator #3 •
Power Deflator #4 • Power Deflator #5 • Power Deflator #6 •
Power Deflator #7 • Power Deflator #8 • Power Deflator #9 •
Power Deflator #10 • Power Deflator #11 • Power Deflator

17   The Biggest "Power Deflators"
     and How to Avoid Them (Cont.)
     #12 • Power Deflator #13 • Power Deflator #14 • A Summary
     of Secrets for Avoiding Major Power Deflators

18   "I'll Work for Nothing"—
     Proof That Power Secrets Work 232

     How Power Secrets Can Work for You Every Day • The
     Power Secret of "Extra Units" • A Power Secret Formula:
     "FCSR+" • Three Steps to Motivation Without Money • How
     Much Extra Work Will Most Executives Do for Another
     $1,000? • Power Secrets Beyond Money • Three Secrets for
     Gaining Power • The "Quality" Power Secret • A Final Power
     Secret • Summary: We Proved That Power Secrets Do Pro-
     duce Progress

     Index 243

1

New Challenges and Opportunities in Managing and Motivating People

"Nuts! I'm going to do as little as possible today," said Ruth S. to her friend Sally L. at their morning coffee break. (Coffee time is often planning time.) "The heck with it," added Sally. "This whole operation is a big fat bore. Say, did I tell you about Frank and Lois at the party last night?" . . . Both Ruth and Sally got very little done that day, even though their supervisor was facing overdue deadlines and was nearly climbing the walls. Ruth and Sally had almost no job interest, a major difficulty in our present world.

An Obvious but Ignored Secret

One of the most obvious but often ignored secrets to power is simply this: The better you truly understand the situation—and especially your employee attitudes like those of Ruth and Sally— the more quickly and easily you can move into a position of powerful motivation. There are several special ways to learn the situation and use it to your advantage. Let's look at the most frequent problems and then some systems that you can use to increase your influence in those situations.

Today, you as manager or supervisor face many tough problems in power procurement. Things are not the same as they were ten or twenty years ago, when money usually did it all. "Get that

23

job done right and you get a raise," people were told. "Do it now or you're fired," was the order, and it worked well.

But no longer. Both the employee's and the employer's circumstances have been vastly altered in recent years and will soon change still further.

Today's worker is much more complex, sophisticated, educated and just plain savvy. Many are also increasingly independent, self-oriented and either not very interested in your organization, or, worse still, downright negative towards it.

It is difficult to get today's workers to accept requests, orders, plans or programs. And even when they reluctantly acknowledge these, it is sometimes still tougher to motivate enough constructive action from them.

The employer, manager or supervisor has changed, too. He or she is also better educated, more complex and sophisticated. But you are also more restricted by rules and regulations from federal, state, city, union, company, manuals, customs, and politics—plus unwritten, even unspoken guidelines. And there's much less latitude, freedom and flexibility now in hiring, firing, raising, promoting and demoting people. In many cases wage money has become so large that it is now watched with an eagle eye. Few managers have much access to it anymore.

The Power Motivation Gap

This has caused the "Great Power Motivation Gap"—as the employees become *more* restless, unresponsive and independent, the employer-supervisor has *fewer* controls and less power over resources than ever before. You have a tougher job to do and fewer old-time tools with which to do it.

But there are secret and powerful solutions. While some doors are closed to you, others have opened, or are at least unlocked if you know how to turn the handle.

There are literally dozens of dynamic, new motivators you can put to your command. We will look at virtually all of these, just as many of the nation's top managers have been doing in situations like the following episode.

Case: "*Most of our people just don't give a damn*," said Perry M., a supervisor, at a national American Management Associations meeting being held in Chicago. "It would almost be better if they were angry, but they just don't care much whether school keeps or not." "I know exactly what you mean," added Dorothy T., supervisor in a retail department store. "Neither the men nor women will make much of an effort. They almost ignore our customers, our policies, won't learn anything about the merchandise, so come up zero when people ask simple questions, or they hide in the stock room!" Other managers further confirmed this with complaints about plant people, salesmen, clerks and service people who had extreme disinterest, demonstrated poor attitudes, refused to accept direction or showed outright hostility. Negative motivation was clearly a major problem. The managers spent the next two days reviewing new ways to improve employee attitudes. They agreed to try several fresh and different approaches, then reassemble back in Chicago in twelve months and report results. A year later the group met again, but this time spirits had greatly lifted. The management reported that employee attitude and motivation had improved dramatically—far in excess of expectations. They had proved beyond a doubt that modern motivation methods, when properly understood and used, can get positive, dynamic results. Those same methods (plus a few other well tested techniques) are all covered in the pages to follow.

Eight Power Advantages You Can Gain

Eight power advantages you will gain by learning employee attitudes are: *First*, you will discover where things are going well and deserve praise. *Second*, this insight will show you where you might spend less effort and so save yourself some time. *Third*, you will discover areas or activities that do need your attention and you will learn where your action will pay off lots more per hour invested. *Fourth*, by being forewarned you are not only forearmed with knowledge but you are able to take that stitch in time and prevent a problem or a disaster. *Fifth*, you avoid the terrible tragedy of dual misunderstanding—where you are expecting one action but the employee thinks you want something else and the project drops between the crack.

Sixth, you identify common ground and mutual understanding that can be the beginning of motivation. *Seventh*, you show you care—another basic start to better human relations, even though you do hardly anything other than simply understand their feelings.

Eighth, perhaps most important of all, you have done your

homework, your research, and you have strengthened your position with your own group. Not only right now (*they know* that *you know* the situation) but for the future, because a problem well defined is half solved. More important, it gives you clues to next steps . . . to goals . . . and to action you and others can take for the good of your company, your people and yourself.

How Awareness of Others' "Hot Buttons" Can Be Your Secret Power

By knowing attitudes, you can often find the employee's hot button— the "on" switch—his key interest. If you make this one of his major assignments, then you almost automatically increase his motivation and results at no extra effort on your part.

Case: Supervisor Ed K. was casually listening to his two clerks Jim and Sally handling customer telephone inquiries. By learning the situation, Ed noticed that Jim found it very difficult and unpleasant to talk with customers but he was excellent at running the memory typewriter and computer addresser. But Sally was not interested in manual skills; she enjoyed giving pleasant, efficient comments and information by phone. Sally really liked to do this and went out of her way to handle calls. So supervisor Ed simply suggested that Sally should be the first one to take calls, with Jim as a back up; he suggested the reverse with the typewriter and addressing. Ed had found their individual hot button and used it sensibly. Result: both Sally's and Jim's motivation and performance went up sharply, at no added effort for Ed, the supervisor.

You can't play the piano if you don't know the keys, and you can't help people solve their work problems, such as those we just saw with Sally and Jim, if you don't know what the troubles are— another reason for, and benefit from knowing employee attitudes.

LLAD: Secret Formula for Learning Employee's "Attitude" Situation

You have seen that you will greatly strengthen your own position and your own confidence by first getting a good understanding of the employee's attitude or state of mind—how he or she looks at the job and the employer.

A simple and effective formula to use in getting this insight is "LLAD," or Look, Listen, Ask, Discuss.

Look at what employees are doing and how they do it. Their actions, facial expressions and even their gestures or "body language" can often speak volumes.

Listen to their openly made comments to you, their associates and customers. Note not only remarks, but choice of words and tone of voice.

In one case, a supervisor followed this suggestion and was horrified to find things were much more serious than she had expected. Walk-in customers were being ignored or offended. But a few fresh techniques were tried and it saved the employee's job, improved customer relations and strengthened the supervisor, herself.

Ask people's opinions about their job. Ask them what they think is good and what is being done right. Ask what's bad and is being done wrong; what needs to be changed. You will usually be pleasantly surprised at how much thought they have given it. And they will be pleased and motivated by your interest.

Discuss things with the employee—programs, ideas, routines. Exchange opinions and suggestions and even review several alternative ways of doing things.

Case: Leo B. was a highly talented advertising writer, who started a small ad agency during the great depression and built it into what is today approaching $1 billion a year. He once said to me, "Craig, one of my best secrets to learning what makes people tick is very simple: I look at things, listen, ask questions and talk it over." This basic suggestion created the LLAD formula.

Three Secrets You Can Use

Here are three secrets for handling the wide range of candor, openness and honesty you will find as you search for an understanding of employees' attitudes. Most of them will tell you their views, feelings and beliefs fairly freely if given reasonable encouragement and assurance of safety from penalty. Others will literally beg you to see their viewpoints or even force these on you. But some either simply won't say or just cannot articulate. Your best technique with the "delugers" is to screen out the key points and let the rest go without much further concern. With the less willing employees you will need a little patience, time and development in order to be invited into their parlor of opinion. And some will never extend the invitation. In those cases you must draw your conclusions largely from listening, simple observation and a dash of common sense.

Four Secrets for Boosting Power
Once You Know "Attitudes"

Clearly, the better your insight and understanding, the more likely you are to accurately learn an employee's real attitudes and hot buttons. Here are some guidelines that will make this easier for you.

First, recognize your advantages in knowing the employee attitude situation. You have just done this by seeing the opportunities to find the "on" switch and key interests.

Second, pursue beyond the LLAD formula by seeing application to what you find. As you notice an area of enthusiasm or high ability, ask yourself, "How can I employ that strength for his goal and mine?" If you don't see an immediate use for some particular liking or skill (such as ability to get on well with people), just tuck this knowledge away. You are likely to find good use for this at another time.

Third, try "exchange positioning," putting yourself in their shoes and looking back at the job. Imagine you have the same situation, problems and hopes that your employees have. Things will suddenly take on a new light and new perspective, giving you new insights. You will begin to think and feel a little as the employee does.

Fourth and last, look in the mirror; observe yourself. How do you look to an employee—not just in appearance but in action? What you wear, and more important what you do, may be perfectly proper, professional and reasonable, but you will help your own understanding of employee attitude and get more thoroughly into the employee's frame of mind by simply trying to see yourself as others see you, warts and all.

These steps will give you new power, new understanding and new knowledge, since you can now work with a structure, ideas and feelings that you see much more clearly, instead of groping in the dark. Your job will suddenly get simpler and easier.

Case: Unions and Small Business Ownership Crusades. Successful union leaders and small business owners have at least one thing in common: they know how to understand people's attitudes and get into their heads. Two such leaders in the petroleum industry made almost a game, a hobby, "cause" or crusade of this. They looked, listened, asked, discussed opinions with their employees and found hot buttons. They put themselves in the other guy's shoes, and they looked in the mirror and tried to see themselves as others saw them. As a result, they gained great acceptance, respect and influence with their groups. The union was successful, and the small business grew, bought out two minor chemical firms and is now on the New York Stock Exchange.

Three Advanced Opportunities for You to Increase Your Power

As you get to know the attitude situation, you should be especially alert for two major challenges because they are important motivation opportunities for you: (1) the strong obvious opinions and (2) the hidden, subtle feelings.

The strong ones are easy: great problems or dislikes with some part of the job or people, or high ability to do things or work with a particular task or team member. You'll get these loud and clear, in most cases.

The hidden, subtle opinions include vague feelings that people often don't even know are really there, such as a resentment of any authority or enjoyment at being one's own boss for some part of the program.

Recognize that man is not motivated by "bread" alone, if we may paraphrase a Biblical statement. And in this case we mean bread as money, of course. The situation is rarely so simple that it can be totally and easily controlled by the mechanical injection of cash, just by itself. Here are three steps you should consider that go beyond money and so help increase your motivational power.

First, consider using some of your hunches and intuition. Management is an art to a large degree, even though some people

would love to have it a pure science where we simply apply chemical "X" or dollar amount "Y" or electrode stimulus "Z." Your
strength and ability increase the moment you recognize that management is dealing with emotion as well as capital, insight as well
as formulas, art as well as science.

*Second, look for "feelings" since man is a human, not a ma-
chine.* Too many modern mechanists attempt motivation more by
moving machinery than men's minds. This is a nifty idea because it
makes life so simple. If only it were true. But it's the lazy man's
solution and it's a cop-out, a phony both for the supervisor and the
employee. Money as a machine is only a partial solution.

Third, consider non-cash interests. Money is necessary, but it
is *not enough*, anymore than air and water can sustain life. They
are necessary but not sufficient. Look for people's interests that
are aside and apart from money—above and beyond—and perhaps
even better and more exciting than cash alone.

Case: Money Is
"Zero Motivator" for a Tyrant

Almost every industry has an example or two of a company
manager who rules like a dictator. One such example is a small but
well known food related manufacturer in Chicago, who for years
depended entirely on money as a motivator. The man was an impossible, offensive, confused, insulting, degrading, demoralizing despot. People quit or were fired, and new ones were hired so fast that
no one really learned his job. The "revolving door" operation became very inefficient, and the manufacturer had to pay higher
wages to attract employees. Eventually, the day came when
hardly any capable person would work for him. Just recently, de-
spite growth in his total industry, his own financial position became so bad that he fired everyone and filed for bankruptcy.
Money alone failed to provide adequate constructive motivation.

Giant Power Opportunity!

*If money is a poor motivator, what will work? Secret: try
starting with hopes and dreams.*

As you review and learn your employee attitude situation you
can easily see the challenge of the "great motivation gap"—*more*

employee resistance, *less* employer power. But you used the LLAD formula to learn more about your people, and you have discovered some hot buttons, and you know that this is not money alone.

How to Look for Hopes and Dreams

Everyone has them. They are usually something beyond food, clothing and shelter. Even for the guy with a patch on his pants, his dreams are more in the way of mental or emotional wants. For example: to believe in something worthwhile, to do something interesting and important, to be somebody, to be accepted in the group, recognized, appreciated, secure, awarded, respected, honored, promoted, to have increased authority and responsibility. *Here your situation*, an employee with dreams and goals, *becomes your opportunity* for motivation because: the extent to which you can help him reach these hopes and dreams is the extent to which you can generate his excitement, enthusiasm and constructive action. Your powers of motivation have increased.

And we didn't say a word about additional money, because many people want these non-cash things almost as much, and sometimes even more, than they want a few extra dollars. They will often work a lot harder for their beliefs, their convictions, their hopes and dreams than they ever would for money alone.

Case: A very popular spray cleaner was a product that started purely as a gleam in Jack Brown's eye. It was a hope, a wish, a dream—to build a successful small business. To have something of his own, that was challenging, important, recognized and respected, to be a key person in his community. He and his son Tommy started in their garage. They mixed the liquid chemicals and poured them into bottles. Tommy's mother pasted on the labels, and they sold it out of the trunk of their car. At times things were rough and they thought of quitting. Money was not the main goal because they could easily earn much more money working for the nearby fabric mills. But they hung in for years under tough, miserable conditions. Their dream and their goal were their motivation. And it worked. The product and the Brown family did reach the levels they had hoped for . . . and far beyond. Today the spray cleaner is a multimillion dollar product.

How to Use Your Secret S-O-S Formula

S-O-S stands for Situation-Objective-System. This is a simple and effective method to plan for motivated action and get it.

Here's how it works: Step #1 you learn your *situation* or where you are now—your problems and opportunities. Then, step #2, you set your *objectives* or where you want to go—your targets and goals. Then finally, step #3, you decide on a *system* or how you are going to get there—your methods or procedures. And there you have it. A simple, three step approach that has worked for thousands of the nation's best managers: Situation-Objectives-System.

You have secretly done a key part: the situation. You have reviewed, studied and measured your employee's attitude. You have found out where it is good and where it is bad. You discovered their likes, dislikes, hot buttons, their hopes and dreams. You have measured the dimension of the problem; you may have found it to be very small, or it could be more serious than you thought. Being well defined, your problem is now partly solved.

You have performed a valuable service to yourself because you are now in a position to build a good motivation program and take the next step: objectives. But you cannot make a truly wise, sharp decision on your goal (where you want to go) if you have not first done your research (your homework) and learned your situation. Also, you can't make sensible plans for a system unless you have good goals. So, you see, each part fits together, hand in glove, and you have now done a good job on your first step, which will make your next move that much easier and more dynamically effective.

How This S-O-S System Can Work in Four Powerful Ways

First, this book organizes the whole story and plan into three easy bites. This chapter covered your motivation situation; the next covers the motivation objectives; and the remaining chapters deal with dozens of motivation systems you can use. So you have your plan right here, right now, in your hands and before your eyes. *Second,* you can use this same S-O-S method in your actual *motivation program,* which you can start this week or next. You can look at your motivation situation, set your objectives, select your motivation system. Plan your work and work your plan. *Third,* you can use this system in almost any program or part of your business life to "work smarter, not harder."

Case example: You come to work tomorrow and your *motivation situation* is that you are facing a disinterested employee, who is even a little negative. You also may have a project that needs to be done by 4:00 P.M. Your *motivation objective* is to create interest within that employee sufficient to wash away negative feelings, generate enthusiasm and get that job done well and on time. Your *motivation method* may be to select one or two of the techniques or methods suggested by the pages you have in your hands right this moment.

Or another case. *Situation:* you are in Atlanta. *Objective:* you need to visit New York today. *System:* take a plane. Your S-O-S method is now yours for the rest of your life. It's pretty simple, and you can use it every day, sometimes every few hours, to solve problems and make progress.

Fourth, you can even teach employees to use this, and it, in itself, becomes a motivating device to them, as we will see in a little more detail later.

In summary, your knowledge of the situation is one key secret to power. We clearly saw that you, as a modern manager, face many tough motivation problems. Some people are disinterested, and others are deliberately negative. You are looking at the growing Great Motivation Gap—with increasingly independent employees, yet less supervisor latitude on wages, budget, hiring, firing and other kinds of clout. It's a serious challenge to you and a *situation* worth your checking out rather closely. A simple technique for doing this is "LLAD," or Look, Listen, Ask and Discuss. This has lots of advantages; you learn where things are OK, places to reduce your time investment, problem spots to work on. Being forewarned, you are forearmed; you can avoid misunderstandings; you discover common ground, showing employees you care; and by defining your problem you partly solve it. You can find other people's hot button, get into their heads, "exchange positions" and see yourself as others see you. You will notice that man is not motivated by bread alone and that management is an art as well as a science.

Look for emotions because people are humans, not machines. Mechanically injecting money into them is not good enough. Hopes and dreams are often more important and is a great opportunity for you to increase your power and your employee's power. By knowing your employee's attitude *situation* you have taken the first big step in the handy S-O-S, or Situation-Objective-System, plans technique. Now you can apply this simple method to reading this book, to your actual motivation program next week and to almost any problem in the rest of your business life, so you can "work smarter not harder." Next, let's take your second big step: setting your *objectives*.

2

Power Secrets of
Using Goals and Objectives
to Get Action

"I know the trouble, alright. That's no big deal. Everybody knows the problem," said supervisor Wally R. "I just don't know what to do about it. I don't know what my most sensible "people-goal" or motivation target should be. Can I really expect to change their attitude from disinterest to enthusiasm? By how much? How soon?" Wally is asking some good questions—questions you have probably asked. The simple fact that you asked is an excellent sign that you are starting to plan your program and have taken a good step in the right direction.

Objectives Are a Key Power Secret

Now that you have measured the kind and size of employee attitude problem you are facing, you are ready to set your most realistic motivation goal. You can decide how much you might change or improve these attitudes (an objective) among how many people (another goal). This chapter will demonstrate secret techniques for using such objectives to increase your own power, your influence and your motivation results.

35

Secrets for Using M.B.O., or Management by Objectives

M.B.O. simply means that you manage, use or apply all of your resources—like your time, money, effort, talent, employees—toward your goal. And only toward your goal. When you are tempted or tricked into directing your resources toward something other than your target, then you are not using M.B.O. Examples: you are just coasting or doing something that is purely an interesting side issue but is not a goal; or you are involved in helping someone else reach *his* goal but not yours. This is not M.B.O. But when your every action, every step, every resource helps you reach your target, then you are using M.B.O. And that has proved to be an effective, efficient, popular and dynamically powerful procedure among America's most successful managers. It works better with every passing year.

Notice that "Objectives" is the middle name of the S-O-S power formula plans method. Objectives are the heart of the M.B.O. system. Obviously, to really use M.B.O. as a tool for serving you to the fullest, you must begin with a goal.

Case: A large pest extermination service started as a very small operation. But they had a dream—to grow, expand and become a strongly established contender in the field. They managed their few resources toward early, modest expansion. And they did grow—slowly, at first, but then they picked up momentum. They made certain that the chemical bug-killers they used were the most effective possible. They used great care in hiring and training service people. Their uniforms and trucks were sharp and clean, their service polite and prompt, their prices reasonable and their advertising convincing. Their every resource was aimed at their specific goal. The service grew steadily, and today not only have they reached their target, but they have become one of the leading exterminators in the U.S. They managed by objectives.

How to Set "Motivation or Power Goal"

Your target—the results you hope to accomplish with your motivation program—should be the end product of your effort.

Decide where it is that you want to go and what it is you wish to do. Your objective should be expressed in terms of who you want to motivate, how much, when and where.

For example: You may have a situation where you have an employee or several employees who are disinterested, perhaps even negative. Your goal may be to generate, develop or create a more positive attitude and then enthusiastic action, right here in your group, within the next two weeks or maybe even today. And you feel that these targets are at least partially reachable when you apply the steps described.

Four Ways Power Objectives Are Useful to You

First, they save you wasted effort. If the action you are considering really isn't aimed at your goal, forget it. You are spending time and effort, but this isn't actually helping you get where you want to go. (For example, revenge or getting even with someone may be somewhat satisfying, but it rarely helps you reach your goal and may actually reduce your progress. It is usually not very practical, which is one reason few good managers use it.)

Second, by concentrating effort toward your motivation objective, you suddenly discover not only that you are making progress, but you are making *more progress* per day than ever before. People are starting to respond, turn on and take action—multiplying your own effort so that while once you were one, now you are two or six or twenty. *Third,* you start to become a smarter worker, not a harder worker. By focussing all your time and attention on your goals, you will find that you can frequently accomplish more with the same effort or even with *reduced effort*. So you do more and you work less.

A *fourth powerful advantage* to you in pin-pointing your objectives is that once you decide what person you wish to motivate, how much, when and where this will help *guide your next and last step* in the S-O-S (Situation-Objective-*System*). And, as Bell Telephone has advertised in recent years, "The system is the solution" to your situation and your problem. By knowing your objectives, you are more likely to select the right tools. You don't use a fly swatter to stop a tank or a cannon to blast a mosquito.

"Objectives" can be your secret word to help you in extra ways, not just in building your own plan, but in dealing with others and in exciting and *directly* motivating them.

To increase your power, ask people, "What's your objective?" Do this especially when they request help, propose a procedure or complain. Ask, "What is it you are trying to accomplish?" Or, "What is your goal?" This is a simple question. Very basic. But it is usually a challenge, even a mild shocker to most people.

The result is often amazing. They will stop. Look. Stutter. And then think, especially if you ask it more than once. And then they, too, will start to clear away some of the rubbish in their own minds and daily activities. They tend to stop or reduce the wasted efforts and wheel spinning that they have been applying to useless projects.

Another Goal-Setting Secret

Next time you see your employee wasting effort, ask, "What is your goal?" You are taking a simple step toward greater power.

Three Secrets to Motivating People with Goals

Setting objectives for yourself and others can be one of your most important, even dynamic, strategic steps. A moment ago we looked at ways to set your goals in your motivation program. Now let's look at how you can move people with *their* own goals. *First, your look at the situation* will give you lots of clues, and most of these will be pretty obvious. "Man, I sure wish people would realize the load of work I do around here to keep this outfit going!" She is telling you one of her goals: recognition. Notice that she is not really asking for less work, but for appreciation in return for doing that work.

Second, sharpen, clarify and focus these hopes, dreams and goals. Don't squash them. They are about to go to work for you and for others. Don't rain on the parade.

Third, build these up. Expand on them, emphasize them and make them important.

How to Apply These Three Steps

Here's how you can apply these 3 powerful steps that use personal goals to motivate people: You might say something like, "You have a lot of strong talents" (you just took step #1 and recapped part of the *situation*), "and I'm sure you want to get the recognition you have earned because you deserve it" (you just took the second step; you focussed and clarified a dream that almost everyone has, sometimes completely unconscious, other times just barely on the edge of our awareness and still other times as a burning want and need). "Let's keep this in mind: fair and full appreciation for your good work—and together we might reach that goal" (you just took step #3; you built up, expanded and emphasized the target, so that it shines brightly in everyone's mind; it is hard to ignore or forget).

Another power secret: show that the action *you* need helps them reach the goal *they* want. *For example:* "That new project you are doing is helpful to the company in several important ways; so if you get it done right and on time, you will surely be recognized for making a strong contribution. I'll see to that."

And this increases your power and your strength because your approval and support are more important than ever. One of the world's most astute analysts of our economic scene, John Kenneth Galbraith, said in his recent TV series, "A truly accepted and acknowledged leader is a person who has made or appears to have made a complete commitment to use his or her abilities toward helping others reach their objectives."

A secret step; try to set fairly realistic goals both for yourself and for others. Be sure they are reasonable and reachable. They should be neither too low nor too high. If the goals for either of you are too low, then there is not much challenge, things are too easy, there is no reach, no stretch, no stimulus for action. The goal is ineffective, either as your planning tool or as a method of motivating your group.

If the goal is too high, then it can either be discouraging right from the beginning (it simply looks impossible, so why try it), or it can generate false hopes and early, phony unreal enthusiasm—and later disappointment when it never happens. This is the tragedy of excessive expectations. They produce a discouragement that can be much worse than if a lower goal were missed.

Example: A starving man is promised a sumptuous turkey dinner, and he visualizes the steaming dressing, the wine, the juicy white meat, the mince pie. But he gets only a piece of bread. He is crushed and perhaps even furious. But if this same starving man is promised a peanut butter sandwich, yet gets only a slice of bread, he is not so disappointed. He missed his goal in both cases, but he came a lot closer in the second situation. He does not suffer the disillusionment and anger of unfilled, excessive expectations. Make reasonable, realistic, reachable promises to yourself and to others. You might exceed these and please many people, including yourself. Don't expect miracles, although you or others have high abilities. Sure, even if they are starving they should reach for the stars and naturally have the hope, the drive and aspiration toward a turkey dinner. But they should keep in mind the realistic goal of a peanut butter sandwich. Or maybe two. Half a loaf is 100% better than starving.

Case: A condensed milk company set realistic goals that motivated powerful action. The dairy division sells fresh milk to stores and homes in a large area of the southeast. Recently, they noticed that sales were at best level in some cities and declining in others. The sales manager was in trouble and so were his route truck supervisors and the drivers. The managers looked at the situation, listened to their routemen, store owners and household customers, asked them questions and discussed the situation. They learned that the routemen were totally unenthusiastic, which often resulted in little or no effort and activity. The problem was lack of motivation. The managers got their heads together and decided to use goals in two ways: (1) as targets in their motivation plan and (2) in stimulating employees.

First, as part of their S-O-S Power plans approach, they knew the situation: low employee interest. Now they needed a motivation objective or an incentive goal—some level of spirit, enthusiasm and positive attitude that they expected to reach with their employees. This would be a guide to selecting some sort of system. *Second, they wanted a goal simply as a direct* motivator to the routemen.

REASONABLE AND REALISTIC GOALS WERE SET

FOR IMPROVING ENTHUSIASM AND FOR RAISING SALES. These were stated clearly and repeated daily the first ten days, and then once a week. Managers showed how their efforts and resources were now being matched with those of the routemen to help those drivers reach their goals. Managers were making a personal commitment to assist in employee goals.

Managers and first level supervisors saw a dramatic improvement in routemen's attitude. The drivers had more of a reason for being and for coming to work in the morning. Managers accomplished their motivation objective. And sales increased well above the modest estimate. As an unexpected bonus, store managers were pleased, stocked and featured more of the company's milk and homemakers wrote letters of appreciation for their on-time milk deliveries. Goals had helped both with (1) management's own motivation plan (by setting reachable incentive levels) and (2) the direct motivation of the salesmen.

In summary, objectives are a key power secret. Once you understand that the situation facing you is employee attitude, then you are ready to take the powerful step of setting your goal or target to shoot at. This becomes the objective for your motivation program. If you "manage by objectives" or use your time and effort *only to reach your goals*, you will gain lots of advantages: you will avoid waste, make more progress, multiply yourself into a team of people and accomplish more with the same time investment or maybe even less work. Also, once you know your *Situation* and *Objective*, your best *System* can now be more easily and accurately selected, to complete your S-O-S plan. But while "objectives" have this first important value to you, that of helping make your most effective motivation plan, they have a second major benefit to you: *directly* motivating people. "Objective" can be your secret magic word, especially when you ask the challenging and stimulating but simple question, "What is your goal?" You can motivate people with their own objectives by *first* looking, listening, asking, discussing and in that way identifying *their personal* targets, *second*, sharpening or clarifying the focus and *third*, building its importance. This increases your acceptance, influence and power, since you become a part of the commitment to reach employee goals, if only through recognition and understanding. Be sure to set reasonable, realistic and reachable goals, since those that are too low are not stimulating and those that are too high are either discouraging right from the start or lead later to the tragedy of excessive expectations.

*   *   *   *   *   *

IF YOU GET NOTHING MORE OUT OF THIS WHOLE BOOK, TAKE THIS ONE SIMPLE SECRET WITH YOU: *REMEMBER TO ALWAYS SET SOME SORT OF OBJECTIVE FOR ANY PLAN*. USE THIS AS A KEY PART OF YOUR S-O-S MOTIVATION PROGRAM . . . AND USE IT AS A DIRECT MOTIVATOR FOR OTHERS. THINK ABOUT IT FOR A MOMENT AT LEAST ONCE EACH DAY. USE ALL YOUR RESOURCES ONLY TO REACH GOALS. NOW . . .! YOU HAVE JUST ENLISTED A NEW SERVANT . . . "OBJECTIVES" . . . THAT WILL HELP YOU ALL THE REST OF YOUR LIFE!

*   *   *   *   *   *

This book can and will earn you thousands of extra dollars and save you thousands of extra hours of otherwise wasted effort. It will provide you with many more dynamic, proven and effective power secrets.

And now you have completed two powerful secret steps in your S-O-S, situation, objective, system, motivation program. In chapter #1 you covered your situation, and in chapter #2 you have just seen how to establish your objectives. These two steps were absolutely key and essential. They are your launching pad because from here on we leave the vital basics of situation and objectives. We will be providing you with dozens of power secrets for your *system* of motivation to reach goals. Let's start with some of the simpler, obvious techniques, such as fear, and then move to some better, more effective and advanced methods.

3

Fear: How to Use It
and How Not to Use It

Fear has long been a powerful secret weapon. For centuries it was *the* major motivator. Even today, as humanist Studs Terkel says, "Everybody is afraid of something." For years, surveys have reported that the highest personal concern in the U.S. is loss of income. But threats of job loss may now be losing their motivational punch, as security programs grow and money becomes somewhat less important. Successful professionals have found easier ways to motivate today's workers—methods that get even better results than trite, over-used bluffs and threats, which can under-motivate and over-irritate. The prostitutes have a slogan "C.Y.O.T.E." "Cancel Your Old Tired Ethics." We may not sympathize with prostitutes, but this same slogan is being whispered, mumbled and sometimes shouted by a growing percent of workers. Secret and powerful ways to motivate without using fear include: establishing rules to the game, understanding each other, discussing problems, goals and plans, personal involvement and developing your own status and prestige to keep yourself in control—perhaps more than ever if your program has a few hidden teeth and remains the iron hand in the velvet glove.

How an Advertising Agency Increased Motivation by Decreasing the Fear Factor

A medium sized black advertising agency decided to hire a "new business manager" (essentially a salesman) to get new clients. The agency had once grown briskly, but had leveled off and showed a decline in recent years; so it needed new accounts desperately. One cause of the trouble was that Bill A., who owned and ran the agency, was a heavy user of threats, fear, humiliation and firing. These had once worked well to whip employees into shape. But today these same methods, coupled with frequent resignations and high turnover, created low morale and low efficiency. (Most employees were trying harder to hide from Bill's wrath than to do a good job.) Bill hired Don D. to get more business, but then used the same tactics on him. Don was a good salesman with a record of many successes. But the threats and humiliation caused him to become demoralized, then partly paralyzed (low output), and after a few months he was ready to quit.

About that time, Bill A. attended a management conference where successful managers reviewed how they had found fear to be increasingly non-productive and expensive in today's situations. Instead, they discovered that use of more professional methods—smart work, not hard work—got much better results, at less cost. Avoidance of fear tactics and threats and mutual analysis of problems, setting rules, discussion, understanding and involvement were the way to go.

At first, like most managers, Bill A. did not completely change his mind or his methods. But he did modify them a little. He partially tested the newer techniques. The response was dramatic. Don came to life. He made more and better sales calls and signed a large new account. Bill used more of the fear-free approaches. Not only did Don get better results and two new clients in two weeks, but most of the other employees improved their performance quality, quantity and job satisfaction. As of this writing, the agency has been able to increase staff substantially and is negotiating purchase of several other agencies. Fear techniques had actually held them back. Better methods generated profound financial, managerial and emotional improvements.

The Fear of Humiliation

Fear of humiliation has power because people hate to be degraded, to lose face among their friends or associates or even to lose face in their own eyes. This dislike of humiliation is almost inborn and instinctive. It even exists among animals. (Did you ever notice a dog slink off with his tale between his legs, while the victor strutted off with "flag" waving in the breeze?) Aversion to humiliation was present with the cave dwellers and among people through history right up to yesterday. Use of this fear as a motivational tool is one of the first devices most managers think about since it is so obvious, simple, dramatic and established. But good managers know that it is a little simplistic to think it will work every time or solve every problem. It's a little like: to get money, earn it; to educate students, teach them; to cure sick people, treat them; to eliminate criminals, shoot them. Fear of humiliation is still effective. It still works. And it will keep on working for many generations. It is the first stage of that great motivational team, Punishment and Reward: the stick and the carrot.

Humiliation can serve you and get you dramatic help, especially when you have people working with you who have pride in themselves. They tend to fear failure and humiliation particularly *in their own eyes.* This *internal* fear grows as people's pride and confidence grows or they become more directed by themselves.

But fear of humiliation is declining in power as well as in result among today's workers. Why? There are several reasons. *First, you are often dealing with average* or above average people. With average or above average people, actual humiliation or threat of humiliation may have been a strong motivator at one time, but today they feel above this and even a little insulted by it. Such a threat often simply causes demoralization and then paralysis. *For example,* they may feel: "The boss threatens to humiliate me, or just did, so therefore my spirit is rotten. I really don't feel much like doing anything. Guess I'll dog it for an hour or so." This is negative motivation.

Second, they may actually resort to a sort of quiet foot dragging or even a little innocent, passive sabotage. *For example:* "I'm sorry Mr. Jones, my typewriter broke. Looks like a staple is stuck in the works." Carried further it becomes rage. Noiseless, perhaps, but still there. Your report or your order doesn't get there quite in time to solve the problem. Key supplies run out, way ahead of time. The form isn't quite right to be accepted by the computer. A message or client contract file gets "lost." The company car won't start. The toilet overflows. Does this sound familiar? Things just seem to "go wrong," one thing after another, and strangely it's very hard to pin the blame because everyone has good explanations and seems equally distressed. It's quite easy for people to see that things go wrong without doing anything. They simply don't take the extra effort to see that things go right. Then who do you fire? You can't fire everyone, and if you do, the same thing can happen to the new group.

Third, withdrawal and resignation set in. The employees don't necessarily keep on with the resistance; they simply start to not care anymore whether school keeps or not. They do only what they must do and begin to eye the door, the life boat and the greener pastures. They make contacts and soon, to their relief and yours, they leave. Good riddance, right? Yes, in many cases. With that kind of attitude you may be well rid of them, whether they were really capable or not. But in effect the fear of humiliation tactic did not really accomplish your goal. It boomeranged. Rather than being motivated to do what you want, too often today people simply resist and then leave.

The Fear of Being Fired

Fear of being fired—it "scares hell out of 'em!" The fear of dismissal is much deeper than the fear of humiliation. Being fired is loss of face, pride and status, plus the big hurt: loss of income.

Case: In one small meat processing plant, the supervisors were each analyzed and evaluated by a management consultation team. Then, on Friday afternoon, one of the managers was called into the front office and fired. After this happened several times, the pattern became clear and fear swept over those who remained. They took to playing everything very safe, doing as little as possible to avoid error, drinking at noon and wearing their best suit the last day of the week in case they had to go around and say goodby. It became known as "Blue Suit Friday." For weeks, activity and progress came to a near standstill. Fear produced partial paralysis.

Just the threat of this shocks and staggers most employees a little. Even the hint is often all it takes. In fact, just the physical presence and observation by the person with the power to deliver the blow—even though nothing is stated, no hint is made, no thought is even in mind—is enough to frighten many people. Firing and the threat of firing are traumatic, sometimes crushing motivators today, and, right or wrong, they will be for years.

As Kipling said, "As it was in the beginning . . . is now official sinning. And shall be for ever more." *But*—and this is a very key "but"—it is losing its punch, power and persuasive dynamism with each passing year. Each survey shows that while this fear is still the #1 concern among a majority of our population, that number and majority is shrinking.

It's the ultimate power weapon, but it's getting obsolete. If and when a manager exercises this option, or even makes this threat, he is playing his ace. He has reached the bottom of the barrel and has used up all his options. Further, if the threat is repeated too often without action it loses effectiveness. Were he now to go back to a lesser threat, this pales into insignificance by comparison and makes his more severe threat of dismissal appear to be a hollow, phony bluff.

Playing the ace eliminates the ace. It is gone. Once a person has been fired, he has little or no remaining concern for his prior employer, who shot his wad. It is *before* the shot is fired that the threat, the fear, has maximum impact. It is the threat and ability, not the action, that has the most power.

Playing the ace, or simply threatening, partly assumes that we are still back in 1950's or 1960's, when a job was "essential." This is rarely so today. Most employees have at least three or four options. *First*, they either already know of another job or can find one after a week or two of restful "vacation." *Second*, they can draw unemployment or even coast for a while on savings. *Third*, they can simply let their spouses support them for some weeks. *Fourth*, many women (and some men) casually leave the labor market . . . retire . . . go back to housekeeping, even if this means a lower standard of living, to be lured back into a job only when something interesting and convenient comes along.

With about 50% of adult females employed, this means an all time high of family units (or people living together) that have two incomes. One job can often be easily dispensed with for at least a few weeks if not indefinitely.

In nearly all cases, being fired no longer means total loss of income. It is simply *reduction* of income down to welfare levels, other spouse's level or a lower paying job. This is a *totally new situation* in the business world.

From the manager's viewpoint, with such a hue and cry being made over "unemployment," it is almost "un-American, un-Godly and unpatriotic" to even allow someone to be unemployed—much less *cause* such a "dreadful" state—even though it is rather obvious that, since millions of low level jobs have for years gone begging, many people are unemployed partly at their own choice, saying they "can't find" a "suitable" job or income.

Is a "good job" desirable? Almost always. Is "just any job" essential? Rarely. Here is the point: All these factors, taken together, pretty well emasculate much of the whammy to today's threat of being fired. Very few adults in America need, want or will take just any job. Nearly all have other options.

Case: A small management consultant firm asked the local college of business for their best senior graduate management student, to work half time. The student was hired, trained and then scheduled to help put on three key presentations for clients. He did fine on the first one, but the next two mornings overslept, missing both meetings and creating considerable damage. The episode did not really bother him since many jobs and other options were easily available to him and he finally took one.

Fear has most power with older workers, not younger. Fear of being fired usually has higher motivation among older people for a number of reasons.

First, they live at least partly in the past or are influenced by memories of back there in the 1940's or 1950's, when job loss actually was a disaster. They are therefore shaped and conditioned with those indelible memories. Fear of dismissal is ingrained and habitual for most older people. Response to a threat is nearly a conditioned reflex, an immediate knee-jerk reaction, favoring the ordered activity.

Second, a person over 40 or 50 usually has deep personal or *financial commitments* that make job loss (translation: major income reduction) a severe penalty. Most of these older family units have only one income earner. They have big mortgages, kids in college; they owe on the cars, boat, plane or cottage. Job loss could mean moving away from life-long friends, church, children or relatives, destroying valuable tap roots that provide spiritual sustenance and important reasons for living. These are matters that may seem "uneconomic" but have a strong bearing on motivation; and they show once again that there are other things just as important as money—often, even more so.

Third, conscientiousness, duty and honor have been drummed into a large number (perhaps most) of older people by church, school and family. This is in fairly sharp contrast to many younger people. The older ones have been taught that it is a "disgrace" to be fired and if that happens it almost automatically meant that it was "mainly their fault." They "have failed" somewhere. Again, this reinforces the power of firing threats.

Fourth, many older people are ignorant of other opportunities for jobs or benefits. They feel it is "disloyal" to look around, inquire or even learn of their rights. They sometimes fear that even this would endanger their vitally needed jobs.

Fifth, they get inflexible, habitual and rut-bound. Then, the rut becomes somewhat comfortable, or they grow around or get accustomed to the lumps and bumps. They don't want to lose their jobs, and even a mild threat strikes terror into their hearts. Most older people are super-vulnerable.

But, the worm can turn. Many older people are discovering that their experience and ethics have wider value than they once thought. They are often the most willing and able workers. Most of these senior folks have seen a lot—from horse-drawn milk carts to moon walks—and have adjusted to thousands of changes. To youth's surprise, one more adaptation by older people is no big deal to them. It is nothing new. Adaptation has been a way of life to many for 40 or 50 years. This, then, reduces the surprise, shock and power of firing threats even among the older group.

Case: A retail store had long been hiring a mixture of young and old clerks. About half of the younger ones had a disconcerting habit of arriving 30 minutes late or not at all (without calling in), or goofing off, smoking and visiting in the stock room. The boss said very little. Most of the older clerks did none of these things except on rare occasions. But then, they were threatened with dismissal, which frightened them. Recently, however, an older clerk simply said, "I am sorry I am late, but it was truly unavoidable. If you feel I must be dismissed, that will be your loss, since I am one of your best clerks and have already been offered positions down the street." The worm had turned.

But youth are more mobile. They have no memory of "the

good old days." Most live in an aura of optimism. They usually have
a family unit with two incomes and have no children in college yet.
While they may have debts for cars, boats, etc., they take these
obligations more lightly than do older people. They may have gone
through a repossession or two and found the world did not end.
Duty, responsibility and dedication to the job are hardly a prevail-
ing conviction to most young people, although it certainly is to a
small percent of them. They are often well informed of opportunities, benefits and rights. Their confidence is high.

But most important, it is possible that a majority not only has
little fear of being fired, but *actually likes change, new situations*,
new friends, new challenges and new locations. Further, many are
convinced that the fastest way up the ladder is usually to switch
ladders, since the opening just above them in their present organizations is often blocked. But some other company almost certainly
has a vacancy. These individuals may frequently change jobs, voluntarily. Thus, just the possibility of a firing threat may be all it
takes to have them fly from the tree. Threats mean little.

*Case: My wife and I were staying at a motel in a city suffering
from high unemployment*—a town where jobs were rare, so job
loss should be a thing to fear. At breakfast, the young waitress
took our order, then disappeared. Ten minutes, twenty, thirty—
and finally the hostess appeared and calmly said. "I'm sorry, but
the assistant manager had a few strong words with your waitress
and she walked out. Now how did you say you wanted your eggs?"
Even when jobs are scarce, many people today do not fear job loss.
And no one seems very surprised.

*Where workers have high confidence, firing is a problem to the
boss*. Today's employees of all ages have increasing levels of self-
respect and confidence. In these circumstances, threats (veiled or
blatant) have somewhat less impact, for many reasons: *First*, the
person feels that he or she is a valuable, constructive employee, so
is very unlikely to actually get the axe. He feels the boss doesn't
want and can't afford to let him go. *Second*, if it should happen, he
or she believes that he can quickly get another job at the same
level or possibly higher.

And so, any use of the firing threat often results in *indifference, then disgust*. Later, resentment changes to resistance,
rebellion, retaliation and finally resignation. The threat hardly
achieved motivation.

On top of that, the supervisor now faces all sorts of *penalties to himself.* There are the possibilities of unpleasant scenes, disruptions of morale, static from the former employee's high-placed friends, union action and grievances. Even without these, he now has an empty slot where duties and activities are not getting done. Schedules are collapsing, and work is piling up. He must go through all sorts of paper work, advertising, recruiting, interviews, tests, reference checks, selection and (when someone is hired) training—plus long, low-efficiency learning periods. And, at any one of these steps, the whole thing may fall apart, and he must start all over again. This can—and does—go on for a year or more. Hardly a rewarding experience.

Net: The threat of firing folks is not all that high powered as a motivator. Firing can be momentarily fun and ego inflating, but in the end it is usually just a lot of work. Both the threat and the action are declining in clout. They can actually be counterproductive, causing more cost and trouble than they are worth. They are usually inefficient and ineffective and should be looked at as "the court of last resort." Since mid-1960, much better ways to motivate have been emerging.

Case: How a Department Head Paralyzed People with Fear

"This part of the office may be bugged," said the foreman to Sam, the new order clerk. "So be careful what you say. You could be going on tape. Some say the boss reviews the tape weekly. If you say bad things, you'll get canned." Some of the problems plaguing the order clerk were caused by the boss himself, but Sam was afraid to say this to anyone at anytime, for fear that the bugging story was true. He discovered that it is easy to say a place is bugged but hard to prove it isn't.

Slowly, work in that part of the office became more conservative. A strange ill-defined fear took hold of the staff. Costs rose; sales, profits, performance, motivation and morale dropped. But then things changed. Outsider Hank R. was appointed as the new department manager. It was immediately obvious to Hank that something was wrong. For some days, no one trusted Hank enough to tell him what it was, but he kept on gently inquiring and finally got the story. The problem was clear.

Hank looked into the matter thoroughly and learned that the

rumors were totally unfounded. He got the group together, right in the supposed bugged area. He candidly explained the rumors and what he had found. Hank stated that he wanted no part of such spy tactics, and if anyone knew now of any bugs or discovered them later, he wanted to know about them immediately—and they would be smashed.

Then Hank outlined the business procedures he hoped to see in the department, set ground rules, discussed the order clerk's troubles and other problems and listened to ideas, accepting some and rejecting others. He clearly stated areas over which he wanted to retain control.

Hank defused the fear situation, treated the circumstances, attacked the problem, and got agreement on the systems and programs for the group. Fear melted away, and dramatic constructive action grew with each passing week. To this day, former employees disagree as to whether the department really was bugged. But there is no argument that new professional methods used by Hank R. generated greatly improved performance.

Power Secrets for Eliminating the "Fear" Atmosphere

If we recognize that fear of humiliation and fear of firing are usually counter-productive, then elimination of these fears works to your advantage. Here are a few ways you can easily do this.

First, treat the circumstances, the symptoms, the hang-ups and uncertainties. If you are not sure about the approach, just ask yourself how you would like to be treated if you were this person. Try to get on a one-to-one basis with people. Find out what's bothering them, what's holding them back, what's got them angry or frozen. Discuss it; listen very carefully; show you really understand what they are saying. Perhaps play some back, just to prove it. Discuss solutions, options and ways to solve the problems. You don't really need to promise anything unless you want to—except that you will listen.

Then attack the problems, not the people. Once you find out what's causing the trouble, try to remove the obstacle or discover who can. Fear usually melts away. People do not hate or fear you. Why should they? They *want* to trust you and like you because you apparently can help them.

Third, aim the program at the goal. Remind them of your

mutual objectives. Discuss ways they can reach these goals. Consider their ideas for action. Pick some methods that make sense to you. Now fear is usually declining fast for two reasons: you haven't made threats, and you are using what stage magicians call "redirection." You are directing their attention to things of value, interest, use and excitement to them personally. Fear is frequently forgotten.

Five Ways to Increase Your Power by Setting Rules of the Game

There are several easy ways you can further reduce fear, avoid fear-type problems and stimulate motivation toward your goals. *First, establish boundaries*, territories, do's and dont's. Give people their own areas of responsibility, and specify which areas do not belong to them but to others, so they know *exactly where they stand*. Psychologically, this usually generates an immediate feeling of confidence, understanding, even appreciation and security.

Second, discuss any remaining or new problems, goals and options. This makes them feel they are not being put down or belittled or facing a threat of being humiliated.

Third, show understanding, compassion and appreciation for their inputs. Some of this may actually be a little stronger or greater than you really feel, but don't play it up and make a phony display. What you are really doing is showing respect for their creative effort and, more important, reducing or eliminating fear. How can you be afraid of someone who shows insight and appreciation for you, while simultaneously encouraging and motivating greater performance?

Fourth, show deliberate dislike of fear tactics, either by saying so or by criticizing some outsider who uses them—perhaps positively stating something about "the great advantages we can enjoy by trusting and feeling comfortable with each other." This has strong implications: no threats and no fear. Or show dislike of fear tactics by conspicuously not using fear when others obviously do in neighboring units or when you are urged by others to use fear. A sure-fire way to eliminate fear in the group is to simply allow small errors to go by with minor correction rather than major humiliation or threats of firing. There are dozens of other ways, but as an easy general rule, simply toss fear out of your bag of key techniques and your discard will soon be known and felt by all concerned. Motivation will nearly always expand.

Fifth, maintain your control of the situation. Some supervisors in an effort to "show they are good guys," relinquish all management. This produces chaos and anarchy, a condition that people dislike and one that actually generates fear, since they are uncertain as to what might happen next. People fear the unknown. They actually want some reasonable amount of control. So do you; so keep it. This in itself will stimulate motivation and also help you to direct it.

Thus, in a nutshell, to reduce fear and increase your motivation and your management of people, follow these five steps: (1) start with rules of the game; (2) discuss problems, goals and possible activities; (3) show that you appreciate these; (4) show that you dislike fear and prefer trust; and (5) maintain your control.

Case: Manager of Bottling Plant
Fired a Whole Department

"You're fired!" said Jack T., sales manager for a soda bottling plant. But he had just received quite a shock himself. Private detectives had reported that most of Jack's delivery truck drivers were stealing products from the company. "Since you see fit to swipe and re-sell pop, you can just turn in your uniform and get your check! You're through!" said Jack to one of the salesmen.

But stealing by others went on. Threats of firing and actual dismissal of several more men had no influence. Eventually, almost the total sales force had been replaced without much improvement. The detectives reported to Jack that the new men were just about as bad. The fear program was getting nowhere.

Then Jack called in the security representatives and a couple of trusted route supervisors and said, "Gentlemen, I'm at my wit's end. I don't know what to do to stop this stealing. Firing and threats of firing seem to have little effect." The detective spoke up. "Jack, I hate to tell you this, but you unconsciously cause part of the problem! Here's why: we find that about 25% of the people are honest, 25% are dishonest and 50% are about as honest as you make them. Frankly, some of your mechanical methods and procedures have not made them honest. You let them be dishonest. In a sense, you actually encourage it! Threats of firing and actual firing are just not enough to overcome seductive temptation."

Then Jack installed new systems that attacked the problems and their causes. He made honesty convenient and stealing difficult. He eliminated threats and firings. He set rules, discussed systems, applied new ideas, showed recognition for good work, yet kept management over key matters. The sales staff performance doubled and doubled again—and other firms actually tried to hire Jack's entire route truck sales force. Dropping fear tactics and using better methods got high results.

Summary: Replace Fear with Motivation

Fear, threats, humiliation and firing have been heavily used for centuries. These will continue, but they are losing their power as the world changes. Workers increasingly respond to fear by becoming demotivated, fighting or quitting. Younger workers, particularly, have high personal confidence and can easily go elsewhere. Replacement becomes a major and expensive project. Firing is often more trouble than it is worth. Other methods are growing in power. To eliminate the counter-productive, damaging "fear atmosphere," treat the hang-ups, attack problems not people and aim the program at your common goals. To replace fear with motivation, set rules, discuss problems and plans, show dislike of fear tactics and appreciation of good work and maintain your personal control over key matters.

4

Easy Ways to Make Respect Work for You

Here are three surprising power secrets. First, a little respect shown to others turns out to be a motivational tool of unexpected clout, sometimes a tremendous force in your hands. Second, the use of respect is not only almost childishly simple but quickly effective and low in cost. A third surprise is that you don't have to do much. In fact, people are often nearly dying to hand you considerable power in return for a little respect. But there are a few techniques you should use, or your best efforts will not only fail but boomerang badly, with harmful results.

How You Can Use "Respect for Others" to Build Your Own Power

A secret hunger exists. Of course, people don't go around saying, "I wish someone would respect me," and yet their actions speak volumes, loud and clear. Their dress, hair styles, cars, boats and homes are all at least partly a bid for respect. If you want to give them the acid test, look at them and ask yourself, "would they do all those things if they lived alone on a deserted island with no one there to impress?" Not likely. They are sending repeated, almost plaintively pathetic, non-verbal messages to "someone out there," saying "I wish someone would respect me."

This is a strong secret desire, not a weak one. Just notice how *much* money they spend to gain recognition and status. How *hard* they try and how *long* their effort continues—from childhood to old age. This is no passing fad, but a strong, abiding, deep instinct. It has existed right from early society where respect from associates had survival value. Loss of that respect could mean being driven from the tribe to perish in the wilderness. Give respect and you fill a deep, powerful need and instinct. You almost automatically become very important to the receiver.

Respect is a proven and powerful performer or motivator of activity over the centuries. As you show respect, you not only satisfy a secret hunger and fill a basic need, but you become a person for whom people want to perform and whom they want to please because that means continued and increased respect. You have used your respect to build your own prestige, power and status.

Case: How a Manager's Respect Motivated Progress

The problem, simply stated, was that a small department of a pen maker felt "inferior." They had low self-esteem, and so it was not surprising that they took little action and made little progress. Motivation was badly needed. Scott R., manager for a major supplier, began working almost daily with this small group. Scott had considerable training and experience, and his supplier company was very large and well regarded.

Scott showed respect for the little division, not only when he was with them, but when he was with other, larger parts of the company and when he was with his own company. He supported, spoke up for and defended the small department. He listened to them, made suggestions and complimented their strengths. He took a sincere, even dedicated, part in their meetings, field visits to dealers, training sessions, golf outings, banquets and other social affairs—always showing respect for each person's activities, decisions and accomplishments.

Results: the small group's own self-esteem began to grow. Their plans became more thorough and professional. Their reputation improved. They became proud of their performance and role with the company. Feelings of inferiority diminished. Scott's efforts were far from the only cause of this. Others took larger but similar roles, and together, their use of respect resulted in substantial constructive motivation. Man is a social animal who nearly always cares about and responds to what people think of him, and what he thinks of himself.

Why Everyone Secretly Wants
Your Approval and Respect

Is respect sought only by a few odd souls? Kooks? Or by a wide range and percent? It is sought by virtually all. Hardly anyone says, "No one respects me and I'm glad, because that's the way I want it!" *For example:* In a recent TV documentary, "Mr. Rooney Goes To Work," Rooney interviewed hundreds of employees, at all levels. In his words, he "discovered that nearly everyone finds some reason to believe what he or she does is at least a little bit special or *important and worthy of respect.*"

In the plush executive suite, the public bar, the assembly line, office, retail store, construction site, fox hole or even the death bed, *people seek respect.*

We live in a world where almost everyone *demands* respect. *For example:* You can get angry at the auto mechanic, postman, housewife, secretary, store clerk or trash collector. You can argue with them. But the instant you show disrespect for their jobs, you've just issued fighting words. The battle flags are out. You have declared war and possibly created a monster, if not a mortal enemy. A word or sign of disrespect, a raised fist, can become a permanent hurt, hate or source of violence. But a kind, respectful word often becomes an instant source of long remembered appreciation.

Many people secretly strive for this respect, but never get it. For example: Archie Bunker assumes respect from wife Edith and daughter Gloria but secretly and constantly seeks it from son-in-law Mike and from his own fellow workers on the loading dock. A clerk seeks it from the supervisor and the supervisor from the boss. But it is only rarely given and seldom in frequency or amount to fill the *daily* hunger. This creates disappointment and frustration.

The "Respect Gap"

Frustration is growing every year as many supervisors and managers, with increased personal conceit and disregard for others, move into higher positions. They show even less respect for employees—at the very time that these people have increased education, confidence and self-esteem, so want and feel that they deserve *increased* respect. Employee needs are up. Supervisor delivery is down. This leaves a "respect gap," a void crying to be filled. This is a golden opportunity for you to stand out and stand higher than other managers, by providing what people crave. It gives you better motivation and management of people, with little or no extra effort.

People actually die for respect from supervisors. A rather remarkable percent of the employees seems to be looking for "their father" . . . or more accurately their "ideal" father. *For example:* TV portrays Fred McMurray, the good old Dad in *My Three Sons*, along with other Dads in the *Waltons*, *Father Knows Best* and similar shows, as mature, intelligent, concerned, stable and interested—both earning the respect of their children and showing respect for those same children, a respect they desperately desire. Subordinates often will pay a high price for this.

For example: nearly all the millions of combat deaths from ancient to modern times occurred at least partly because the warrior wanted the respect of his commander and his companions. He did not want to be thought a coward, though coward he may have been. He would rather die in honor, to retain respect, than live in dishonor and disgrace.

In business, many a manager will and does work beyond sensible rules of good physical and mental health—excessive hours, bad eating and drinking habits, extreme anxiety—to gain and keep respect from subordinates, peers and supervisors. A large percentage of fatal heart attack victims in the 40 to 60 year age group falls into this category. They died with their boots on and they died largely to win respect.

A Three-Step Formula for Showing Respect

To what extent should your respect be genuine? The respect you show does not have to be of the deep seated, dedicated and religious variety to be effective. They key is an easy three-step formula: *First*, it should be at least reasonably sincere, true and honest. *Second*, it should be emphatically stated in a manner that is clear and understandable. *Third*, it should be fully developed—well filled out, not emaciated. An attempted show of respect that is artificial and dishonest, mumbled and hidden, puny and shrivelled is almost worse than none at all. It nearly becomes an insult. On the other hand, "You are doing a really good job, John. A check of many parts of your work proves this. I want to state my appreciation loud and strong to you, for all to know and hear." This is usually powerful medicine, generating favorable motivation.

People are amazingly sensitive. They can smell a phony miles away. If a supervisor trys to con or manipulate employees with artificial respect or with fake flowery words, the employees feel it and know it immediately. The effort doesn't motivate them, it demotivates them. They are not easily fooled.

Sincerety increases your power. Pick something for which you can really show respect, something they will recognize as correct. Be both emotional and logical. Try out your statements, perhaps quietly to yourself. If you really are sincere, but it doesn't sound that way, then either forget it for a while or change your approach, or you'll create more problems than you solve.

Secrets for Displaying Your Respect to Build Your Power

There are several simple, easy and relatively natural steps you can take. Most respect starts with a statement. But *first, list strengths* of the person you have in mind. Naturally, you want to know for what and why you might show any respect to begin with. So get some facts. Find out what the person does. Among these things, list those actions he or she does well. Pick these carefully, making sure they are items the person and associates will find believable and acceptable.

Second, express these simply and clearly. A complex or confused statement either is a totally unreceived, and so useless, message or sounds like you might be making a joke. This would have very negative results. Instead, recognize a fact and even give the employee a reputation to live up to. Say something like, "John, we notice that you have one of the best records for accuracy and quantity in our entire service unit this year (a fact that he and everyone else probably knows). We not only appreciate this, John, but we would like your advice as to how we can help others do the same." This has the ring of truth, particularly since you went further than just a compliment. John will believe you respect him and will usually be somewhat motivated, pleased, and even enthused and turned on.

Note that John's name was used freely, frequently, prominently and pointedly. We live in a society where people too often are "non-persons" or numbers, yet at this same moment thay seek individualism, identity and respect. Further, world famous people influencer Dale Carnegie says, "A person's name to him is the most beautiful sound in the English language."

Third, pick a right time—not a forced and phony moment, but an occasion when recognition is natural, such as when you are visiting with the group or something good has happened or you're recognizing others. Poor timing reduces motivation. Good timing enhances it.

Fourth, there are many ways to show respect other than a statement of praise. Sometimes these non-verbal expressions are even more effective: just listening and accepting opinions or statements, giving these real consideration. Avoiding criticism, condemnation or telling the employee he's wrong, treating a person as your equal or, in specialized matters, your superior. If you are clearly wrong on something, admit it promptly, clearly and emphatically. These usually generate notable respect motivation with very little effort from you.

How Showing Respect Builds Power

A major problem, or perhaps the great barrier to the manager's use of respect, is often the belief that the supervisor is reduced, lowered or somehow demoted by showing respect for peers or subordinates. "Hell, if I'm nice to those guys, next thing you know they'll walk all over me."

This is not at all true, if done right. When you show respect, you gain immediately in at least two ways. *First*, you show the group or the individual that you are a human, reasonable, concerned *friend* who appreciates them. In short, a rare cat . . . filling a real need.

Second—and this can be very important—you automatically place yourself at an increased level of *authority*, responsibility and power, when you pay a compliment and show respect. To most people you must be a person of substantial rank to take such a step.

To other people, you must be a "BIG" person in heart, humility and generousity to do such a thing. Either way, you gain. Either way, you are more important, more influential and more desirable to know and to serve.

A third point to consider is that you can and should end up with increased control, by not going too far, but instead by using a middle ground. Many supervisors think that there is no such mid-point—nothing between "haughty executive position" on the one hand and "kissing their muddy boots" on the other hand. Your best bet is to step down in the mud, shake their hand, get some dirt on your shoes (you won't get infected) and then climb back out of the trench. You made your point beautifully, but you are still the supervisor, a bigger one.

More Secrets You Can Use to Gain Power Through Respect

Here are some of the most effective techniques for motivating with respect that are used by successful professionals. (You'll note there are a lot of rererences to "I" in these, but always followed closely by a reference to "you.")

First, "I am listening to you." Here the supervisor or manager simply stays quiet. This can be rather easy, since people frequently have urgent things in mind. They are often ready to talk, and they mainly want someone to listen. You don't have to do much, just be still and look into their eyes. Follow, understand and nod. This alone builds motivation.

Second, "I have confidence in you." Another easy, natural step. You have already listened, and now you are standing behind your people. Did we say earlier that people look for the ideal father? You are being just that, respecting them, believing in them and in what they told you; so motivation increases.

Third, "I know you do well on your job because I have seen the figures." You are not only mentioning a specific, but you show you cared enough to do your homework. Your sincerity increases because you went beyond simple words. You really took time to look into a person's performance. Some people's hearts melt, right here. At the least, they appreciate what few "fathers" bother to do. You made an effort. Your motivation power grows still further.

Fourth, "I am proud of you." This means you are openly

endorsing the person, or appear to be. You are standing up to be counted and even staking your hard earned reputation on him. If other expressions develop little positive reaction, this one almost always gets up at least some steam. If you have any regard for yourself, how could you possibly not respect and value someone who says, "I am proud of you"? Here is an ideal blend of logic supporting your position plus emotion or human dedication. You have applied a near ultimate accolade of respect, usually producing strong motivation.

Three Extra Secrets Why This Increases Your Power

If you are familiar and feel comfortable with the mechanics of how these tools work, you will usually find them easier to use.

Your respect builds confidence. When you show regard for a person or his or her status, "turf," position or performance, you are reinforcing his own hopes, dreams, beliefs and even convictions. You support him, you join him, you are one of his tribe, team or army. Instinctively, he wants to regard you as a friend and usually has a desire to repay you with some sort of support.

You also build his reputation, his status. It is a matter of great pride to employee "A" if manager "B" shows respect to "A." People "C, D and E" all see this, and their regard for employee "A" goes up. Further, if manager "B" happens to be a person of some status, importance or authority, then this builds "face" even more strongly for person "A." Still further (and here's some of the pay-off), "A" now wants to support and build supervisor "B" to look as good as possible. Then "B's" respect has still greater value, and "A" looks even better in the area of "face" or reputation with "C, D and E."

How Your Respect Becomes
a Self-Fulfilling Prophecy

You'll recall that the philosopher said, "I think, therefore I am." Well, the self-motivator says, "I think I can, therefore I really can." Your respect helps people become more self-confident, to believe more in themselves. This is a major step toward constructive action. The thinking can make it so.

How Bassett Furniture Used Respect to Become America's Largest

The problem was simply one of numbers. Bassett was only one of four thousand furniture makers, many clustered in the Southeast. Bassett was founded mainly by a few folks from the hill country and the Piedmont area. Many felt a great unfulfilled need, a hunger for respect, recognition and status.

The Bassett family realized that and, over a period of years, trained their employees in a wide range of skills. Together they developed their own new ideas and listened to the suggestions of the employees. Managers showed respect for employee innovations, efforts and accomplishments. A fierce loyalty, dedication and devotion developed among them because they realized their supervisors were sincere in their regard. Employees put forth great effort to earn, retain and enlarge the respect they craved and enjoyed. The supervisors lost no power by their expressions of respect, but, in fact, gained in status and influence, at very little cost in time, money or effort.

They built a growing confidence, reputation, pride and a habit of success. They told their people they were winners; the employees believed this; and in time they became winners.

Today Bassett is the largest furniture manufacturer in the nation. Respect shown people in a little town tucked away among the low green hills of Virginia helped generate a self-fulfilling prophecy.

Summary: How Respect, a Power Secret, Builds Your Influence

When you show simple respect for people, you satisfy a strong but secret hunger. History proves that this has motivation power. Nearly everyone wants your approval. Many try for this, yet never get it. And today's manager often gives *less* respect while the employee feels he or she deserves *more*. This creates a "respect gap" that you can fill and use to gain motivation. Your respect should be as genuine as possible. It can build your power, if you acknowledge really worthy performance. Express this simply and clearly, picking the right time and showing respect in several ways, both verbal and non-verbal. Done right, this should not humiliate or weaken you, but add strength. Say: "I'm listening, I have confidence. You are doing well, I am proud of you." This builds the employee's self-conficence and reputation, and it builds your influence and often becomes a self-fulfilling prophecy.

5

Practical Secrets for Using Meetings As Powerful Motivators

Many top managers have discovered the power secret of effective meetings. Gatherings of people, properly planned and presented, provide strong motivation. But this usually means doing a little groundwork and then checking during the meeting to see that it is geared towards stimulating action. Simple mechanics need to be carried out correctly. To begin with, miserable surroundings can shoot the whole effort down in flames. You should start the meeting with a highly effective motivational tool: "common problems in our mutual situation." There are easy techniques to do this effectively. Next, you can build mutual goals. Take people to the top of the mountain and let them enjoy the breathless and exhilarating view of what might be. There are techniques that encourage them to paint their own picture and decide on their own hopes, dreams and rewards. There are methods you can use to encourage such goal setting, and these methods often bring more motivation than you had expected. Then you can stimulate strong development of programs, plans and schedules—and you can motivate people to take aggressive steps to reach goals. You can lock up your whole project into an action-charged schedule when you use the right re-cap techniques. This chapter should give you at least a dozen such powerful motivation secrets. Here is a case history which, though it involved a large company, can give you practical proven methods you can use even for meetings of three or four people.

Case History: A Soap Manufacturer Plans a $20 Million Brand

Situation: One of the world's largest and best run companies (according to several surveys, including Fortune's "500") for some years had been watching the deodorant market. A large part of the nation's 70 million homes were buying underarm deodorants, and the annual dollar volume was in the hundreds of millions. The company decided to introduce a contender in this product area.

Objectives: Now . . . the big project was to get insight into problems, targets, plans, schedules . . . and generate constructive action—in short, to use a meeting to motivate. And to develop concrete dollar results. In this case, the goal was to generate at least $20 million in factory sales the first year.

Strategy for the meeting consisted of several steps: (1) A meeting plan was reviewed with Curtis B. (brand manager designate) and Jim K. (advertising agency account executive). They outlined, on one page, a "pre-meeting summary" of the situation, the problem and several goal options. This had a valuable motivating effect on the meeting, as you will see. They also listed ideas and a simple agenda. Much pre-meeting debate went on over this. The desire to cover everything in the first meeting, to cross all the t's and dot all the i's, took time and conflicted with the need to limit the meeting to one day. Curtis and Jim needed several hours of planning to juggle and fit all the items into the time available. Some pet subjects had to be trimmed back and some dropped, especially if there was going to be time for discussion, idea exchange, input and "two-way streets." Jim K. was the chief "chopper," insisting that items be trimmed or taken out so that the meeting would work well. (2) Mechanics were checked. A large, beautiful conference room was reserved. The room was comfortable, quiet and away from phones, and it had a flip chart and facilities to pin up drawings, show slides and write lists (on a chalkboard). (3) Seven team members were carefully selected, invited well ahead of time, confirmed with a short note and rechecked by phone a few days early to be sure all could attend.

But the meeting began as a disaster! The best laid plans did not fully materialize. One key member could not be there, but sent a substitute. Two were sick at the last moment and sent no delegates. The beautiful meeting room got pre-empted by a more important group. The agenda was not typed in time. The meeting had to be held in a very small room with poor light, bad ventilation and rickety, hard chairs. But cool heads, common sense and determination had some influence.

The meeting began with the outline of the problem, opportunities and some optional goals. The "pre-meeting summary" held the group together and gave them a vital beginning point. Eventually, the agendas arrived. Jim and Curtis encouraged discussion and agreement as to the central problem, and this was written on the chalkboard. The leading brand became the "one to beat and the one to hate" . . . but also the one to watch. Slides were shown of that brand's packages and store displays. Goals were discussed. Since there were several options, this resulted in much discussion, interest and involvement . . . generating increased motivation. A goal of 10% share of market was agreed upon as the group objective. Ideas were listed and accepted for strategy to reach the goal. The jobs were divided up. Even those not present were given parts to play. A time schedule was outlined. The meeting closed with a verbal re-cap by Jim K. and Curtis B.—covering the problem, goal, plan, delegation and schedule.

The next day, Jim K. drafted a summary of almost two pages covering the highlights they discussed in the re-cap. Particular emphasis was on facts, goals and a schedule as to who did what, when and where. This was sent to those attending, and to those who had planned to attend, plus various supervisors and others. Recipients were told, "If anyone wants changes in this material, please let us know promptly." Only one absentee requested an adjustment in his assignment. Otherwise, all accepted. That locked things in.

Results: A long series of projects and research was done including brand name and package design tests. Initially, the package selected was a cream, with roll-on and aerosol forms to follow later. Some test markets were opened, and the brand exceeded the 10% objective. The product was then introduced into major parts of the U.S. and finally nationally—developing over $20 million in sales. It all started with the use of a well planned and executed meeting that motivated highly constructive action.

Secrets for Using Meetings to Build Powerful Action

Every year or so a researcher comes up with a fact which seasoned professional managers are painfully aware of: "Meetings are both the most productive and the least productive devices of modern business." They sometimes generate highly effective action. Yet, other times they take up two or three full days a week and simply pour huge quantities of expensive man-hours down the proverbial rat-hole. The major difference between the successful meetings and the disasters is one word, "planning."

Seven General Power Secrets for Meetings

Your meeting plan should include at least these seven subject points. If so, you will enjoy much better motivation, effective use of valuable time and positive results from all concerned.

1. Your problems, situation and reason for the meeting.
2. Goals to accomplish at meeting.
3. Methods appropriate to reach these goals.
4. Agenda of subjects to discuss. Perhaps with time limits.
5. Attendees carefully selected.
6. A call for preparation before the meeting.
7. Acceptance, confirmation and follow-up of attendance.

Let's look at each of these:

1) *Your problems, situation and reason for the meeting.* Here you simply ask yourself, "What are the conditions or difficulties facing me?" You might want to make a short list, if only in your mind. Then you should decide why you are using the meeting technique. That is, why not use some other device? If the meeting looks like your best approach, fine. Go ahead with it.

2) *Goals to accomplish at the meeting* are additional things to consider. What is it you want the meeting to do? Inform? Discuss? Make a plan? Motivate? Perhaps all of these. When your objective is clearly in mind, then you can design your program to reach your target.

3) *Ideas for methods or projects to reach your objective* should be listed ahead of time. *For example*, your goal may be to plan and motivate. Some ideas for doing this might be to encourage suggestions and get agreement on several of these. In that case, your plan should include time for suggestions, discussions and commitment.

4) *An agenda of subjects to discuss*, even a simple one page list is usually very helpful and motivates the group toward doing

the things you itemize. It's strange how a list is a compulsion to most people, pushing them toward checking every element. If you include a time for each item (such as 9 A.M. for facts, 9:30 for goals, etc.) this often motivates more rapid action, since participants know their time is limited.

Case: One group that switched over from an unstructured meeting to use of a simple agenda found that they doubled the output of their monthly meetings.

5) *Attendees are worth giving careful thought.* Generally, you should invite only four types: (1) contributors, (2) endorsers, (3) action takers or (4) folks who need to know. Avoid over-attendance by duplicates of these or just the curious, the spectators or "professional meeting attenders." An easy way to be sure you have invited the right people is to ask: Is there someone expected who can contribute, endorse or act in each part of the program? Second, look at every prospective attendee and ask: Is there a good reason for this person attending? Third, have we missed any key person? In this way, you can be more certain that you are motivating the right people with your meeting. The most common error is inviting too many people—including some who just attend to enjoy the show as a sort of break or diversion from other work.

6) *A request for attendees to prepare* before the meeting is an exceptionally useful motivation device. They spend *their own time* doing their thinking, rather than using super-expensive meeting time. Here you simply include a request saying something like, "Please come to the meeting: (a) with any suggestions you may wish to offer; (b) with any questions you may have to ask of others; and (c) prepared to answer questions you think people may ask in your general area." Such a request starts a suprising amount of thinking, since each attendee now knows these points have been asked and all know they may personally be expected to contribute. This makes for a lively, better prepared and more highly motivated meeting.

Case: A sales manager who used to send out only a brief meeting invitation note started adding a one paragraph description of "this week's key problem." Meeting attendance, enthusiasm, motivation and results greatly increased almost immediately.

7) *Acceptance, confirmation and follow-up* are simple steps that you should consider to increase the commitment and involvement of the attendees. This might be done by phone, by letter or in

person, making sure they have the invitation and the agenda, and plan to attend or send a delegate. This has the added motivational value of reminding the group, showing your personal interest and often stimulating more pre-meeting preparation.

Seven "Mechanical" Secrets for Building Power with Meetings

Here we are talking about such routine things as the room, seating arrangements, heating and cooling. In the excitement of planning a meeting, these basics are often ignored by unskilled managers—but not by the successful professionals who long ago learned (sometimes the hard way) that bad room facilities can ruin a meeting.

Case history: I once held an important meeting, involving many thousands of dollars, to be held in an open area near the client's production line, in Orangeburg, S.C. On the day of the meeting, some guy nearby was banging on large steel industrial drums much of the time. It was not only disturbing but disastrous. The meeting was a total failure.

Mechanically, there are dozens of things you should be sure are working in your favor. Here are the seven key elements:

1) *Comfort.* Be sure the table and chairs are at least adequate, the room reasonably well lit, ventilated, heated or air-conditioned, close to coffee and restrooms but away from phones, traffic, typewriters and people banging on drums.

2) *Supplies.* Have paper, pens, extra agendas and ashtrays available. People sometimes forget to bring their agendas. These help stimulate and guide interest. Also, as people "turn on" they often want to make notes and smoke.

3) *Speakers.* If you have guests scheduled to make a presentation or talk to the group, make sure they know the audience, background, objectives, their subjects, how much time they have, when they go on and key points to make in motivating the group. A good device is to hold either a practice session or at least a brief "walk-through" of the presentation. A rotten, off-key, out-of-sync speaker can ruin a meeting. But a good one can build big motivation, partly because he or she is a third party, who has no apparent axe to grind but can speak about key points you pre-selected.

4) *Graphics.* Psychologists say that about 80% of what we learn comes through our eyes. So if you want to impress, convince and motivate the group, try to have at least a few pictures, graphs, slides, films, charts, samples, displays or something to look at. (Incidentally, this visual impact is why a live speaker is so much more effective than a tape recording—and why visuals or handouts often multiply the value of the speaker.) Be sure you have proper light, projector, screen, cards, wall plugs, etc. Double check all of this at least twice beforehand. If and when equipment fails, you will lose the spark of enthusiasm. When things go well you double the excitement, input and motivational flame.

5) *Begin by stating the purpose* of the meeting; give a clear expression of why you got together and what you hope to accomplish. Be sure this is thoroughly understood.

Case: One supervisor pinned up a sign saying, "Our goal for today: fewer rejections, more break time."

6) *An opportunity for discussion*—for opinions both in favor of and against an idea or proposal—is another way to stimulate and motivate people. It develops excitement, starts creative juices flowing and gets personal involvement. The best time to do this is after an idea has been suggested. Just say something like, "What do you folks think of this?" A key factor: be sure to allow enough time for discussion during the meeting. People do not like to be "talked at" for 40 minutes. It is much better to present ideas for 20 minutes and let people ask questions and give their opinions for 20 more minutes.

7) *The simple mechanics of keeping discussion on track* and on schedule have surprising motivational value. People who want to get up and "have a go" at things get quite frustrated at wandering, meandering, aimless, time wasting meetings. But they turn-on to well ordered, reasonably controlled ones. This means you should sometimes step in and say, "Folks, we are getting a little off the track. Please, let's get back and finish this subject, or go on to the next item."

Another Power Secret:
Label Your Problem As "the Situation"

Here's an excellent and easy motivation tool: definition of the problem, the enemy, something to hate; description and discussion of the thing that is causing the trouble.

History, politics, sports and business all have thousands of examples here. To motivate people, find a villain. The sharper and clearer the image, the stronger the psyched-up feeling. People do not function 100% by reason; it's more like 50% logic, 50% emotion. Sometimes it's nearly all one or all the other. (Just as a person probably does not succeed 100% on his own, but, as Machiavelli says, "about half by ability and half by luck.") So start with reason and move to emotion.

Millions of people have been motivated to incredible heights and sacrifice by focusing attention on "the problem." In the Crusades, people died for it. Soldiers fought tyranny; police fight crime; agencies fight poverty. Each highly motivated group nearly always has a vibrantly clear image of "the problem." You can stimulate similar action, drive and determination as you develop the living picture.

Case: A baked goods company holds regular meetings, where they show Nielsen graphs of progress made by competitors. This nearly drives attendees up the wall with enthusiasm to get out and do better.

How can you build a crisp, clear image of the problem? Begin with the group. After you have reviewed the situation, ask the group members what they think is the key problem. Listen to them. Don't agree too quickly, at least not until you hear suggestions that closely match the facts and the major trouble as you and others know it.

Now, when they get closer to the real problem, *show strong agreement* with at least that part of their statement that matches the true situation. *For example*, "Right, John! I sure agree with the part where you said that our problem is to improve customers' awareness and opinion of us." John may also have said, "Our problem seems to be that we have a poor computer credit print out." But if you know this is mostly wrong or only a minor side issue, you simply don't mention that when you give him your strong support and agreement.

Next, someone else may add a suggestion. If it is totally out of line with facts, ignore it or simply say in a pleasant tone of voice, "Well maybe. What other ideas do we have?" Encourage and listen for the next suggestions. When someone says something that does fit well, then again provide your rapid and strong supporting agreement. The group members are building your mutual target, "the problem." They are handing you the parts of the enemy. You are applying judicious editing and putting it all together. But in the end it is totally made up of their contributions—ideas they submitted and you accepted.

Now, get emotional, deliberately. You've been logical long enough. Build some steam, excitement and enthusisiam concerning the problem. Particularly, try to find some element of the situation that really seems to be hurting, perhaps both your group and other people, like your customers. This can greatly increase motivation. There are few things that excite people so much as a problem or danger or "enemy in our midst," whether real or imaginary, that needs correcting. (Like "gas guzzlers" or stream pollution.)

Secret Ways You Can Focus Attention on "Their Goals"

Once you have agreed on your mutual problem, then you should promptly concentrate the group's attention on the goals you wish to reach.

Your job should now be getting easier, because finding the solution to "our" problem can now become "our" goal. Ask for the group's opinions on this goal. *For example:* "Don't you think a major target should be to make people aware of us?" Few will disagree, based on the earlier discussion. "Shouldn't another goal be to build a favorable image of our company, products and services?" Again, you should get agreement. "And surely, another should be to try and equal or exceed the leading brand." How can they argue? This is motherhood, baseball and apple pie. Note that these are strongly "leading" questions. They suggest and almost demand the answer.

Listen for suggestions. Some members of the group may recommend that "awareness should be our first target." And that makes sense, since you can't have a good image until your customers are at least aware that you exist. Others may say, "Next, let's get a good reputation." Agree with them, if it fits a reasonable pattern. Others may say, "Then our objective should be to beat the top brand." And again, this is reasonable, since you have awareness, then a good reputation, and then you can get sales volume beyond the leading brand. Notice that your concentration on a goal has motivated strong interest. If you also show respect for the goal suggestions made, you will usually turn on increased group enthusiasm at no cost. Again, you are motivating without money. But you also gain in other ways.

Your respect and the resulting activity will generally stimulate increased thinking, involvement, desire and competitive spirit. This can result in better designed goals and larger objectives, which they, the group members, spontaneously and on their own have set for themselves. They are reaching for the stars and have made a far stronger commitment than if you, personally, had set the targets. It now becomes "our" goal, theirs and yours.

Power Secrets for Using
Programs and Plans in Meetings

Up to this point you have reached agreement on "our problem" and "our goal." The next logical step is to *make plans* to reach that target. If you followed a method even close to that outlined in the first part of this chapter, chances are the group is already starting to suggest plans, steps and programs. In fact, that's a common problem you should guard against; meetings that start out with people suggesting strategies long before anyone ever agreed on "our" real problems or the "goals" we want to reach are off to a shaky start.

If you see that sort of thing happening, your best bet is to say something like, "It's good to think about programs but this will be easier if we first agree on a few facts of our situation and our objectives. Then we can look at plans to help us get there." This usually works pretty well.

And then, the time has come to speak of programs. If these are not already pouring out, you can usually release the flow by saying, "Now, what steps should we take to reach our objectives?" This generally gets at least one or two ideas. If these have any merit at all, you might jot them down on a board or flip chart. This will usually stimulate more.

Have a check list on hand or in your head. For example: the five W's are often a natural action plan outline. Who should do what, when, where, why and how. You might ask, "Do we need new systems in the way we purchase or package our product, or present our service or promote our group reputation? How about price, product design, public relations, advertising or customer location? Introductory offers? Sampling? Customer opinion of company or brand? Dealer or distributor opinion of these? Market test programs? Budget plans? Quality control? Supervision? Legal elements? Records and forms? Salesmen and production training? Delivery? Displays?" These are just a few thought-starters for your list.

Divide and delegate your questions among those key people who have charge of those areas. For example, delegate product and quality control questions to the production person, and advertising, selling, publicity, sampling and market tests to the sales and marketing manager. Break the projects down into manageable elements. Then talk to those people. Ask their opinions and suggestions for action.

The Schedule Secret— How It Builds Motivation Power

At this point you have identified "the problem" and "our objectives" and together you have selected "strategy" elements for your plan and program. Now all that remains is to build a time frame—a schedule.

The essence of a schedule is who does what—and when. It should be a practical list of reasonable steps and reachable dates.

How to decide "who" does what: Go to the division of projects that you wisely made among people—the step you just took in dividing and delegating questions. Certain people are clear and obvious choices to handle specific projects. They are even thinking of and maybe discussing these assignments among themselves or with you. Production and purchasing people are thinking about product. Sales people are thinking of selling. Bookkeepers are thinking of records. You might say something like, "Each of you has your own area of expertise. Now please think about what steps you feel you should take." Such techniques usually start personal commitment without making a big issue of it.

How to set "when": This can be fairly simple. Decide as early as practical what it is that has #1 priority—what probably needs to be done first. These are often the things that are the most difficult or take the greatest lead time (like product or package or service design, displays, some kinds of advertising), or that must be done before other things can happen (like budget appropriation). Then when you start trying for agreement on date schedules, pick the long term lead time projects first. "Production manager, when can we have product?" or, "Package supplier, when can we have design and finished supplies delivered?" Let them tell you. Then adjust to fit realities or urgent needs.

Schedules have secret power because: (1) Now you have *agreement* as to who does what and when. (2) Now each person has a *target* to shoot at and a deadline to meet. (3) Each one knows exactly *what action* to take next as opposed to wandering around aimlessly wondering what to do. But perhaps most important, (4) each person knows that *everyone else* is aware of his schedule and is depending on him. If he fails, he fails out there in front of God and everyone. If the project collapses, he just might get the whole blame. It's musical chairs, and he doesn't want to be caught standing when the time runs out and the music quits.

Further, schedules get people even more deeply, personally and directly involved in action, boosting their insight, enthusiasm and motivation. There is an old Chinese proverb: "I hear and I forget. I see and I remember. I do and I understand."

A Final Power Secret to Meetings: the Re-cap

The most successful professionals end the meeting by going back to the objectives. They restate the purpose. They briefly summarize what was decided about problems, goals, strategy and schedule. They close with a statement as to the next steps each person should take. This buttons things down and clarifies the picture. People leave with a good feeling and understanding of where they are now and where they are going to go next.

The following case history, while it got large results, really involved only a dozen people and can apply to meetings of much fewer people and smaller projects. The case is given in fairly broad detail and scope so you can easily see and select elements you might put to practical use. The case does not necessarily follow every detail, in order, as described in the previous pages, since few actual cases do that—any more than you should do it. Examples often have unusual or unique aspects and imperfections, just as your own situations will have, but the case will give you a dozen workable ideas.

Case History:
How Meetings Produced $30 Million

Situation: A large percent of the population was becoming highly conscious and concerned about weight, figure and calories. So this soft drink was designed to taste good but have almost "0" calories. It was introduced in many markets with good success, but one large area with a population of over 20 million had not yet been opened. This territory was managed by a new supervisor, Scott R. The opportunity here was great. But the problem was that most of the employees in that market did not believe that consumers in the area were ready for or interested in such a product. Employees also did not believe they knew how to handle such a massive project. Scott did considerable checking and market research, which showed that (1) the market was receptive, but (2) the employees were certainly right about one thing: the company was far from ready to launch such a major program.

Objectives: (1) To get fully prepared. (2) To introduce the product into this large market successfully. (3) To reach a sales level of $30 million retail. (4) To use a series of plans meetings to prepare and motivate all employees.

Strategy for meeting and plans: This was a two step program: (1) Scott planned and held meetings with people in other older markets who already knew how to accomplish the project. (2) Then he had meetings with people in the big new market who were needed to do the job. The first meeting series with those who "knew how" involved group sessions, questions and answers. Scott simply "sat at their knee," asked their advice, listened carefully and recorded their comments.

Then the big "plans meeting" was designed. The several prime supervisors, managers and foremen were invited from the following: plant, sales force, accounting department, advertising department, quality control, chemists, treasurer, purchasing, agent, transport, truck loaders, dispatchers, suppliers, lawyer, etc. The meeting room mechanics insured good comfort, isolation, quiet, light and ventilation. A one page confidential agenda was provided several days in advance, showing subjects to cover: objectives of the meeting, problems, goals, strategy and the role of each person.

People were asked to think about this major new project and come to the meeting prepared to (1) contribute some suggestions, (2) ask questions and (3) answer queries from others. By meeting day, the preparation, interest and enthusiasm were already at a high level.

First, the problem of low sales and missed opportunity was strongly emphasized. Soon everyone present could see where this was depriving them personally—and their families—of bonuses, pay raises and security. Two competitors were shown to be the brands most seriously hurting company progress—they were "the bad guys." Fear was used, but not in terms of threats or humiliation. It was used in terms of danger from a problem; it was used to motivate isolation of the key troubles that needed resolving. Soon, there was strong agreement as to the situation, the key mutual problem and the competitor.

Goals were reviewed by the group. An objective of a $30 million sales level was tentatively accepted as a working target.

Then came decisions on action plans and strategy needed to reach that goal. Each area was discussed, to match each person present: plant, sales, accounting, advertising, quality, funding, purchasing, supplies, law, etc. Each manager made suggestions and asked questions in these areas . . . finally agreeing on the steps to be taken. The meeting lasted a full day, plus half of the next day. But in the end, everyone knew the problem, goal, strategy, his role and the general time schedule. This developed a strong sense of confidence in the total team and in oneself—plus a growing enthusiasm and conviction that, together, they could reach their objectives.

The results: the schedule was followed fairly closely, although unforseen problems (these almost always happen) caused some changes in time and methods. The program was launched. The product and package were developed and produced. Delivery and displays were made. Advertising and sampling started, and sales volume exploded dramatically—just as those who "knew how to do it" said it would. Scott and his group did not hit the goal of $30 million in the first year, due to weather, sudden, unexpected, strong competition, some dealer problems and other unforseen difficulties. But the second year exceeded goal (which may show that things don't always happen quite as fast as we expect, but if we don't plan for action nothing much happens at all). In this case a

well prepared and properly executed meeting, well developed programs, confidence and enthusiasm motivated hundreds of people to
get the job done.

A Summary of Power Secrets
Using Meetings to Motivate

Your plan should outline the meeting's problems, goals, projects, agenda, attendees, preparation and follow-up. Mechanics
should include a check up for good facilities, supplies, speakers and
graphics. You should start with "the purpose of the meeting,"
allow time for discussion and make an effort to keep things on the
track. Find the key problem. Get agreement on goals and methods
to reach these. Then outline a time schedule and close with a re-cap
summarizing key points, decisions and what each person plans to
do next.

6

How to Use Planning and Time Management As Key Managerial Tools

Plans and time management are two major secret power sources. Small group problem solving is an interesting and exciting technique, all by itself, that can greatly motivate people. It does this by getting them directly involved in planning their lives. There are dozens of techniques you can use to do this. And, they work even with only one, two or three people, not just in large, formal meetings. One of the key secrets is to start by getting the problem working for you, not against you. Then you can use techniques to build your status and influence and establish mutual respect between you and your group—this usually has remarkable motivational power. You can generate ideas, options, alternative courses of action and a ranking or evaluation of these ideas. Then, once you have a ranking, there are simple ways to make practical application of the secret S-O-S formula. You can take the "situation" and apply it to your "objectives" and get the person or group to build his or their "strategy." If you just use a couple of these techniques and secrets, they will help you firm up next steps, build pride, confidence and enthusiasm—not phony enthusiasm, but real conviction that the people concerned can do the job. They suddenly know "where we go from here" and they believe in it. You have made

81

them personally involved. Then you help the group planning by suggesting several ways to manage their time,
so that they don't work harder, but work "smarter"—
getting more done per hour invested, at no extra work.
More than that, this better management of time can
change work attitudes and even re-cycle difficult
obstructionists into "born again" disciples, preaching the
gospel of enthusiasm and motivation in your belief. We
will look at how this works, the secret mechanics you can
use and the practical application of these ideas in real life
cases.

Case History: Respect and Priorities
Get a New Soap Package
and Sharp Sales Jump

Phil J. got a telegram: "Urgent. Our detergent sales off 8% in
each of three Midwest markets. Find cause immediately. Prepare
plan within ten days."

A research man was sent to check these various markets.
Over and over the dealers said, "Your competing brands have
plastic bottles, not glass like your product. Women like the plastic.
So do we. So we feature it on displays. Do you want to know what's
hurting your sales? You just found it!"

At one giant supermarket, the manager took the survey guy
down one aisle to see one of the bottles that had just crashed to the
floor. "How would you like to try and swab up a pint of thick
detergent with a bucket of water? Get the message?"

A plans meeting was held at the home office. The researcher
recommended a switch to plastic. "That will cost over $1 million!"
the brand manager said. "But our objective might be a 4.5% share
or $10 million increase." The problem, goal and options were clear.
The research analyst's proposals got high respect and consideration. They made their plan, set their priorities and carefully managed their time to execute their program.

Results: a plastic test market was recommended and opened,
and share hit 4.8%. Later the package was introduced nationally
and reached these market levels within 18 months. Years later, the
brand is still near that level, recording profits, largely because the
little group was motivated with the situation-objective-systems or
S-O-S plan. The group members were encouraged to manage their

time and efforts in the light of objectives. They exceeded their goal, reaching the $48 million retail sales level.

Power Secret: "To Solve Our Problem, Let's Make a Plan!"

Sometime in the next week or two, you will want to motivate just one person—to convince him, stimulate him and evoke an active, positive, constructive response from him. One of your very best bets is to use the planning procedure. People like it and respond well, once they get started and see how easy it is. Begin by saying something like, "let's make a plan and start with a brief look at our problem, goal and steps we might take."

"Why make a plan?" he may ask. Answer: "You wouldn't build a house or a garage or even take a trip without a program. A man without a plan is a ship wandering aimlessly without a port. Columbus didn't just sail, he sailed west."

There's Secret Power in Problem Review

Anytime you want to begin motivation of a person through planning participation, one of your easiest pathways is a quick look at the problem. There are various reasons why this works, and several techniques you can use.

First, it works because a short review of the situation is the natural place to start. It makes sense, chronologically. It is probably the reason or at least one reason why a plan is needed in the first place. Your best technique may be to say something like, "Let's you and I take a brief look at the problem facing us and see if we agree on the situation, OK?"

Second, chances are that the person, or small group, is *already thinking about* the problem or difficulty. They may have already jumped into the system. But if they did that, they certainly must have already considered the problem. And so you both really are on the same wave length, looking at the same problem and thinking the same thoughts. Your comments are likely to meet with recognition, familiarity and acceptance. Your technique might be to say something like, "It looks like our problem is basi-

cally low sales, or low profit or high cost or low spirits, and one of
the problems is a defect in "x" or "y," does that make sense to
you?"

Third, problem review is both an easy thing to do (since you
start from things already known) and it is *a launching platform* to
next steps. It permits the good feelings of early agreement and
solidarity before you march onward. Your technique: "Good, then
we agree on our common enemy, the brand to beat, or problem to
solve, so now let's look at goals and steps to take."

Recognition of common "objectives" should be fairly easy at
this point, since you are united as to the key trouble, and targets
are usually some statement about solving the trouble. You can toss
out some goal possibilities for the person's consideration. You will
usually get immediate agreement on at least one or two.

Now move to "system." Suggest some possible steps or options, in view of the problem and goals. Or, ask for their strategy
ideas. You may even say, "You were suggesting some steps a little
earlier, before we agreed on problems and objectives. Do you still
like those steps? Shall we include them in our plan?" If you ask this
question with honesty, fairness and a level voice, you will usually
get a response like, "Yes, I still think we should change our package, or launch new publicity, etc."

Your Respect Secretly Magnifies Your Power

Showing respect for ideas immediately gives you all kinds of
advantages and motivation spurs, needles and even rockets. Here
is where we can take chapter 4 on "Respect" and apply it directly
to practical personal or group planning for added motivation.

Show respect to each person. Why? Because most people have
a secret hunger that you can satisfy in return for their cooperation.
They want the regard and appreciation of their peers, associates or
supervisors. You can give this, at almost no cost, and it is easy to
do. One technique is to simply listen and be considerate, gracious
and polite. This is especially easy and effective, as you see and
select ideas that have merit and agree with them. The fact that you
listened and respected their thoughts often means as much as your
agreement. (Conversely, you can agree in an unpleasant degrading

way . . . "I'm surprised you had the brains to think of that" . . . and gain nothing. Even lose ground.)

Your show of respect should not humiliate you, but strenthen you. You might say. "Your statement of our real problem sure sounds right to me," or, "I agree 100% with you on our goals," or, "that idea of yours for a solution seems darn good." Many pseudo-sophisticated supervisors think that means you are showing weakness, since you "aren't leading, ordering, directing or dictating to your inferiors."

People who think that are neither good manager/supervisors nor well informed in human motivation. The highest authorities of government, management and even religion long ago discovered motivation power when they praised their people for proper action.

This has two advantages: (1) reinforcement of the people you praise, so that they do more of the same. They encourage others to do so and they all become more enthusiastic, stimulated and motivated. (2) Others watching all this are suddenly motivated to go along with the approved idea, think constructively and become more supportive of you and your position.

There is an old cliché: No one ever stood so tall as one who stooped to help a child. This is particularly true today when those who show respect for people and desire to help others are consistently ranked by annual surveys at the top of public opinion. When you bend to help a subordinate, others see this.

The "option power secret" of listing feasible choices stimulates the group. Encourage suggestions for alternative or optional steps to solve mutual problems and reach mutual goals. This has a number of advantages.

It shows you will listen and are open minded and receptive. How many times have you heard someone say, "I tried to tell him, but he just wouldn't listen." Perhaps you have said the same thing yourself. If so, you know how frustrating, even infuriating, this can be. And you also know how great it feels when someone finally does listen. You can make other people feel this way too. They turn on and become enthusiastic about you and your common goals.

Listing options stimulates creative ideas. It can and often does generate the one new, strong, unique concept that dramatically solves the problem. This idea may never have been born except for the fact that you let it happen.

Case History: A Cleaner's Unique Package Generated $20 Million

A creative group, headed up by Jim J., was asked to plan a new package for a liquid detergent. Most of the ideas were for a standard, ordinary, blow-mold plastic bottle. But Jim J. asked for options; open minded, opened ended thinking. This stimulated all sorts of creative ideas, including a little miniature green industrial drum. This package was pre-tested and found to be unusually well received by consumers. It was introduced with tested product, name and advertising. Sales soon exceeded $20 million—at least partly because Jim J. called for various options and created an atmosphere that allowed a strong concept to be born.

Listing all options helps the strong ideas "pop out" into prominence because they look so good in comparison with weak ideas. Poor ideas, in that sense, are actually a help. So you are wise when you resist the temptation to say, "That idea is so silly let's not even consider it." Instead, list it anyway. This makes the stronger approach, perhaps your proposals, become even more attractive.

Listing options generates personal involvement. The other person or people see that their ideas are not only being heard and considered but are becoming a part of the program. And so they, personally, are becoming a part also. They become more directly and more emotionally committed instead of being a kid outside the candy store window with his nose pushed against the glass. This provides motivation of people at almost no cost to you.

A Secret for Setting More Potent Group Participation

But we haven't yet derived all the value from listing options. We can carry this a giant step further by putting these options in order of priority. This works in several ways with various benefits to you. *You can look for at least four advantages:* To begin with, putting options in 1-2-3 priority makes sure you concentrate on first things first. If you later are only able to do the first or second item, you at least took care of the most important projects. Many studies show that 20% of your projects account for 80% of your results . . . so you want to do *the right 20%*, by focussing motivated effort.

The second advantage is simply the flip side of the coin. *You avoid throwing away your group's money*, spirit and effort on what might be useless activity with little or no advantage—a total waste.

Third, you create order out of chaos. And this all alone has substantial motivational value. When people can see the pattern instead of confusion, can see the start of the string rather than an endless ball or tangled mass, can understand the problem, it becomes less frightening and forbidding. We tend to fear what we don't understand and trust what we do.

As a fourth benefit, a mountain of work is discouraging, but breaking it down into parts 1, 2 and 3 makes it *much more manageable*.

Here are four secret steps to powerful assignment of priorities, or, as some top people say, "prioritizing." (One works as well as the other.) These four steps follow a pretty natural sequence that you can use almost without thinking.

1) *Discuss each option briefly*. Encourage the person or small group to mention advantages and disadvantages. This will quickly begin to tip some options toward the favorable or unfavorable group.

2) *Now ask the small group to give each option an A, B or C grade*. Since you discussed each, this won't be difficult, except that some items may not be clearly good or bad, but a mixture. If so, you may have already solved this problem: give it a B.

3) *Feel their feeling*. Keep your antenna tuned, your eyes and ears open to pick up their reactions. They may give several items an A, yet clearly feel negative about one of them. Or other items a C, yet show all sorts of favorable vibes towards one.

4) *Suggest a second look or revision*. "Hey, do we really want to give that one item an A? If we feel unsure, should we slide it to a B for now?" Or, "Should we move the one good looking C up to a B or A?"

This business of assigning priorities greatly increases personal or small group participation because it stimulates with both logic and emotion through: (1) criticisms, compliments and defenses of *ideas*, plus (2) *feelings*, spirit, enthusiasm and dedication to the emerging plan.

Warning: Try to avoid giving too many projects an A priority, or subordinates will have more projects for a day or a week than they can possibly do. Then they, not you, will decide what is important (perhaps making some seriously wrong guesses), and you will lose control of your program.

A Secret and Powerful Application of Your S-O-S Method

You can now see that we have followed the little formula rather carefully and yet with relative ease.

The "situation" was checked out when we reviewed the problem in the first paragraphs of this chapter. You confirmed the key conditions facing you and the trouble to be solved. It's surprising how many people forget this simple, yet obvious step—an easy step that pays big dividends.

Your "objectives" for the group program were also reviewed, so that you are all pretty well facing in the same direction, oriented to the same target.

Now your "systems" have been selected by listing your options and then picking the most important by deciding on priorities.

The Power Secret to Saying "Look at That! You Made a Plan!"

Now, you can say this to the person or small group. Their interest will almost always jump even more at this point, for several reasons:

First, they usually did not even realize they were working on a plan. In fact, few would know what "a plan" was if it bit them on the nose. Those who did realize what was happening often forgot the overall picture as they became engrossed in the parts. They awake with a start.

Second, the statement was *"you* made a plan," not *"I* made a plan." It becomes *their* creation, *their* brain child. *Pride* of accomplishment, paternity and ownership bubble to the surface.

Third, you have now given them a reputation to live up to, just as world famous people influencer, Dale Carnegie, urges. You have annointed them with a skill, an ability that is believable and proven, right there before their own eyes. They can hardly deny it, and they don't really want to. On the contrary, they want to believe it.

For example: Someone may ask you for your opinion about management or about a person and then give you real evidence that you are right, saying, "You have keen insight into management and people." You would feel pretty good about this statement and want to believe it, since it has just proved correct, right before your very eyes.

Case: How a Major Soap Group's Plan and Time Management Solved a Tough Problem

Ken G. found his job in danger. As an advertising account executive for one of the world's best known bath and facial soaps, he had to see that his small staff made a really complete collection of competitive advertisements, analyzed them, and prepared a detailed report scrap book to be sent in on time every quarter. It was a large, tedious, dull job that got low priority and so was usually incomplete, poorly done and late. The client was furious. "Ken, you either do this job or resign and let someone else do it" was the message, one that most managers get occassionally.

Ken called his little soap account group together and outlined the problem and goal. Some of them were not very strongly motivated, since they sort of hoped he would fail, be fired and they might get his job.

Ken asked them for system suggestions and listed their ideas on a card. One thought was to employ an outside clipping service to help gather the ads, which was the most laborious part of the project. They agreed that this was the "A" priority. Ken picked up the phone and asked the client if this could be done. To his surprise, they readily agreed. He had followed his group's suggestions and gotten it approved, and now they were more involved.

Each accepted a part of the remaining task, on a carefully managed time plan. They had followed the situation-objective-system (S-O-S) procedure. It worked so well that Ken not only kept his position but was given a promotion, and within a few months one of his team actually was moved up to his job. Small group planning and time management got highly favorable results.

A Secret Inquiry
That Nearly Always Gets Action

"Where do we go from here?" This is a pregnant question. At first, members of the small group usually won't think about this, even when you say, "Look at that, you made a plan." For a moment they will bask in the warm glow of success and personal pride of accomplishment. But then their thoughts will almost naturally, even automatically, swing to, "Now what?" And someone will ask.

That is why you are well ahead of the game and the thundering herd if you already know "what happens next," or at least have an idea. At this point you can easily steer people east or west. But once they start to move, turning them to an alternative direction could be difficult. Like the first scratch on a new table, the initial suggestion is usually long visible, because first impressions are lasting.

In short, this is "the psychological moment." It would be a little foolish, even wasteful, to let it go. The iron is hot. The metal is fluid. The pour is ready for the mold. You can be the mold, the shaper, the pointer, the director. They are ready; so move quickly.

Have a few steps in mind. For example: "Since we've agreed that "A" should be our priority option, our first step is to take care of that next week." You will rarely find an argument; instead, you usually get strong agreement. "Then we can do "B" the second week and "C" the third." And it's done. A schedule is set. "Now we all know where we go from here—a question that was bugging some of us." (For further detail on scheduling, please have a look at chapter 5, under the section titled "The Schedule Secret—How It Builds Power." This covers scheduling in a formal meeting, but can partly be used here as well.)

The Powerful Secret of Using "You"

Right here you have another opportunity to easily increase motivation, personal commitment and enthusiasm.

First, simply re-cap the idea that "you know our problems, our objectives, and our programs that make up our plan." This reminds them of what you have done, fixes those ideas firmly in their minds and makes the whole, overall program come together in an easily understood picture.

Second, emphasize their ability. "You did it, and you can easily do it again. Since it is your plan, you can make your own adjustments or a new program. Any time you feel it is needed we can get together to make a plan." Now they not only feel more comfortable but more confident.

Third, be sure they understand that it was and it is group effort, working together—with in-puts from everyone and with your guidance—that generated and built "the plan."

The Power Secret of Using
Time Control for Management by Objectives

The time has come to do things, to stop talking and planning—to start taking real steps. And right here is where the whole thing can turn to rat dirt as people squander time and wander off aimlessly in six different directions. There are simple steps you can take to avoid such waste.

First, try to develop their own sense of time and urgency. This is a key project that can be fun, exciting and rewarding. Explain that time is highly elusive, mercurial, slippery and fleeting. Time is life, irreversible, irreplaceable. "To waste time is to waste your existence," says Alan Lakein in his book, *How to Get Control of Your Time and Your Life*. To master your time is to master your life and make the most of it. If you can build strong feelings here, it can be powerful motivation.

Second, explain the M.B.O. program idea in a few sentences. For example, perhaps you can employ words to this effect: "Let's consider the famous M.B.O. method, Management By Objectives. This means that we will manage our time so that each and every step we take is aimed specifically at our objectives. That way we don't waste any of our effort on useless work. We won't spin our wheels. Each step will pay off. So we make good progress and we do it at the least cost to our time and effort. We work smarter, not harder."

This almost always has the two way effect of first building enthusiasm—since it sounds logical, yet also has an emotional appeal—and second, concentrating that valuable, newly generated enthusiasm toward the goals to be reached. And so the whole team benefits.

Third, give your people a practical list of time management guides. You will usually be surprised at how well these are received, since most employees worry about time. Yet, like the weather, nobody does much about it.

Twenty-Seven Time Management Tips

Here is a list of powerful time secrets that worked well for office, laboratory, sales and service people at a wide range of companies:

1. "Value time, for that is what life is made of." (Ben Franklin).
2. Everyone wants some of your time. Give it carefully. Especially your best hours of the day.
3. Start with a list of projects for that day.
4. Set priorities on your daily projects, A B & C.
5. A's are things that best help you reach your goal.
6. Code just the "must do's" with an asterisk or circle.
7. One easy approach is to separate your papers into A B & C piles.
8. Be a "self-starter." Don't wait to be prodded.
9. Try to do A's first. (You can stand almost any tough job for at least a few minutes.)
10. Do hard jobs at your best time of day.
11. Avoid seductive B's and C's. Easy and fun, but less vital.
12. Remember, 80% of progress will come from your top 20% of your projects.
13. Change priorities when you must.
14. Multiply yourself. Use the phone, dictation unit, delegation, notes and short meetings.
15. Learn to use travel time, waiting time and spare time.
16. If phones or people bug you, find an empty office or the library.
17. Keep asking yourself, "Is this the best use of my time?"
18. Think positive. Avoid self-pity. Believe in yourself. Psych yourself up.
19. Avoid boredom by switching the project order around.

20. Reward yourself. For instance: do an easy task after a tough one.

21. Allow time for interruptions. (Then you won't climb the walls.)

22. Take occasional breaks. Recharge your batteries. Waste a little time. This is actually "constructive"—or planned and controlled—waste.

23. Avoid long phone visits. Say, "I have another call waiting."

24. Learn to "skim read." Discard useless material and projects.

25. Write plainly, simply, clearly. It's easy and fast.

26. Avoid long answers. Writing a note in the margin and returning it is often enough.

27. Measure your results, not your actions.

This will usually step up at least some of your small group, often dramatically. At the very least, it will give almost 100% of them a heightened sense of time, its use, value, limits, resulting in an increased sense of urgency and fewer wasted minutes. And it will also generate greater effectiveness, efficiency, action and spirit.

How Personal Planning and Time Management Motivate

The steps you have just taken motivate in many ways. First, your review of the problem generated excitement and personal relevancy. Second, the look at your objectives focussed attention and commitment. Third, the priorities simplified things and created understanding. Fourth, your personal or small group plan generated direct involvement. Fifth, you have now all agreed on a road map to progress and a track to run on. For many people, these steps alone are enough to precipitate almost irresistible, immediate and constructive action.

Sixth, you have done even more than that. You have generated an urgency for this action, an appreciation that *time is limited*, valuable and fleeting.

But seventh, and perhaps greatest of all: This simple, practical process of planning and time management creates a whole new "can do, will do" work attitude. It often changes the doubters, feet draggers and obstructionists into "born again" converts who not only enthusiastically support the program but often become the strongest disciples, preaching the gospel of better planning, management by objectives and effective personal time control. This is high motivation, indeed. And it saves you lots of work. Other people will often say things, do things and open doors you could not personally unlock without great effort.

Case: Pharmaceutical Manager Used Flip Chart Plan for $100 Million Program

Chuck E. could see the problem building. Reduced sales of the drug product line in his department. The cause was equally clear: growing competition.

Chuck asked three of the company's marketing and purchasing advisors to visit with him informally and do some planning. (I was one. But in all candor, while I played a substantial role in most of the histories cited in this book, in this particular case I was mainly a sounding board, chart marker and observer who took a few notes.)

Chuck suggested we make some rough draft statements on a flip chart. He started with *"problem review"* and listed four problems. We each added one or two, ending with about eight items. We all agreed that this was a good picture of the situation.

Then we jotted down a few objectives, such as new sales and profit volumes for the next few years. Several times the observers disagreed with Chuck. We all discussed the pros and cons. He listened and made changes. There was mutual respect for each other's inputs. Chuck had very large objectives in mind; at one point he wanted the new business goal to total $200 million, but on closer look at the investment needed, he agreed to scale down to "only" $100 million.

Various options for strategies and systems were suggested by each of us. Chuck and I listed these on the chart. Then we looked at priorities. Some projects obviously were low in importance or had to wait for others, so got a "C." Others were clearly first steps or more important and got an "A." We recognized that we had followed the Situation-Objective-System, or S-O-S, procedure and now had our own plan and our schedule.

Time management methods were used to move the program along. We did first things first. Each step was carefully directed toward our $100 million goal.

Results: the program flip chart and document were presented to the Board of Directors. During later consideration of the program, some emergencies came up and the plan was postponed.

Eventually the program was cut way back, modified and applied to another line. Even then, it developed volume of about $12 million at a good profit level. Planning and time management had motivated highly constructive action.

Case History: How a Consultant Motivated with a Plan

Wayne J., a management consultant, had a small client in the auto service business who was in deep trouble. Sales were low, and profits had slipped into losses that were eating up his meager finances. Bankruptcy seemed only a matter of time. Wayne reviewed the *situation* with Jim F., the owner, who had lapsed into discouraged inaction. Together, they located several key problems. For one thing, they had lots of money tied up in expensive tires and gasoline, which were selling less every month. Meanwhile, the repair and general servicing activity was growing. Yet the little company had only one mechanic besides Jim. And the company was not well equipped.

Wayne and Jim agreed on two key *objectives*: (1) increase sales by 25% in the next six months, and (2) reduce costs by 10% in the same period.

The system agreed upon was to change their little newspaper ads to emphasize service and repair, and to train the one gasoline and tire man to become a mechanic. Wayne and Jim both felt personally involved in the new program and Jim, particularly, recognized that now he had a track to run on. He also felt the urgency of time and the need to plan for each week and month. Most important, Jim was steamed up and enthusiastic about the plan.

Results: While they did not cut costs by 10%, they did cut them by 5%. Sales increased by 20% and the little company became profitable again. A plan and time management had achieved productive motivation.

Summary: The Secret Power of Plans and Time Use Can Motivate Major Action

Review the problem, recognize mutual objectives and respect individual strategy suggestions. List these as possibilities or "options" for action. Allow creative juices to flow. Then categorize your options according to priority in order to focus on "doing first things first." Rank things as A, B or C. Apply the S-O-S formula. Develop maximum personal involvement by each team member. Apply M.B.O., or Management By Objectives, to aim every single step toward your goals. Give team members time management guidelines mainly aimed at making the best use of each hour and day. If all this is done properly, you'll always get increased involvement, commitment and excitement and motivated, constructive action.

7

Secrets of Using "Work" As a Powerful Motivator

Here's a powerful secret you can use this week. People hate work, you say? Surprise! They love work, *if it's the right kind.* (Just threaten to take it away and see what happens!) Work assigned properly can be your best motivation tool. But it must be meaningful to the employee. And it must be "doable." Many people are actually attracted to tough jobs, as a challenge. Some live to work, becoming work-aholics. Even animals want to and love to perform and work. America's "work ethic" or work challenge is powerful motivation in itself, if it is done right. But approached improperly, it is a de-motivator and trouble maker. We will look at some secret systems that will help you employ the work interest of others to increase your power and reach your mutual goals.

Case: Fire at the Government Office; People Donate Labor

"A three alarm fire last evening, Christmas night, destroyed portions of a government office downtown. Clean-up has begun," said the TV announcer.

Next morning, most of us went to work dreading what we might find. We were lucky; there was little direct fire damage. But there was no heat and light, and there was serious smoke damage from thick, black and greasy chemicals that destroyed papers, furnishings, plants, phones, typewriters and calculators and even got into file cabinets and desk drawers.

The boss suggested that we all bring buckets, rags and detergent if we cared to come to work next day. Otherwise stay home on administrative leave. Either way, all would get full pay.

Here was a great opportunity to loaf. Government workers are not famous for dedication to hard work. And yet, to my amazement, the next day nearly everyone showed up in old clothes, carrying rags, buckets and soap. Clerks, secretaries, officers, chiefs and director. They began to clean, and it went on all day. Hands got red and sore. Next day, everyone reappeared and repeated the performance. This continued every day for nearly two weeks! White collar folks did tough, dirty, unpleasant physical labor and did it voluntarily!

But this was meaningful work. It needed to be done. Everyone wanted it to be finished so they could go back to their regular work and get on with their business and personal *career goals*. The mess was interfering with their objectives. While this was work they had little experience with, still they were able to do it. It was not pleasant, but employees felt it was better than doing nothing, sitting at home and getting a dole. The mess was eventually cleaned up, and normal activities were resumed promptly and efficiently. Meaningful work was a major, even dynamic motivator.

Here Is the Secret to "Meaningful Work"

Dr. Scott Meyer, top motivation researcher at the University of Texas, says, "If you must boil things down to the simplest bottom line basics, you come to 'meaningful work,' and that means work that helps a guy achieve his own personal goals."

So meaningful work begins with hopes and dreams, a cause, goal or several objectives. These are often unstated, unwritten and even unrecognized targets. We all have them, to one extent or another. Subconscious, secret desires or open, frank, clearly stated ones. And somehow, it seems that the more precise and clear that goal is, the more meaningful our work becomes *if* it helps us to approach this goal.

Thus the first secret of meaningful work might be to set, sharpen and *emphasize the goal*. Encourage employees to recall, think about and concentrate on their own objectives, right from the beginning. Keep reinforcing and reminding them of their target. One simple way is to find out what their goal is for that month. "Since we want to make, sell and process 20 account reports a month, let's remember that is about one a day. Let's see, we are a little ahead for the month but did none the last two days, so we should really produce today." Make a game of it. "We lost a little last week, but we'll win a bundle this week."

Second, check to see that it's a mutual *objective.* Be sure that their goal matches your goal and so becomes "our" goal. This has a strengthening and multiplying effect of work as a motivator.

For example: "The *company* goal is 20 reports a month, but your *personal* goal is to roll up a good reputation that will help you get an assistant or promotion. If you do 20 reports, this will make you look darn good on your record." Here you have two goals stimulating the same work. This becomes a powerful motivator.

If goals conflict, the group action is seriously reduced. *Conflict example:* If your boss says, "while you are doing the 20 reports, the company's and your goal, I'd like you to attend that two day meeting so at least somebody shows up from our department." His goal thus cuts into your time to reach your objectives.

Third, be sure the work, the plan, the efforts really are target oriented, aimed at the objective with each step and each accomplishment moving the group closer.

For example: Going back to our goal of 20 reports, be sure that each page is really needed. Also, some people hold lengthy, almost unrelated discussions about a report, then get discouraged because the total job takes so long. The extended visits did not really help toward the goal; they just burned up valuable time.

Surprise! It's Often
Your Best Power Tool

The mere existence of any type of labor to be done sets off action among some people. But when the work looks like it will help reach their goals, it not only motivates these same people more strongly, but suddenly stimulates and activates a great many more of the group. Whole armies move under those conditions.

So, the work must appear meaningful. The effort must have practical application toward satisfying some want or need among employees. And it must *look* like this. Appearance is the key. *For example:* While the work assigned may be highly goal oriented, it just might not look that way. The employee simply can't see the connection between the work and the goal. This is one of the most common errors in motivation.

Some examples: The clerk neglects a procedure because, "I can't see what possible good it does. It seems like wasted effort." A production line worker says. "Reporting the units packed each hour is nothing but a pain in the neck." Communication has broken down.

Here is where you should build a simple, clearly stated bridge of "reasons why." These will let you connect the driving force of a desired goal to the work action that needs to be done. This bridge acts as a catalyst, switch board or co-ordinating connector, joining the "force" with the "task." When they really recognize the connection, jump back out of the way. You're about to have a motivated team like you never saw before.

One good technique: "The answer to your question is that if we do this new procedure it will not only secure our jobs, but increase chances that some clerks will get an assistant."*Another good approach:* "If you want to reach your personal goals, you must take at least a few steps, and this job program is one of the simplest, most direct moves you can take to get your reward." Relate, hook-up and tie their action to their benefit.

Meaningful work is more important each year because today people feel more in control of their lives and have career goals more often than ten or 20 years ago. A little reminding, reinforcement and revitalizing make these targets take on new shimmer, shine and glow. Suddenly anything that helps the employee reach these goals—like work—becomes important to him.

"Are You Kidding? People Hate Work!"

Don't they? Well, they don't really hate it. Not all work. Just certain kinds. They mainly hate work that (a) seems *pointless* or of no contribution to their fun or objectives, or worse still, (b) that seems to be blocking, *interfering*, stealing or destroying their goal. Surprisingly, unpleasantness has almost nothing to do with it. The fact that the job is routine, dull, boring, long, unpleasant, even miserable or painful is not the pivotal point. It's a minor issue. We all do such tasks every day and do them fairly willingly since they help us to reach our objectives.

Conversely, we balk, resist and fume at relatively pleasant activities that interfere with our goals.

Examples: The salesman drives hundreds of long dull miles and boring hours only to be rewarded with a disinterested, offensive and sometimes hostile prospective customer, resulting in "no sale." In all, a mighty unpleasant experience. But if you even threaten to close his territory, he howls like a wounded banshee.

The commuter packs herself into subway, bus or freeway. The trip is dirty, cramped, long, boring, uncomfortable, hot and irritating. She often gets up a half hour early just to meet the schedule of bus or carpool, but still she values her job highly.

The store clerk is subject to seemingly endless hours of walking, standing, stooping and stretching until legs and feet ache with pain, yet many consider the job as an important career that they hold for most of their work lives.

The plant, assembly line or production worker sometimes operates in cramped, noisy, dirty conditions, where improper light causes eyestrain. Yet, if you threaten less overtime, he threatens mutiny.

The executive must attend dozens of poorly planned and presented meetings that are long, dull, boring and often pointless. Meanwhile, his mind twists in pain at the thought of the projects piling up on his desk, projects that he must now take home over the weekend. Yet he considers his job important, vital, challenging and a source of pride.

The list could cover hundreds more examples of "unpleasant" tasks, aggressively executed because they clearly help achieve personal goals.

Now let's look at the flip side: where a pleasant activity interfers with work and objective.

Sam, a wealthy and influential business associate, takes Joe, an employee, to lunch at an especially nice restaurant, as a grand gesture because he hasn't seen Joe for a long time and besides it is Joe's birthday. They linger over a cocktail and order a big lunch. Sam reviews old experiences and exciting new activities, criticizes old enemies and tells the latest jokes. He is full of compliments. about Joe and his job. A couple of hours fly by. Everything is lovely, right? Wrong. Joe has an urgent, important and highly favorable report to send his boss that afternoon that would normally take three hours. He now has only two. The report would substantially advance his career goal, but he feels obligated to sit in heavenly surroundings while his gut steams and boils. This is an exaggerated example of something that happens almost every day—pleasant prospective opportunities that try to seduce us away from our committed course.

Conclusion: Employees willingly perform pleasant and even unpleasant jobs that help toward their personal goals. Yet they strongly resist pleasant action that interferes with these goals. People don't hate work, per se, just the wrong kind of work. The key is job/goal linkage. The pleasant or unpleasant factor is only a mildly important side issue.

Case: A recent nation-wide study covering one full year showed that "far more absenteeism is caused by pure boredom than by illness." Managers are either reluctant, afraid or unable to provide meaningful work; so employees simply stay home. They have little motivation to do otherwise.

Work Has Most Power
When You Use These Three Secrets

Here's how to create or generate these circumstances. *First, assign work people CAN do* all the way to completion. Few things cause as much discontent, distress, frustration, misery, even anger as assigning a task that a person is simply unable to do, even half way. This has stolen the time, enthusiasm and effort that they could have used in some other way to reach their personal goals. It has left them with nothing—no progress, a loss, disappointment and perhaps criticism.

Here are some examples: A clerk who has been asked to type an impossibly involved letter. A salesperson trying to sell a complex product to a much more sophisticated customer. A manager who has been "tossed in way over his head, to sink or swim"; so he mostly drinks. Net: to motivate with work, be sure to give employees things they are ready for and able to do. Then don't expect miracles.

Second, LET them do it. Now this may sound like a strange statement. Of course, the supervisor will "let" them do it. After all, he wants them to get the job done, doesn't he? Sure he does.

The problem is that sometimes he wants it so bad that he is tempted to over-supervise, breathe down their necks, over-direct, over-watch, stifle. He may give so many directions that the employee doesn't know which way to turn. Or he may set impossible deadlines or give many additional assignments without realizing that these literally do not let the employee do the primary job that both he and the manager want to get done. In addition, the supervisor won't let the employee explain this overload and learn what should be done first. A common obstruction to motivation is unconsciously not letting employees perform, a charge even good supervisors passionately protest. A strong motivation step is to put employees in the position where they not only have the ability but are also *allowed* to perform.

Third, give them jobs they like, if you can—or at least jobs that are or can be made to look attractive. You can build attractiveness mainly by emphasizing the contribution they are making to their company, customers and toward their own personal self-satisfaction and personal goals. This attractiveness factor may seem to contradict what we just said about unpleasantness not being very important. But note, we said it has "almost" nothing to do with it, and we concluded that employees willingly perform pleasant, and even unpleasant, jobs that help toward their goals. Obviously, given a choice, they will usually be more willing to do the pleasant rather than the unpleasant tasks. Note how a youngster says, "OK, I'll help you with the dishes. You wash. I'll dry." As long as they are volunteering, most will quickly choose the job that appears to be easier, although it may not be.

How Difficult Jobs Attract People

This is not at all unusual. Many women—certainly not all, but thousands of them—are now agressively seeking tough work on pipelines, railroads, in the desert, arctic, tropics, coal mines, trucking, construction, foundries, lumbering, farming, shipping, high iron and many more areas, while rejecting clerical, sales, union, factory, management and executive trainee jobs. This hard work obviously doesn't scare them, but helps them reach their personal, financial, social and psychological goals. Work, and even hard work, attracts people.

How the Man Who "Died and Went to Hell" Left You a Power Secret

There is an old story about a guy who died and awoke surrounded by luxury. He was amazed and, at first, much pleased. His every request was granted until he asked for some work to do. This request was denied. "But why?" he asked. "Surely this can be given to me. After all I am in Heaven, am I not?" The reply came back, "I am sorry, Sir, but you didn't make it." Nothing to do, is "Hell."

How do you apply this "desire for work"? There are several easy steps you might take:

First, go ahead and assign work. Don't hold back. Don't be shy or timid, but don't be a martinet or tyrant, either. *For example* you might say, "John, here's a project where we need your help. These reports are just the sort of thing you do beautifully." Be sure that's true and include the implication that John's action helps you, the team and him to reach mutual goals.

Second, don't worry about an occassional gripe or beef. Listen and consider, but change course only if these become stronger, repetitive or there is good reason, both emotionally and factually. Complaining is a popular indoor sport not to be taken too literally. It is often done out of the natural desire to get a better deal . . . on the assumption . . . "it doesn't hurt to ask."

"Pavlov's Dogs Loved Work," Says Peter Drucker

This world famous management consultant tells audiences that the dogs Pavlov used in experiments would run ten miles per hour on the treadmill and get a dog biscuit. When released from their cages, they ran *toward* the equipment, not away from it. Even animals like to work, if it helps them gain their private goal.

Tom Sawyer treated a big fence painting assignment as a special privilege, as well as fun. Soon, others wanted a chance at it. Eventually, Tom had motivated half the kids in the neighborhood to paint the fence.

In both cases, Pavlov's dogs or Tom Sawyer's friends, the job appeared to help accomplish their goal. It was (1) something they *were able* to do, (2) something they *were allowed* to do, and (3) something that *seemed like fun*. Thus, it motivated both humans and animals. Love of work is basic.

Gaining Power from
People's Secret Dislike of "the Dole"

Some people who are eligible for unemployment benefits abuse and rip-off the privilege. However, most who use it apply it fairly and properly, according to private and government investigators. But the great majority of the proper users wish it were not necessary. They would much rather be employed. They resent it and even hate to be on the dole. The gross abusers, loafers and rip-off artists are a tiny minority. They just seem big because their action is so repugnant to Americans, another indication of our fierce dedication to work.

Most working people, as well as the unemployed, dislike welfare. They hope they will never get there. So we see that people both on and off the dole don't like it. There are many reasons: (1) the desire to work, (2) the "work ethic" of early America coming down to us in a really not very old society, (3) the feeling that to be unemployed for any reason is at least partly the fault of the individual, and (4) the fear, humiliation and distaste of facing others who did not lose their jobs and so "must be better than me" and who naturally conclude that "I am inferior to them."

Proof of "dole dislike" is seen in the fact that many people will gladly work for only slightly more than they could get on unemployment or welfare roles. Some will work for the same or even less.

Three Secrets for Challenging People with Work

This can be done in a few easy steps:

First, avoid putting them down. On the contrary, appeal to their pride. Even shame them just a bit. *For example:* "Some folks in the other division say you probably can't do this job. But I don't quite buy that." Or, "The other divisions seem to be able to do this, but maybe they are just lucky. I sure don't believe they are any better than our team." Or, "You are about the best production line people I ever saw. I know you can meet our deadline."

Next, try to get a commitment. For example: Perhaps say

something straightforward like, "Surely, we can do it, can't we?" Or, "Are we good enough to do the job?" Or, "Is my belief in our team at least part right?" Or simply, "Can you do it?" Try to get a firm "yes," preferably, a resounding yes, a strong personal commitment.

Third, extend the challenge. Reach for the stars. You might not get them all, but you may get a few. *For example:* You might say, "Right! I agree with you! We can do it! And with that kind of an attitude we'll do a darn good job. Maybe break a few records. How about shooting for 25% more than they are asking and really making those others look silly? Even if we don't make it, we should come close. Shall we at least try for it?" It's hard to say no.

Ian's Multi-million Challenge

Ian N.'s boss said, "Ian, we want you to do one of the toughest sales jobs there is. Take a new, unknown liquid household cleaner product, advertise, merchandize, promote, sell and push it until you outsell our competitor's top product. And Ian, you'll have to do it with a low budget."

This was not a simple routine assignment or just another job. Here was a long, difficult, irritating, frustrating, seemingly hopeless task—a David and Goliath affair with Ian as David . . . using a pretty small sling-shot.

Ian called his three-man group together and issued the challenge. "Most of the other employees know about our assignment and can't help laughing at us. They are sure we can never do it. But we are not about to roll over and play dead. After all, other sales groups have reached volumes close to this competitor's and at times exceeded them. If those guys can do it, then by God we can do it too, and maybe we can do even better. We should shoot for "$X" million in volume, nationally."

The group prepared careful plans and new ideas. Ian insisted that the product, its name and all the advertising be thoroughly pretested with housewives—a long, difficult, unexciting process. But the group responded to Ian's challenge and took each tedious step.

Results: the product went into test markets supported by a well researched program, aggressive management and well informed salesmen. Sharp growth was realized. When it was introduced to the national market, it exceeded the competitor's products and went over the multi-million sales goal.

A tough, laborious, difficult job, plus a challenge to employee pride, had motivated a team's personal action and generated millions in sales. It has since become a legend in the field of modern marketing.

Case of the Warehouse Production
Clerk's Inventory Chart

Donna B. Did a good job handling simple correspondence, phone calls and files for one of the small warehouses in the Southwest.

But her supervisor, Arnold M., had a problem: They were forever running out of one model or another of their tape recorders but ending up with too many radios and TV sets.

So Arny discussed the problem with Donna and suggested a big wall chart they could display, showing current stock quantities on each model, each month, in different color felt pen numbers.

This was a new and different sort of assignment for Donna, and it seemed a little scary, even confusing—as well as adding to her already busy work day.

But Arny showed her how to do it, emphasized what a real help this would be to him, the warehouse crew, their customers, and pointed out that this would make her more appreciated by "the big boss."

Donna went to work. She made a much neater, more attractive and more thorough chart than Arny did and even thought of some improvements. *Results:* She was recognized by higher management (one of her goals) and the system was adopted by many other distributors, to the benefit of warehouse teams and customers.

Summary: Work Can Be Your Best Power Secret

What did we prove? We saw that people don't really hate work, just certain kinds. Work can be the greatest single motivator, if it is meaningful work—that is, work, even hard work, that helps the person achieve his own personal goals, work the employee can do (is capable of doing) and may do (is allowed to do) and likes to do. "Hell" is having no job and nothing to do. Pavolv's dogs loved work. Tom Sawyer's friends begged for it. People hate to be on the dole. Most will rise to the challenge when someone says they can't do it or that others can do better. They will usually try to reach for the stars. Conclusion: beyond any doubt, meaningful work greatly motivates most people.

8

How to Get Through
to the "Heart and Mind" of People

Proper use of "Heart and Mind" is a powerful secret
used by some of the world's most influential managers.
And it's really pretty easy when you know a few basic
steps.

Case: Fred J. was in a dangerous situation. Fred
had the kind of problem many managers and executives
face today. Unless he could come up with an improved
selling program on a line of foot products, his good paying merchandising job would soon go to someone else.
Fortunately, Fred recognized that the heart and mind of
a person are powerful producers of dramatic results. He
knew the heart and mind would stimulate ideas with
brainstorming, challenges, the "five W's," goals and the
A.I.D.A. formula (Attention, Interest, Desire and Action). Fred got a little group of advertising, sales, production and purchasing people together. He applied
these techniques and ended up building a display and
merchandising program that saved both the brand and
his job. A few months later Fred won an award, a pay
raise and a promotion. Let's take a closer look at Fred's
methods and see how they can serve you.

What Is the Secret Power in "Heart and Mind"?

Heart and mind are simply short, basic, everyday words for
two of the most potent internal hot buttons, turn-ons or power
switches within this great animal we call the human being; they are
emotion and intellect.

First, think of those emotions that motivate constructive action: *Hope* of success; *fear* of failure; *spirit* of enthusiasm; *love* of self, of others, of life, of accomplishment. These are positive, dynamic, pleasant, rewarding, emotional feelings. If we stimulate, excite and develop these positive vibes in others, then we turn on an incredible force, the kind that conquered nations and the same kind that built multi-million dollar fortunes. Neither of these great accomplishments happened without spirit or emotion. Henry Ford said, "Anything is possible with enthusiasm."

The second part of this duet, intellect, should be considered by those of us looking at motivation, as "the use (or apparent use) of facts and reason to get logical, favorable results." It's the flip side of emotions. While emotions are hot and fiery, intellect is (or is supposed to be) the cool, calm, calculating, analytical, synthesizing and constructive side. This has practical use when you turn the team's tough, hard light of logic and facts towards solving your problem. In a sense, intellect channels emotional power towards constructive results.

Example case: "By God, we've absolutely got to get our suppliers to deliver on time! And they better start doing it by next week, or I will take some extreme steps with them! And also some action with people right here in the company!" Dismissal is clearly implied if not stated openly. (Here is an emotionally charged situation.) But the subordinate co-ordinator in the department cooly reviewed the matter and found the three main needs were: (1) longer lead time or early order placement, (2) an agreed upon schedule for delivering half the order in three weeks, the rest in six, and (3) reminders or follow-ups at weeks two and five to see that things were on track. The new system worked just fine. Logic, or system, had meshed with emotion and motivated successful action.

How Do Heart and Mind Generate Secret Power?

As you can see, heart and mind are sort of a two-way whammy. They are both catalytic and synergistic, as well as mutually reinforcing. One feeds the other. To use these for motivation, try to establish both a factual base and emotional enthusiasm, openness and dedication in your group. Openness here meaning "open mindedness" and willingness to think new, try new, accept new. Then when you have established some heart and mind (emotion and logic), build on which ever of these is the most promising or easiest. Here are *two examples:*

First, note the next few television commercials. Few of us really like commercials, but they motivate millions every day in a very efficient way. They work. Most of these are made by people who have spent their lives both studying and practicing motivation. You can often learn a few things from them that you can put to practical use. Note especially the nationally advertised goods and services, as opposed to local ads for banks and car dealers. Note how the commercial opens with a grabber of either heart or mind. Then it goes on to develop that emotional or logical concept: the excitingly beautiful person you desire or desire to be and the reasonable, factual, intelligent way you can manage to reach this goal. That sixty second commercial often packs in half a dozen appeals to both heart and mind.

Second, one of the most successful advertising professionals who ever lived, Leo Burnett, started out in the 1930's with three people in offices equipped with used furniture. "Leo, you'll end up broke and selling apples on the corner," someone told him.

"No, I'll give them away at the secretary's desk." And he did. 40 years later, dozens of receptionists still do. The company's billings are over $500 million.

When I was a young account executive, Leo once told me, "Craig, to motivate people use emotional appeals that sound reasonable. People are basically emotional, but they like to appear logical. For maximum effect, fire both heart and mind." *Example:* If you talk to a new car buyer, he or she will give you a dozen reasons (logic) why he bought it. But the real reason may be that he thinks he looks good in it (emotion). (Industrial psychologist Dr. Ernest Dichter, an old aquaintance, says that people don't just ride in a car, they feel they are wearing it.)

Here's How You Can
Secretly Stimulate Powerful Ideas

When you seek concepts to build logical and emotional motivation, you should look to your own group as a good resource of ideas and as a resource of self-stimulators and self-motivators for the group. There are several easy ways you can turn on people's creative juices, and, surprisingly, most people have gallons of such juice if you know how to tap the keg. If you do this properly, you can get a four way split on these thoughts (both logical and emotional); then you'll find ideas both practical and far out.

First, create a permissive atmosphere. This is fairly simple. Just "permit" things or "allow" things. The juice won't flow unless you let it. Show you will. An easy way is to say you want ideas and then welcome any and all. Even ideas you don't like. The way to avoid being stuck with having to accept some bad concept is to simply not give it much recognition. Just ask, "What other ideas do you have?" The key point: don't rain on the other person's parade, or you'll shut off the flow of things that can help you. Don't kill the goose with the golden egg.

Second, set some reasonable limits. For example: You might say, "We want *any ideas* for a retail store banner to sell this new tape deck, but it should be aimed mainly at young executives and managers. And avoid bad taste. Within those wide boundaries, anything goes. For example, we want logic or emotion . . . far out or practical."

Third, let one door open others. If an idea doesn't seem usable but may have some small advantage or even a fresh new approach, encourage development. "Hey, let's build on that idea. Where else might that take us? How could we modify, twist or adjust your idea? What similar thought do you have?"

Fourth, encourage really "wild" ideas. This pulls out all the stops. It drops the bars, and the flood of restrained thoughts can pour out. People often get long nurtured concepts off their chests. An easy way to do this is to say, "Hey! Let's get wild! Think wild! Out of sight! Strange. New. Exciting. Different. Fire off anything that comes into your head, even if it seems wrong, foolish, nutty. Maybe it will lead to something!" Again, be careful. Don't criticize, or you douse the pyrotechnics. Let them explode. You don't have to love it all. As you go along, you can re-shape some of these into practical programs. And these "hypo" the suggestors. You gain two ways: with ideas to stimulate others and ideas that motivate your group.

Case example: Three young managers were trying to solve the problem of an uninspired sales team and felt that a product improvement would help. They believed better or easier application of the liquid cleaner would make a big difference. Someone suggested an attached cleaning rag. Another thought a soaker-dabber on the cap might be better. Their supervisor said, "Let's develop that idea." And they ended up with a trigger action spray bottle that dramatically motivated sales people, dealers, house-wives and sales action.

"Brainstorming": A Powerful Secret to Serve You

What we have just been looking at and considering is a system that works and gets results. It's called "brainstorming," and it has served hundreds of the most successful professionals in today's management.

If you followed and at least partly accepted the ideas just discussed about stimulating emotional and logical ideas, then it will be easy for you to apply these simple mechanics that will serve you well in motivating people through their hearts and minds:

1. Call it "brainstorming." This has exciting images.
2. Start with the idea that "brainstorming is fun." This encourages freedom.
3. State a goal, like "new ways to improve client service."
4. Emphasize that : "No one is wrong; let's consider everything."
5. Record almost everything, even nutty ideas.
6. Later, rank these. Pick the "goods," "fairs," "poors."
7. Stimulate and excite; encourage total participation.
8. Encourage both emotional and logical thinking—heart and mind action that motivates the group.

Case example: A little group of sales and advertising people was trying to think of a program to sell a small quantity of beer that had been put up in wide mouth, stubby bottles and had poor sales. They got together and said, "any suggestions are welcome within the bounds of a small budget." All sorts of logical and emotional ideas were tried, both far out and practical. Someone suggested "Big Mouth," and they started to play with slogans and jokes like. "Open your Big Mouth, today" and "put your sweep lips on my Big Mouth," and others. They settled on Big Mouth as their lead theme, and it not only sold out the small stock but required many additional runs and hit new sales records. Brainstorming resulted in both a motivated team and motivated customers.

Challenging Secretly Builds Your Power

When you create, generate and psych-up a brainstorming session, you are challenging the group's spirit and intellect. In effect, you are saying to them, "Can you do it? Can you say what you think and how you feel? You all have good constructive thoughts—hopes, dreams, compliments, gripes, suggestions—that you spout off at bull sessions. Let's hear these now. Put them to use, to help us all. Let's solve our problems and figure out ways to make some progress." This challenge helps you and the group in several ways:

First, you draw out personal feelings that give several immediate benefits. Many people are "just busting" to tell someone their thoughts; and these are often constructive ideas.

Case: The warehouse fork lift truck operator for a soft drink wholesale distributor suggested a new way of stacking pallets that would save 40% of the space. "Why didn't you suggest that before?" his boss asked. "Because, this is the first time anyone would listen," the operator said. Milk home deliverymen saw sales were low on their route trucks; so they quickly suggested adding a line of fruit juices that proved a major contribution to spirit, motivation and income.

Second, it can be a pleasure for both the group and yourself—just pure fun. None of you may get a thing out of it but enjoyment. And that's not all bad. Leo Burnett liked to say, "The day I don't get some fun out of my work is the day I look for another job."

Third, it can be interesting, stimulating, even exciting as ideas unfold and sparks fly. Emotions stir, enthusiasm builds, and concepts bounce around. The initial idea may not be usable as it is, but it can often be modified into something more practical.

Case: A home building construction worker noticed that a huge amount of time was being spent shaping and assembling windows and door jambs on the site. He suggested that the wood milling equipment be put on location to save time. A study of the plan showed this to be impractical, but the idea led to the in-plant prefabrication of the units before the material left for the job site. Last year over 85% of all such units were done that way. An initial idea was impractical, but when modified it generated major progress.

How to Put the Five W's
Toward Building Your Power

Now that you have the pot boiling and ideas are being generated, *it's time to give these a little guidance* and give yourself a little control. The five W's can serve you here as a handy, simple device: Who, what, when, where and why. You might ask: Who has an idea for better client service? What product or system changes should we make? When should we do this? Why will this help us? Where should we start on this project?

You accomplish several things by asking such questions. First, you stimulate and encourage action. Second, you channel it into usable directions. And third, almost without anyone realizing it, you are helping others and yourself to build an orderly management plan or program; note how you covered the five W's in a way that can be written, refined and executed into a going operation.

As an extra bonus, these questions often give you added *power to probe* for and uncover hidden ideas, even passions that may have been locked in some people's heads and hearts. Perhaps you find some of their secret likes, preferences and loves, their hot button, the switch that turns them on.

Case: How a Steak Chain "Challenged"
and Five W's Stimulated Employees and Sales

A steak house chain in a section of the Southeast had a seriously low sales picture. They called in Bruce R., a consultant, and within a few days one typical problem was obvious: "No heart, no mind," or rather "no practical use of employee spirit and ideas to achieve motivation."

Bruce discussed this with the president and the top officer group, who all quickly agreed but could see no solution.

Then they decided to run a test. Bruce formed a task force

of three people and *held a "brainstorming" meeting* with the 20 employees of just one restaurant unit. The task force permitted, requested, encouraged and stimulated all sorts of ideas from the group for sales building. Some were pretty wild. Then Bruce and his team challenged the employees to get more practical and to answer the five W's for each idea.

Result: Wheels started whirling in peoples' minds. Even the bus boys came up with better ways to speed service. Hearts and minds turned on. They were involved. A few had been furious at some foolish, obsolete procedures and knew much better ways. The task force then went to all the other units. The programs that were generated were tried. Every week, for the next 20 weeks straight, the sales exceeded both the preceding weeks and the same week a year ago. Staff was increased by 53%. Clearly, the use of a challenge, the five W's and an opened attitude developed heart and mind motivation, with highly constructive results.

Employing Others' "Heart and Mind" Techniques to Increase Your Power

Up to this point we have seen how to use "heart and mind." We saw how to stimulate the flow of emotions and intellect. Now, you naturally want to avoid just toying aimlessly with ideas. You want to fully harness these to help make progress toward your mutual goals.

Stimulate "group heart," group emotions and group feelings, not just the heart of one spirited individual. Encourage that one valuable person to set fire to the others. Encourage these others to catch this fire. You can do this initially by allowing, approving, even praising suggestions and then getting a bit enthused yourself.

Next, keep closely tuned in with your eyes and ears and instincts. Catch the group feeling, the trend, the consensus, the direction in which they are moving. The steam and motivational energy is growing. Now guide this toward your goals. If they are getting excited about promotions, then aim this at the sales problem you must solve by posing questions and asking for ideas in that area. If they are getting creative, then guide this toward the service improvements you need.

Stimulate "group mind" in about the same way, to build new thoughts and useful concepts aimed at solving your problems and so reaching your objectives. Well reasoned ideas, facts and logic are often a bit easier to guide toward your goals just because they are a little less emotional. For example, "Your idea for a computer automated dress or shoe rack in the store may be a little expensive. How could we do it at less cost. Some sort of revolving carousel?"

Your Secret Objective

As you initiate "group heart" and "group mind," you will often see both the emotional commitment and the idea action begin, but then sputter or stay at a low level. If you can keep this spark alive and fan it into a burning flame, you will have generated a powerful engine of heart and mind to help you reach your goals. There are three simple steps you can take that will further fire up this heart and mind machine:

First, a little common, garden variety respect. The fact that you are interested in their feelings and ideas is a good start. You can expand on this simply by really listening to them. Even listen to the foolish comments.

Second, focus on the common problems, troubles, difficulties and obstacles that "are hurting us all, cheating us and ripping us off." A common enemy unites and makes people's blood boil; and this leads to further action.

Third, provide work. Outline projects that must be done to eliminate the problem and reach the goal. A group will usually get enthusiastic when action is needed, understood and assigned. Your contagious confidence in the group and their ability to plan and execute a solution is a further stimulus stoking the engine. This confidence can become another one of those self-fulfilling prophecies.

Secrets for Using
the A.I.D.A. Formula for Power

Professional motivators have devised a little formula that works well in building enthusiasm of both the heart and the mind. A.I.D.A. standing for: *Attention, Interest, Desire* and *Action.*

Attention can be gained with your simple but forceful and

provocative question, statement, mention of the problem or some major benefit they can have in the near future.

Interest is developed as you touch on or mention how the problem hurts the people involved and how the goal can be achieved by them.

Desire can be generated as you detail or elaborate upon practical ways to solve the problem, with particular emphasis on personal enjoyment of the many benefits.

Action is stimulated by a call to "Take some steps immediately. Do it now! Today!"

Examples: Successful motivators use this formula, with strong effect, thousands of times a day. Just note the next TV, newspaper, magazine or radio ad, or church sermon or political talk. Chevy starts by telling you, "Monte Carlo will make you proud." Polaroid says, "The Minute Maker is under $25." Bell tells us, "Home is wherever there's a phone." Kodak says, "I wanted everything in my pocket." TWA has "Twice the flights as any other airline." They got your *attention.* Now each builds your *interest* and *desire* by showing you how easily you can achieve your goal and then all the lovely benefits you can enjoy. Finally, they call for *action,* now. "See your camera dealer today." Attention, interest, desire, action, the "A.I.D.A. formula." They hammer you and me and millions of others with it every day, and they have done this for many years. Rigid, scientific tests show that it generates billions of dollars in sales of goods and services. You, too, can use A.I.D.A. to reach your motivation goals.

Secrets for Building a Powerful "Gung-Ho" Team

By now you've pretty well "done it all" with your group's heart and mind. You stimulated emotion and ideas with brainstorms, challenges, five W's, enthusiasm and the A.I.D.A. formula. To wrap it up, you want the group to be a unified, aggressive team working toward your common goals. Here are a few easy ways to do this:

First, know your resources. Understand your people and your physical supplies, equipment, facilities and budget. *For example:* If you have talent and resources for executing a selling program, but not for doing statistical analysis, your way is clear. Go for the sales and forget the statistics.

Second, get involved personally. Take the "heart and mind" ideas and spirit; then fit these to a suggested course of action. *For example:* discuss problems and solutions. Give and take ideas and feelings. Get consensus. This gets your own heart and mind personally into the action. Be human, said Shakespeare, for one touch of humanity makes the whole world one. The team will soon take off somewhat on their own, partly because people resist inaction.

Third, reinforce your common goals by occasional strong reference so the target shines clearly in everyone's mind. This is an easy step that comes naturally and is usually welcome because people like to think of their reward. Effective leaders of yesterday's armies and today's business never let the goal image fade.

Fourth, continue input of spirit, pride, "face," reputation, enthusiasm and encouragement of personal dedication. "You've gotta have heart," the old song says, and you gotta keep that heart pumping with input of excitement and emotion.

Fifth, keep efforts focussed properly so that every action gets you closer to the target. Avoid wasted time and effort. This is true management by objectives.

Case: Heart, Mind and A.I.D.A.
Build Gung-Ho Team

The problem was not a crisis, but simply a common one where nobody really cared very much. In a small wax division all ten people were just sort of living day to day with a static, slowly declining business. About all they could look forward to in the distant future was the possibility of being transferred or just getting out and finding a new job or eventually losing this one when the division was closed.

Then a new manager, David T., was assigned to work with the wax group. Dave was familiar with motivation through heart and mind. And he promptly recognized that neither spirit nor intellect was being applied to the problems at hand or to the motivation of the group.

Dave's first step was to get the financial facts of the situation. They were worse than he had thought. The business was dying at an accelerating rate. He decided to use the A.I.D.A. formula: *attention, interest, desire, action.* Second, he called a meeting and displayed a giant sales graph with a big, red, jagged line sloping downward to disaster. He plainly stated the personal significance of this trend as it would affect the group.

Third, now that he had their *"attention and interest,"* he elaborated and expanded upon the troubles they all faced if the trend continued, and particularly the benefits they would enjoy if they changed the picture *(Desire)*. This is the same approach the ads often use. (The misery of headache solved with a change to Anacin . . . and "happy days are here again.") Dave encouraged their comments and ideas, suggesting plans and personal participation in the general discussion.

Fourth, Dave called for *"action"*, for spirit, belief, conviction and commitment. He challenged them. "We all have a tough job to do, but we all know how to do it, and I have complete confidence in each one of you that you will succeed." He knew his resources and his people. He got involved, personally, with the goal and the spirit, while he focussed their effort.

Result: The team developed all sorts of "heart and mind"— emotion and ideas. These were built into an aggressively executed business plan. The sales trend was reversed, and the brand continued on for years after it ordinarily would have perished. A business and jobs were saved by applying heart and mind motivation to activate a group and build constructive action.

Summary: "Heart and Mind" Generate Secret Power

Both of these can and do motivate us all, every day. Perhaps one of the most powerful motivators is *a combination* of heart and mind. People use this successfully, thousands of times a day. People's own heart and mind can be their own best motivators, plus generators of spirit and ideas that build constructive business actions. Stimulate the "mind" partly by permitting and hearing ideas, even wild ones within limits, letting one door open others. Brainstorm with a goal where nothing is "wrong." Record ideas, rank these, and stimulate more. Challenge people to supply the five W's toward the goal. Build "group heart" and "group mind," spirit and ideas, by reviewing the problem, and the work to be done and by showing your own personal confidence. Build "heart" or emotion with the A.I.D.A. formula; know your resources, get involved and focus inputs of emotion and constructive ideas. The result is a "gung-ho" team.

9

Power Secrets
for Using Delegation Effectively

Delegation can be one of your most powerful secret motivating tools. But, there is plain old "delegation," and then there is "effective, modern delegation." And only such effective delegation will really be a dynamic motivator. Once you understand it and get a feel for how it works, you will make a rather happy discovery; it not only takes no extra effort on your part, but it actually reduces your work load by using other people's inner drives to take on tasks that help you reach your goals. So, with less effort you get greater accomplishment. As the current cliché goes, "Less is more."

This chapter outlines the "five W" secrets of delegation, particularly the "what" and "when" and demonstrates how this helps you reach your goals by turning others into self-starters. You can then easily see how to put a person's desire to "be somebody," along with their thirst for authority and responsibility, to work for you. You will also see how to use the "pride formula" to increase employee motivation.

Jim D., Jay M. and Scott R. all had the same problem: little or no team action, low group performance. Each person was in a widely different business—a retail hamburger chain, management consulting and a bottling plant. But Jim, Jay and Scott all used delegation methods—almost exactly as outlined in the next few pages—to motivate; and they got positive, favorable results far beyond their best hopes.

Delegation's five W's. The five W's is a proven quick and easy way to get a clear picture of something, especially an idea or concept like delegation that can be vague and a bit slippery.

1. The "What"—Four Secrets to Powerful, Modern Delegation

Let's define delegation here as assigning a part of your activities to someone else, so they take your place in that particular action. To protect yourself, you should consider at least four things:

First, ask yourself, is this something I can *safely* delegate without disasterous results? (Example: you could delegate payroll preparation to a good accountant, but probably not to a file clerk.)

Second, do I have a right to delegate this? (Example: you might delegate payroll check preparation, but you probably can't delegate payroll check signing.)

Third, does the recipient or second party accept the assignment? If not, delegation never really happened. All the delegation in the world doesn't mean anything if it is not received, acknowledged and agreed to. (You threw the ball but no one caught it.)

As a *fourth* precaution to the what-gets-delegated question, be sure you *do not delegate too much* and end up giving your job away. Delegate but don't abdicate.

Case example: One executive found that he had many written inquiries arriving at times when he was either out of town or otherwise tied up, and he could not answer for days. He worried that those writing him would interpret the delay as indifference. So he asked his secretary to send a brief acknowledgment of each inquiry, indicating that a more complete answer would be made within a reasonable time. She agreed and performed well. Note: This was a *safe* delegation since it could hardly cause trouble but, in fact, avoid it. It was a *right* and reasonable act to delegate since it didn't put an unfair task or undue burden on the secretary, so *she accepted* the assignment. But the executive *did not delegate away* his entire job, merely a part of it, retaining the key decisions and answers to be made by himself at a better time.

2. The "Who"—Secrets of
Selecting Your Designate

You are the one who must usually take the first step. You decide what part of the job can be parceled out and who might accept this assignment. The key to who-gets-delegated is largely a matter of willingness and ability; you should delegate to someone who will take the assignment and someone who can really do it to your satisfaction. Incidentally, if you are employed by someone, then you, yourself have already been delegated or assigned to a job that your boss either can't do or doesn't want to do.

3. The "When"—Three Secrets to
Power in Timing of Delegation

There are several key rules of thumb here. *For one*, delegate when you have more assignments than you can reasonably handle. An over-worked, over-loaded manager is a situation crying out for delegation. *Second*, delegate when you have some assignments that are simple, easy, annoying, well below your top ability. World famous consultant Peter Drucker says, "A manager should always work at his highest skill" (if he is to maximize his value, contribution and salary). So delegate and get rid of your simple activities, giving them to someone else: a subordinate such as a secretary, clerk or other person in your group. *Third*, avoid delegating until you know what you are doing. Know the consequences of your act and how the delegated activity should be performed. Otherwise, you could be giving out assignments that will cause you unexpected problems. *Fourth*, delegate when other persons can do the job nearly as well or even better than you can, such as typing.

Case example: Kathy R., a manager of a three-person department, was asked by her boss to handle four new one-time projects. One was rather complex. The other three were fairly routine. Kathy called her group together. She explained that these were more added chores than she could possibly do, so delegated one of the simple tasks to each employee, who could perform them as well as or better than she could. Kathy was careful to explain

that she would keep the toughest one for herself to do and offered
to help anyone else who needed it. The group was well motivated,
and the projects were all done far more thoroughly than if she had
tried to do them all herself . . . and with far less work for Kathy.

4. "Where" to Delegate for Maximum Power

Normally, at your place of business or at least at a location you
can reasonably watch. Delegation across long distances, such as to
persons hundreds of miles away can sometimes work, but often
falls apart due to lack of easy communication and supervision. Says
comedian Flip Wilson, "What you sees is what you gets." And if
you see nothing, that is about what you are likely to get. So your
best bet is to delegate where observation and contact are convenient.

5. Power Secrets of "Why" You Should Delegate

First, it frees your time to do other, more important, more
productive things. *Second*, it is usually more efficient, since the
person taking on the delegated task can often do it better than you
(like typing). *Third*, this has a strong motivating influence on employees. Since we have now come to the main point of this chapter,
let's look at how delegation works, how to delegate and a true case
illustrating these points.

How Delegation Secretly Helps Build Power

The major ways delegation helps you are that it divides up
large, sweeping assignments into small *manageable jobs* that can
be done one part at a time. *Second, it permits specialization* so
that when you split up the job between yourself and someone else
each of you can now learn more about one activity and do it better
than you ever could if either of you tried to do it all yourself. *Third,
you build interest*, enthusiasm and drive in people accepting the
delegated assignment. They become involved, a part of the operation, an important part. *Result:* They are turned on. They work
harder and better and contribute more toward your mutual goals.
You have put the simple idea of delegation to work for you to help
accomplish things for you and your organization.

Power Secrets for HOW to Delegate

There are dozens of ways you can delegate, but each one is usually some variation of three basic methods: the "honor" approach, the "assistance" system and the "assignment" technique. Each one ends up with the person doing more but also feeling more important.

The "Honor" Secret

The "honor" secret simply bestows an apparent honor or recognition on the person. *Example:* "Mary, you are the only one who really knows how to assemble this unit. Let's put you in charge of that function."

The "Assistance" Secret

Here you candidly admit that you need the person's help, which is really no big deal since that is why the person is hired to start with. "Bill, we really need your assistance on this. We almost can't do it without you. How about keeping this set of records up to date on sales and purchasing." Note: it's a question made as a statement. Note also that Bill probably feels more important.

The "Assignment" Secret

Here you simply nominate, request or assign a project. *For example:* "Sam, I can't go to the meeting tomorrow. Will you please attend and take a few notes so you can tell me what was said." Again, it is phrased as a question but made as a statement or mild directive . . . and it makes Sam feel more important.

How a Hamburger Chain Manager Used Delegation to Solve Problems

The situation faced by Jim D., unit group manager, was largely low activity, low sales, low morale and low motivation. Jim's group of six units was part of a chain of 300 hamburger outlets. Each unit was well designed and had an attractive, tasty menu of food and drink at least as good as competition and sometimes better. But the employees were spending most of their day watching traffic drive right past their door. When a customer did stop in, there were mistakes, confusion, delays and disappointments. Sales were poor, and if this continued, units would have to reduce staff and perhaps close down.

The objectives, as agreed upon between Jim and the employees of each unit were: (1) to get more customers, (2) to improve speed and quality of service and, most important, (3) to convince the customer to come back again.

The strategy decided upon was delegation. "John, you have a natural ability at sales. How about if we designate you as Vice President of Sales Development." His job was to work with the headquarters and take steps, locally, to attract customers, such as by getting hand bills with special coupons to all nearby homes and businesses. Each team member was delegated to specialize in one part of the operation. "Mary, I need your help to operate the grill." "Sam, how about you serving soft drinks and keeping records."

Results were seen within a few weeks in at least five areas: (1) morale improved greatly; employees were now more important; (2) activity was greatly increased; each employee had a goal, as assignment; (3) more customers were attracted by the Vice President of Sales Development; (4) each customer was served more rapidly, smoothly and efficiently with properly prepared food; (5) a larger percentage of these customers was pleased, and so as the days passed they came back. The units prospered. Staff was not cut back, but instead it was expanded, and several members of the team won awards and promotions. Delegation of specific job segments had generated the motivation needed to make big progress.

How to turn others into self-starters. If you can turn people on as the manager did in the hamburger chain, you clearly have much more going for you than you do if their switch is off. But how do you throw the switch?

The Three Power Steps

There are three secret power steps: First, recognize that a surprising variety of people will get enthusiastic when you give them the *right strokes*. Don't count anyone out. Sometimes the greatest troublemaker or least enthusiastic person becomes your best ram-rod and pile driver. In fact, seasoned managers deliberately keep a weather eye open for the seemingly unlikely. Their very ornery, negative attitude can well be a hidden stifled cry, "I want to *be* more and *do* more!"

As a short case example: Juana N. was a good secretary, who felt able to write letters and to do other little things. This was not recognized; so she became unenthusiastic. She was really saying, "I can do more." Then a press release was needed for the local newspaper. Her supervisor said, "Juana, I need your help. How about taking a try at this." She jumped at the chance, did a fine job, expanded her assignment and eventually won awards.

A second step you can take is to solicit volunteers actively, yourself, whenever and wherever it makes sense; and see what turns up. Here again, the very act of asking for help may spring loose someone who was on the verge of offering their help, anyway. (Just like Juana N.)

Now, third, "fan the flames." Once you have someone even remotely interested, recognize that beneath that cool and casual attitude may (and usually does) lie a small volcano of potential enthusiasm and motivation. It's often hidden, a bit. After all, you don't always show all your cards and interest; and so why should they? Answer: they don't. So the hot coals are often there. Feed them with your approval. They want that; they seek it; they crave it. And for you, it's cheap, easy, and gets a large return on your investment of time and effort.

How to feed them with your approval. Simply show or state your positive feelings about their spark of interest. You might just say, "I'm glad you're interested." Or, "You'll do well in that project." Or, "You always do a good job in that area." Or even, "That's great! Our whole group will gain from your help!" This is what psychologists call "positive reinforcement of favorable response."

Why people secretly want authority: To "BE" somebody. People have cravings and all kinds of wants. These are certainly food, clothing, shelter, sex, recreation, inspiration and others. Not necessarily in that order, depending on the person and the situation.

But above all they shout out, "I want to be me!" Yet, even before that, young people, especially, first ask, "Who am I?" Now, what is it that this person is really asking? The answer is, they want to know, "Where do I fit? What is my role? What is my part in this big, complex and wonderful world? What can I do to be accepted, wanted and loved by my equals?" In pure and simple terms that most all of us have experienced, they have "an identity crisis." They don't know who they are: they don't like it; and they want to know.

They have a real problem. But you have a real solution. They want to know who they are. You can tell them. You can fill a craving, a yearning and a deep desire. Not one you made up, but one that is already there, pleading to be filled. And, by filling it, you gain help, support, enthusiasm and motivation. A multimillionaire recently said, "To really succeed, find a need and fill it."

Case: Some time ago there was a TV commercial for "Hush Puppies," showing a country boy putting on a pair of shoes and saying word to the effect, "At last! My feet can breathe! Now I can go to school. I can BE somebody!" Note the importance of the last goal . . . the ultimate. He can BE somebody. Now most viewers, of course, were not country boys, and most of us laughed a bit at this comment. But secretly we all want to be somebody. Each of your people feels just like the boy in the commercial. They want to be somebody. If you help them to be this somebody, you gain not only their support and enthusiasm, but you gain their long term loyalty. And you have used delegation to build powerful, supportive motivation.

Power Secret: Help a Person BE Somebody

You can do this easily enough by simply using the two things we just discussed: *first*, basic delegation, building an importance and a role in the working world; *second*, generating an attitude towards being "a self-starter," perhaps by feeding them with your approval. As a *third* element, you would be wise to emphasize the value of their assignment. This helps the person become even more important in his or her own eyes.

Authority and responsibility are secrets to constructive power. Now that you have caused someone to BE somebody, how does this help you? *First*, it helps because you have created, generated and awarded power, prestige and status. You built position and a step up, where before there was none. You have bestowed a purple mantle, a laurel wreath, a gold bar of responsibility. *Second*, the simple fact that you personally did this is clear and abundant evidence that you *can* do this. Therefore, you are or must be at least fairly important, powerful and worth serving, since you can give out the goodies. *Third*—and this is a much more subtle, less obvious, more hidden thing—you have established, developed and built a new and powerful feeling, an inner glow of happiness, a feeling of self-satisfaction and self-admiration, of beauty and inner peace. You have bestowed a gift beyond price, a thing that money cannot buy. Even double the wages could not necessarily do what you just did. When you bestowed the authority and responsibility, you lit the fire of self-esteem, of enthusiasm and of motivation toward your mutual goals.

"I Am the Head Knocker!" or the Pride Formula

The pride formula is simple: "Pride plus responsibility equals action." You have developed pride because you delegated something, almost anything, and made someone BE somebody. Then you bestowed the gold bar of responsibility to ignite that inner glow of self-esteem. You have touched off a motivating fire and pointed it in a direction. Is it any wonder that now you get action? When a person feels proud and feels responsible to respond, that person is almost always going to act.

Case: A famous story provides an example of this. A group of soldiers had been causing a lot of trouble: inaction, resistance to orders, obstruction and fights. Then their leader picked out the biggest, toughest, meanest, most difficult, most vocal, most able of the group and delegated him as "The Head Foreman," the "Top Sergeant." Suddenly, the picture changed. The group took a new look at the situation. The new sergeant took a new look at the group, and he took over. He ordered obedience, performance and productivity. "And if that don't happen, heads will get knocked, because I am the *Head Knocker!*" And he got the results he demanded. What had happened? Pride in himself plus responsibility to do a job—both delegated to him—generated real action towards needed goals. The system worked.

This is purely an example of the formula functioning in it's simplest form. This is not to suggest "head knocking," but merely to show how pride and responsibility are a powerful mixture of delegated elements. They almost always explode into motivated action. The steps to delegation, of course, are not always this simple, easy or clear—especially in dealing with non-militaristic, modern, free-thinking, independent, educated, even sophisticated workers of today.

Using the "Territorial Imperative"

The "Territorial Imperative" is a popular concept that hit the newspapers and magazines in the last few years. Basically, it means that all of us want to be in charge of our own area, some space, some land. It becomes important, even imperative, to us. All of us occupy some space at work: a desk, a chair, an office, a bench, a sales counter or a work station of some kind. We sort of "own" this. It is ours to use and work from. The territorial imperative idea developed from scientific observation of birds, where it was found to be a strong *basic animal* drive.

We don't really own our territory, of course. It was delegated to us. But it still becomes a part of our own personal world and our daily lives. We feel comfortable there, at home and friendly. Even if we are not exactly thrilled with our job, even if we don't much like our job, we have grown accustomed to its face. Or as prisoner Jean Val Jean says in *Les Miserables*, "My very chains and I grow friends." This territory can be geographic space, or it can become an area of responsibility. It becomes a sort of personal possession. For example, did you ever notice how you bristle just a bit when someone uses your desk or work space or gets into your area of responsibility? With some people this resentment can grow into a very strong and even unpleasant confrontation. Then, we have what is sometimes called a "turf war" on our hands. Such wars are very common to animals at nearly all levels, not just us human critters.

Your power increased with delegation. If you assign an area (as we discussed in "How to Delegate," above), the territorial imperative can quickly take over. It can act as a powerful, natural, basic human, even animal, instinct to motivate people to attachment for that area which in turn relates to or is aimed towards your objectives.

For example: "Hey Joe, why don't you be Vice President of Packages?" Here is an informal, almost jocular type of delegation. It is often made completely in jest; purely as humor or good natured kidding. People in the organization know there really is no such thing or title as "Vice President of Packages." And yet, in many, if not most every instance, the person so "delegated" nearly always takes this at least half seriously. Here we see the power and attraction that delegation has for people. Delegation is often not at all like pouring water up hill. Quite the opposite. It is a pebble or rock or boulder poised on the side of a mountain that will roll into action with very little encouragement.

The small joke: "Why don't you be Vice President of Packages" and the action this often motivates are an example of both the pride formula (responsibility has been lightly but plainly assigned) interlocking with our friend the territorial imperative. And we're off to the races, chased by a rolling boulder of high kinetic motivational energy. Your power has increased.

A word of warning: this kind of little joke, like most business jokes, is all too often treated, at least partly, as a serious statement, and sometimes it is taken as a formal assignment. It's strong medicine, so don't toss it around too casually. *You* might be kidding, but the other guy isn't. He just got promoted to a new "territory" of pride and responsibility. He will act and expect you to approve such action.

But it is a strong secret tool for your motivation kit. It lets you apply the powers of delegation in a light hearted, easy, fast, friendly way without being heavy handed or dictatorial.

From "no one" to V.P. in one day. Jimmy F. was foreman of a small plant. He took great pride in keeping the production line and storage areas clean, painted, lighted and sharp. The linemen were supposed to push broom during down time, but they usually pushed more coffee than trash. Then one day Jim said to Cliff K., "Hey Cliff, I'm going to promote you to Vice President of Sanitation. There's no extra pay . . . but think of the prestige!" They both laughed, but Cliff's was more of a chuckle. That afternoon, Cliff was behind the broom nearly every possible minute, and the next day he came to work wearing a little black leather bow tie.

Ten Power Secrets

In today's complex world, there are lots of ways to foul the gears of delegation and cause slowing or even break up on an organization team. This is particularly easy when the would-be delegation motivator tries to dive in full force and accomplish everything at once. He often makes matters worse.

But there is an easy way to create delegation action and motivate people. Let's break the job down into a few simple, manageable chunks.

Power secret one: take a good look at your situation. Do you have the kind of conditions that suggest or even cry out for delegation? *For example:* do you have many more projects than you can reasonably handle? Are some of these much more simple than others? Are they the kind that others might even do better than you can? And are there people available who obviously can do these things or just might do well, if you give them the chance? Or, if you are uncertain, are these the kinds of tasks and people where it's worth a try, where failure won't bring any big disaster or even a small disaster, but merely a correctable delay? If these conditions exist, you have a situation, opportunity and resource that is "green and go" for delegation.

Power secret two: pick a goal or objective for yourself. It might be, "I want to delegate preparation of all routine ABC reports over to John Smith or Suzy Jones. My objective is to get him or her to take charge of this activity completely, so I can use that part of my time to better advantage."

Power secret three is easy, because it consists of several simple moves. Obviously, your first one is just to ask for volunteers to do this specific job. "Who wants to buy the supplies? Who wants to sell the coffee? Who wants to keep records?" Or direct your question to a certain person. "John, which of these tasks would you like to do?" Or even, "Mary, would you care to handle the phone calls and paper work?"

Right away, you will usually have volunteers, people who like to do these things, have done them and may be afraid that if they don't volunteer for these activities they will get something less pleasant, or, worst of all, something they can't really do.

Power secret four: but what if you can't get a volunteer? You abandon this approach, right? Wrong. The really smart operators always give the volunteer approach at least a second chance, maybe a third. The theory, which has proven realistic, is that many who won't volunteer the first time are simply holding back, waiting for the initial wave of people to move in. Many employees who would like to volunteer—and that probably includes the *majority of the population*—are still a little slow to step forward. They don't want to be last, but they still don't want to be first. America is mostly folks in the middle.

So you ask again. Even suggest, "Hey, Sam, I'll bet you would like this project." (Don't call it a job. That sounds too much like work. Projects in school were usually things of a few hours or few days.) Often very capable people are waiting to be approached. They are thinking "Why don't they ask me? Don't they believe I can do it?" And then there is the occassional hard-nosed cat who says, "If they won't bother to ask me, I won't do it."

Power secret five: You can always shame them. "The mail room group has already found someone who is willing to call customers for orders. Too bad we don't have some people who can do that." Or appeal to their pride, "We probably have the best outfit around here, especially in buying and recording. Now, who's willing to take a crack at doing the purchasing or record keeping?"

Power secret six: go back to that sense of responsibility, importance and pride. "Whoever handles the customer contact is going to be my right hand man and probably the most important member of our team. But I'm only interested in someone who really wants to do the job."

Power secret seven: Notice the strong red line of "RESPECT" running through all of this—the respect the person gets for "being" somebody, the ego building feeling from saying, "Yes, I can do this." Respect is reflected when you ask, "Would you like to do this?" There is respect when you say, "Who's willing to try this?" And when you say, "Whoever handles this job is my right hand man."

Power secret eight: But what if no one volunteers? You have several further options. One is to build up one or two people. Tell the group how capable each of them is. Express the hope that one of them shows an interest. That is pretty strong stuff. It's hard to hold out against. You are now sort of creating a competition between two people and again using the "pride" element, a factor never to be underestimated.

Power secret nine: Another option is to simply come right out and ask. "Joe, would you handle this?" The danger is that Joe will decline. Then you must either retreat, confront or cajole. Cajoling

is your best bet, with an eye toward retreat. "Joe, you might do a
great job and I'd be proud to work with you on this. But, maybe
someone else could do as well or even better. Bill, how about you?"

*Power secret ten: If all this pussy footing around doesn't
work,* ask the one you really feel is best to sit down and visit with
you, privately. Then say something like, "You are obviously the best
suited for this. You would do a good job and gain credit for both
yourself and the group, if you do this." It could be that you are in a
position to order the person to do it, but it is almost always better
to at least go through the motions to get his or her personal agreement or commitment. A cliché covers this: a man convinced against
his will is of the same opinion still. Try to get them to believe in it
and want to do it. Even if you must, in the end order the action. It
will pay to be pleasant. Winston Churchill said that even if you're
going to execute a person, it doesn't cost anything to be polite
about it.

Have you noticed the S-O-S system you have been following in
this whole series of steps for building delegation activity?

First, you looked at your situation to see if things were ripe
for delegation. *Second, you set an objective* for yourself, in terms
of what you wanted others to do. *Third, you planned a system.*
You sought out volunteers. Then, if that didn't work, you made a
direct request or finally a specific assignment.

Case History: How SCORE Used Delegation to Help Build the World's Largest Consulting Group

The problem: In the United States there are about 10 million
small businesses, most of whom have management problems. Few
of these firms can afford to hire consultants. But the nation also
boasts a valuable natural resource of about one million retired business owners and managers. And so SCORE, or Service Corp of
Retired Executives, was organized. For years the group has provided free counsel to small business presidents, although in many
cases the local SCORE chapters were highly inefficient.

The solution was outlined by Jay M. and other SCORE leaders. They recognized that there were literally millions of firms who
desperately needed help and that there were many basic jobs the
SCORE chapters needed to do if they were to provide that help.

The chapters needed good recruiting, client case assignment, publicity, quality control, training programs and policies. In most chapters of ten to 100 or more counselors, these jobs were all done either by the chairman alone or by just a few members. Jay decided that delegation of these tasks would motivate more action, and better, more efficient performance. Jay and other leaders urged chapters to delegate these various parts of the overall activity to individuals or small groups who could specialize in recruiting, assignments, publicity, etc. Soon, hundreds of chapters across the country recognized the power of delegation and started to use it.

The results: This was obviously a situation crying out for delegation. Far more work existed than could be done by any one person or even a small group. And some of the counselors could do it better than their leaders. Many members were willing, even eager, to accept delegated responsibilities.

Suddenly, previously inactive members began to feel more involved, more needed and more important. They started to "BE" somebody in addition to what they already were. They became motivated—self-motivated self-starters. Little teams formed, such as for recruiting or publicity. These teams were often made up of people who had done this kind of work in the past and liked it but had never been asked to volunteer to do this. Now they had authority and responsibility, an increased inner glow of status, power, prestige and self-respect. Pride plus responsibility generated action. More small business owners were served, in a far better manner than ever before. And a surprising, totally unexpected thing happened: suddenly, thousands of prospective counselors, who had not been attracted by the less structured, less organized operation of the past, began joining up. Many of these were men and women of unusual talent, enthusiasm and energy. And SCORE with over 8,000 consultants, became, and still is, the largest management consultant organization in the entire world. Delegation became the spark plug, firing motivation efforts that influenced millions of businesses.

Case History: How Production Team Delegation Solved a Sales Crisis

Situation: Plant Manager Scott R. had organized a major summer selling event to build increased sales volume for a bottling plant. Added income was desperately needed, or else the plant would have to close down. Scott's plan was to feature root beer. A large newspaper, radio and TV advertising program was prepared, scheduled and contracted. But a week before the event was to start, the root beer flavor concentrate still had not arrived at the plant for production. The shipment had been lost. Without a supply, advertising would run with no product to sell, resulting in a major waste. A bad financial situation would suddenly become a disasterous one. As the week ran out, a grim silence fell over the little company.

Solution: Here was a situation that almost allowed for nothing else but delegation by the plant manager. Scott could not personally produce the product himself, nor could he order it done if the production team elected to head for the hills on their weekend. As the crisis began to appear on the horizon, Scott generated a strong delegation climate by explaining the situation and objective to the production team. They were delegated to be "The Task Force" to do whatever they could to help the common effort. They accepted. The group now knew they had been given specific "territory" to care for. They knew the results of failure and understood that it all fell largely on their shoulders. Other employees recognized this and respected them for it. But when late Friday afternoon came and no supplies appeared, Scott and his people quietly went home, realizing that the game was lost.

Results: Then the vitally needed concentrate suddenly arrived late Saturday night. Sunday, Scott just happened to stop by the plant to pick up some papers. It was working full tilt! Overtime! Free! Without pay! "What the hell's going on here?" he asked.

"The concentrate came in! We're running off cases of root beer like there's no tomorrow!" said the production foreman, in an obviously high state of enthusiasm. And there they were, the full production crew. They had come in Sunday morning to work on their own. They were going to "BE" somebody, the "guys who saved the day" and maybe the company. They felt it was their responsibility. This responsibility linked with their pride generated action. They knew the problem, and they knew the objectives. On Monday morning, the trucks were delivering thousands of cases of root beer to hundreds of stores in the huge metro market area. The ads appeared that night, and sales volume took a giant step forward. Jobs were saved, and the future brightened. With a warm glow of self-satisfaction, self-esteem, self-respect and self-motivation, the

production team stood ten feet tall in the eyes of their fellow workers, their families and themselves. Delegation created motivation
that brought many rewards to a desperate company plant.

Summary: Delegation Can Be
a Great Power Secret for You

You have just seen how even fairly good delegation can be one
of your most effective, most dynamic tools, a tool that not only
takes no extra effort on your part, but cuts your work by applying
other people's wants and drives to help you hit objectives. We
looked at the five W's of delegation, especially "What" to delegate
(mainly things others can do well) and "When" (when you have too
many jobs, especially simple, tedious chores). We saw how this
helps you reach goals by breaking big jobs into manageable chunks
and by getting people involved. You can delegate with the "honor"
approach, the "assistance" system and the "assignment" technique, as they did in the hamburger chain. Self-starters can come
from surprising sources if stimulated by your approval, because
people strongly want to "BE" somebody, to have an identity, authority, power, status and responsibility. The "pride" formula of
pride plus responsibility almost always touches off action, especially when someone can say, "I am the Head Knocker or the Vice
President of this territory." When you explain the problem, the
goals, get volunteers and show respect for them, your delegation
steps usually develop strong help for you in reaching your goals.
We saw Jim D. with his hamburger units, Jay M. with consultants
and Scott R. with a bottling operation all face the same problem of
inaction. All used delegation methods reviewed here, and all enjoyed dramatically successful results.

10

Coaching and Guidance:
a Powerful and Overlooked
Management Tool

Alfredo B., brand manager for a world famous brand of pen, had three of those common, everyday problems facing many small group managers: Low team enthusiasm, low action and low sales. This did not seem very important to most people in the company, but it did to Al, because it not only threatened his promotion and bonus, but it also endangered his job.

Al looked into the matter and found that everyone believed the pen display was the main problem. It was not liked by the company salesmen, retailers or prospective customers.

He called his little group together and outlined the problem. Al delegated his assistant Manuel to develop a better display. Manny was interested, but uncertain about how to proceed. Al could have said, "Figure it out for yourself, Manny. That's what you're being paid for." But instead, Al decided to use some contemporary and well tested coaching techniques. He explained some ten basic do's and dont's for pen displays. Then he demonstrated, with competitive units, just where these were followed and where their own display had most of these, but missed several key elements. Al encouraged Manny to sketch out a couple of drafts, while they were talking, applying the ten basic rules. Then he suggested that Manny spend the next few days doing some further sketches with the design and sales people, reviewing these with retailers.

Manny did just that. Then he and Al discussed the strengths and weaknesses of each new sketch. They agreed on changes and some new ideas. Manny put himself into the project with growing interest and vigor.

In the end, a sparkling, dramatically new display was produced. The little group became highly enthusiastic, highly motivated. The display generated wide acceptance, increased sales and renewed consumer interest in the brand. Al's coaching and guidance had built new motivation, new sales levels and increased personal rewards.

Al and Manny gave us several power secrets: they showed us that coaching and personal, team spirited guidance are strong motivation. They are often overlooked in our natural desire to give quick orders and get quick compliance. The pen case history shows (and we will see in the next few pages how) that the "Ex-Dem-Pra" formula of explanation, demonstration and practical work gets results. It has worked for millions, especially after the people being motivated see that "work" is not an end in itself—not "just something we do," but a means toward a goal.

Here you will also see some positive suggestions for practical, dynamic delegation and development of constructive action without abdication of your authority or control, but, in fact, building your position, power and prestige.

Coaching: Its Power and How It Secretly Motivates

Coaching is the understanding of people, problems and goals plus mutual development and testing of solutions. Perhaps the key differences between directives or orders and coaching is that an order simply demands an action or result without much concern for method or involvement or trial. Coaching reflects insight into the person's situation and ability as it matches up to some goal. Coaching gets very concerned with method. But most important, coaching reflects a sympathy, an empathy, a sharing, a "we" spirit, a "let's-do-it together," a "we'll-solve-it-if-we-work-as-a-team" attitude. Coaching uses criticism only to the extent of saying, "Well, that approach didn't work for us; so let's try a different way." This is constructive criticism that shows you really care and that you need help and co-operation. Coaching is not saying, "Boy, are you a slob!"

Since folks secretly fear "strangeness," coaching should start out with what we know, what we face and what we want to do. These things are not strangers to us. Then we can move on to ways we might do this. Looking at these procedures eliminates the aura of uncertainty, suspicion or surprise. It builds familiarity and comfort with a concept and enhances interest, developing motivation.

Insight leads to respect and liking. When we understand a subject, we tend to enjoy it. When you know and understand a person or hobby or sport or business procedure such as accounting or writing or selling, you tend to feel more comfortable doing it. Strong insight is a further motivation towards activity. Coaching builds such increased understanding.

The major goal of teaching and coaching, however, is not really just to implant fact "A" into employee mind "B." It is to build an *emotional* climate and condition, to sell interest, desire, enthusiasm and action. The best teachers don't teach; their students learn. The effective teacher or coach motivates the employee to learn. As the cliché goes, you can lead a horse to water, but you can't make him drink. The coach convinces him to learn and to act.

If you think back to your favorite teachers, that is exactly what they did with you. They were not just teaching. They were coaching and motivating. In the end, it was you who did the learning. You can do the same sort of coaching motivation with your people.

The power secret is good "technique," applying a few simple methods. It ain't what you do says the old slogan, but the way that you do it. This means use of the system and approaches that have proved effective. Bauer and Black has a sign in the conference room that reads, "If you would succeed, you must do those things known to cause success." And this applies to small groups as well as large. Let's look at some of the most successful coaching techniques.

A Secret Formula That Always Improves Your Power: "Ex-Dem-Pra"

This stands for "explanation, demonstration and practical work." It is a coaching system that is always effective except for rare, abnormal conditions (such as physical or mental illness).

Explanation is your first step. This simply means description of the key items in the problem—the basic goal—and the few action steps a person should take to accomplish this objective. Recognize reality, analyze the aggregate, and synthesize solutions. Get it all together and tell 'em what you want done. Use the five W's: who, what, when, where and why.

Demonstration means to show them. Do it once or twice. Or just do a small part. Or describe in detail how it can be and has been done. Perhaps you can use pictures, sketches or diagrams, so they can see, hear and feel the solution. Tell about actual cases. *For example:* You may want a written or accounting report prepared in a certain way. Sketch out the form with pencil lines drawn to represent lines of words or numbers. Give a few key words at major points. Or you might want a sales presentation, or a production part assembled in a certain way; do it. Go through the steps, describing them as you do them. The most successful coaches say, "Never ask a person to do something you can't do, or at least don't understand well."

Practical work is a step regretfully too often ignored, with costly motivational penalties. Let them do it. Explain and make sure they feel and understand that it's OK for them to make mistakes. You expect them to. Everyone does just as you did. The important thing is to make those mistakes now, when it doesn't matter. Then correct these, practice some more and get the feel and the habit of doing it properly. Ask and encourage them to start slowly, seek a system and polish it to perfection. Make it become second nature to do it right. Only then should they increase the speed.

Here's Proof That "Ex-Dem-Pra" Coaching Has Secret Power

Ex-Dem-Pra coaching has motivated millions, particularly over the last 40 years, in war, colleges and businesses.

In war—during World War II, Korea, Vietnam—and in between, Ex-Dem-Pra coaching was used to train and motivate over 20 million service people in the U.S., plus about 100 million in Germany, Japan, Russia, England, France, Cuba, and among Chinese communists, the Vietnamese, the Viet-cong and others. *For example:* every machine gun squad of four men was told how to assemble and disassemble the gun, then shown, and then allowed to do it themselves, over and over again. It is a proven technique to generate maximum proper action with minimum coaching time and effort.

Thousands of colleges, here and abroad, use some version of Ex-Dem-Pra coaching with millions of students. This is particularly true with the professional and graduate schools of business, medicine, music, art, journalism, architecture, law, sociology, engineering, aviation and others. Who ever heard of a dentist or a pilot who had not had the profession explained and demonstrated, then been encouraged to try each step a few times on a test basis?

And yet, Ex-Dem-Pra is ignored in business by many lower or first line supervisors, while it is used extensively among higher level executives in millions of firms. Why? Because the more successful managers learned long ago that good coaching; (a) is easily learned, and (b) often motivates people better than any other technique. But first line managers rarely use Ex-Dem-Pra because: (1) they have never heard of it; (2) they don't think coaching works; (3) they feel it is too bookish or school like, unsophisticated, simplistic, corny or somehow beneath them; and (4) they haven't watched top managers closely enough to realize they are doing some version of Ex-Dem-Pra coaching motivation much of the time, with excellent generation of action.

As further proof of Ex-Dem-Pra's secret power recall, there is an ancient Chinese proverb: "I hear and I forget [explanation]. I see and I remember [demonstration]. I do and I understand [practical work]."

But, "work" is not the same as "results." This is another power secret. Some managers get the impression that the purpose of coaching is mainly to create activity. Not so. Action is certainly one objective, but rarely the major goal. The real purpose is results—something of value happening. Employees often miss this point.

For example: "I made more than my quota of sales calls. No, I didn't sell anything, but I made the calls." Or, in other cases: "We made up all the reports and products. Well no, we didn't send them out. Were we supposed to send those to someone?" "My people sure are hard workers. Here every day on time and leave on time. We may not win any prize for successes, but we get an "A" for effort. We give it the old college try." In all these cases, there was a lot of action but little or no real progress.

Diagnosis: The coaching motivation was cut too short. It didn't go far enough. The Ex-Dem-Pra got things started, all right. Action took place. The project was explained and demonstrated, and the employee may even have performed some practical work. But the coach did not tie in Ex-Dem-Pra with the real goal, purpose or objective for the activity. The employee naturally equated work with results. Work became an end in itself, not a means to an end. The game became: "Big effort, little result." The solution is for the coach to equate the activity with the target and make it emphatically clear that the activity is merely a way of *achieving that goal.*

But what if they finish in half the time, or with half the work and effort? Does this mean the work is less valuable, since results were achieved at costs in time, money and effort much lower than anticipated? The coaching motivation was simply more efficient than expected. The person or the team is a living example of "working smarter than harder"—or at least working more effectively.

Case: A Car Dealership Coaching Motivation
Ex-Dem-Pra Cured "Big-Effort/Little-Results" Pattern

"You can take that new car and stuff it up your nose!" said the furious customer. His face was red, his voice trembling. His anger was so overwhelming that he was clearly close to violence.

The manager stepped back a little. "There, there, sir. Let's look into this and see if we can't take care of you."

"You've taken care of me all right! Oh man, have you ever! Four times! And this time is worse than ever! One more time and it will be junk!"

Since this was the sixth irate customer that day and things had been like this all month, the manager obviously had a problem. Sales, profit and morale were down seriously. Jobs were in danger of being abolished.

Steve R., a consultant, was hired. He interviewed the three department heads who each supervised a half dozen people. Steve got to know each manager and the managers' assistants. He listened to each person's gripes and frustrations in not being able to reach their goals.

Key problems were located. For example: in one case the service write-up man at the gate tried hard and worked hard but was poorly coached. When a person drove in and said, "There is a noise in the water pump; fix the pump," this was done, only to find that the noise was still there. And so was the irate customer. Mechanics strongly felt that the order should have described the symptom and let the mechanic, not the customer, prescribe the therapy. The order should have read, "check noise." Other similar problems were located. Severe personality clashes had developed from all directions. Morale, action and performance all fell sharply, making matters worse and clients madder.

Steve and the manager decided on a series of coaching motivation sessions. They worked together with each group as a team to improve customer service. They discussed errors, misunderstandings and new methods. Motivation started to grow. Each person slowly became more concerned with learning solutions instead of cutting up other people.

Once new systems were worked out, they were explained to everyone. Steve, the manager and the department head demonstrated these to each individual employee. The gate man and the others practiced their new methods. Everyone understood that just new ways and major effort were not good enough. Results were what counted: satisfied customers.

The new systems were introduced. They did not produce miracles overnight, since a bad reputation proved tough to live down. But complaints did decline immediately. Sales, profits and morale soon went up to healthy levels—a vast improvement from the earlier situation. Within a few weeks, coaching motivation had saved morale, jobs and a medium-small sized business.

The Coaches' Power Secret

The better, more successful, seasoned coaches learned long ago—often the hard way—that they cannot simply practice Ex-Dem-Pra, tie it to an expectation of results and walk away assuming that all is peachy.

To build power, good coaches assist, then follow up. Without over-supervising or breathing down anyone's neck, they complete the Ex-Dem-Pra routine. They stand back and let things happen. But they *come back and check* to see how the coaching motivation "took," how well it worked, what happened and with what specific results. "Follow-up" has almost become a *secret success technique*. It is a magic phrase in the better companies. The good manager does not delegate and then abdicate by walking away.

"Love me or hate me, but don't ignore me," said the philosopher E. Julia. And strangely, most employees feel about the same. To be treated as if they were abandoned or do not exist is the most unkind cut of all. *For example:* Most Canadians have been a bit ticked-off at U.S. companies for excessive economic and political domination of their country. But what really infuriates them is that most U.S. citizens don't even know that the Canadian is angry! He is being ignored! He feels the same as most employees who would rather be complimented or corrected or coached than ignored; and he will respond with much greater spirit and motivation. They want to know someone cares about them.

The follow-up power secret: A price of success is eternal vigilance. Additional coaching may not always be needed, but rechecking and observation constitute an essential technique. They are a form of communication, and, as world reknown consultant Peter Drucker says, "Communication is one of modern managers' greatest failings." Watching permits you to spot small problems and take simple steps for correcting these. "The best doctor is not necessarily the one who makes the most accurate diagnosis," says the old medical slogan, "but the one who quickly sees and corrects inaccurate decisions." And most important, watching reinforces and supports, and reassures the employee that someone cares, while refreshing or rebuilding the coaching motivation.

Four Power Secrets for Handling "Coach's Surprise"

This is somewhat in contrast to the situation where you went to the employee to motivate correction of some difficulty. This time he brings the problem to you. Your goal is still the same: to motivate action that gets desired results. But your technique should be different because you have been handed a "coach's surprise." The employee currently knows something you do not. Perhaps he or she knows a lot more than is said. There are at least four steps you can take that are fairly easy, since they form a logical and natural time sequence: study, ask, support and follow through.

First, study the problem. Strongly resist any temptation to panic, ridicule or criticize. Ask short, basic, nonemotional, impersonal question—just questions that show you are seeking constructive facts and information. Be sure you really have a problem. Ask the five W questions. "You say you are getting a lot of rejects?" (You are confirming and restating.)

"When did we notice this? How bad is this? What is our reject level now compared to normal? What do you think may be causing this? Where does the trouble seem to be coming from?" Notice that these are calm, non-accusing questions that employees usually don't mind answering, even when they are partly at fault. They show respect and mutual concern. They show a "we're-all-in-this-together" attitude, not a "well-where-did-you-goof-now" approach. Your objective is to get the facts, without flipping the emotional apple cart.

Second, ask the employee for suggestions as to how the problem might be solved. Mention the facts and ask how the situation might be changed or corrected in the future. Listen carefully. You are building the coaching motivation system by developing the explanation part of Ex-Dem-Pra. For example: "Do you think the cause might be that they change instructions on us? Did that new spec sheet revise our procedure enough to create the trouble? If so, how can we change our product? What if we made it shorter or lighter? Can we do that by adjusting our start-up orders?"

Note that steps one and two (studying and asking) give you important time and data to overcome the "coach's surprise."

Third, suggest the best method and explain how it might be done. This should be generated out of the facts and employee suggestions plus what you know, plus your own management judgment and common sense. For example: "From what everyone has said, including the new specs, we clearly need to take two steps: cut the size and improve our own inspection."

Fourth, complete the Ex-Dem-Pra coaching motivation by actually taking and showing the necessary steps as closely as possible. Then invite each person involved to try out the new system and get familiar, comfortable with it. Even adjust the procedure to fit the person or condition, where that is indicated.

To solve "coach's surprise," you have studied, asked, suggested and followed through—completing the Ex-Dem-Pra coaching system.

How to Coach When
He's Doing Pretty Well

The key words in these situations are: "very carefully." Your major objective here is to keep things steady as you go, not to rock the boat or mess things up. Successful, professional coaches have learned long ago when to keep their muddy fingers out of the watch works—to leave well enough alone—and they resist the amateur's perennial temptation to tamper with a good operation. There are usually many other coaching needs and opportunities that will give you a much larger return on your investment of time.

Time management expert Dr. Alan Lakien says that an easy way to help you decide on allocation of your hours and days is to occasionally ask yourself, "Is what I am doing right now the best practical use of my time?" Heavy coaching of the good performer is rarely the best investment. Consider these steps:

Avoid over-coaching or over-supervising. This has a tendency to smother, inhibit and annoy people, particularly the good performer. They know they are doing well and, unless they ask for help, they tend to resent any major dose of advice. It reduces their initiative and can easily be taken as an insult.

Simply observe what they are doing, for two reasons: first, for your own information, as it may affect others or help you coach people, and second, in case you see any major errors that need immediate attention, or minor errors that can be treated if the employee is receptive to the advice.

Suggest very lightly, casually and briefly if and when they seek coaching or an opportunity comes up, such as general discussion of the project. Then do it as a suggestion. "It sure looks like you are getting a lot done on the Zepher Drug account, Sam. I notice they put in a new line of cosmetics last week. Do you think you should ask them if they want cosmetics included in our accounting service?"

Provide a little direct help. Actually work on a small part of the program, as the opportunity comes up. This has several advantages: you get a better feel of the thing; you set a good example; you show leadership by doing; and you are coaching by demonstration. "If they do want us to include the cosmetics records, Sam, I'll set up the forms here, so they'll be ready for use when you get back."

Case History: How a Division of an Aluminum Company Used Coaching Secrets to Build Powerful Motivation

"Hell, my dauber is down, and I don't care if school keeps or not," said one of the packaging linemen to the records clerk. And that pretty well summarized the attitude of most employees in that small, ten-man division.

Doug R. had recently been hired to head that division, and he quickly recognized the problem. It was basically low morale and low performance based on low motivation. Doug also saw lots of procedural problems on the packaging line, where things were getting messed up and greatly contributing to the general despondency.

Doug decided on coaching as his best bet to generating motivation.

He took the first step in the program by learning more about the problem and finding several potential solutions. (He strengthened his position by taking the simple expedient of checking to find how other division heads solved these same packaging problems. No sense re-inventing the wheel.)

Second, Doug let everyone know that he had studied their situation and would work with them as a team, so that together they could solve their problems.

At this point he thought of having a long meeting with all the employees but scratched the idea in favor of several short discussion sessions with one or two people at a time. These proved to be far more relaxed, friendly and constructive.

Before the meetings, he reviewed new procedures with the group foreman and revised the system to make it as practical and workable as possible. Then Doug presented the system to the small group. He asked for their ideas of how this could be improved and then put to work. He got suggestions in both areas, picked out the best ones and described a system to the group. (Explanation.)

Next, he and the foreman or he and one of the better employees performed the new system. (Demonstration.) They actually walked out onto the line, ran off some packages the new way and packed them in shipping cartons.

Then they all took turns practicing the new approach. (Practical work.) The same lineman who had so plainly expressed earlier discouragement suggested a change in the shipping carton that would make the procedure even more productive. Then another lineman had an idea for a double flow on the package line so two workers could work, one on each side.

When they ran into problems Doug was ready. He stepped in, and together they discussed possible solutions and tried these. Once things were going well and no real problems were present, he mainly lay back in the weeds and watched, offering minor ideas when circumstances required.

Results: The Ex-Dem-Pra coaching system, used to aim action towards results with or without the presence of problems, worked well. It not only developed greater team work and greater efficiency, but dramatically increased the motivation of the group so that now they really did care that "school kept," because they saw results, gained self-satisfaction and felt that it was partly their "school."

Summary: Coaching is a secret and powerful motivator if properly done. The key is avoiding the put-down, working together to understand and solve a problem, plus building a desire to learn and try solutions. Show you care about them and you need their help. The "Ex-Dem-Pra" formula has proved highly effective in war, college and business throughout the world. It is often foolishly ignored by the first level manager but widely used by the top professional. It must be aimed at goals, since work is not the same as results. And even then a manager should not simply walk away assuming performance, but should watch and follow through. He should be ready to step in and study things, ask, suggest and follow through when his team has a problem. Then he should step back, watch closely and suggest rather lightly when they are doing well. Such coaching has and can provide strong, pleasant and excellent motivation that is rewarding to both the employee and manager.

11

How You Can Triple
Your Communications Impact

Every day, communications have a powerful influence.
Yesterday, your friend Bill was deluged with over 2,000
messages: advertisements and news items. Chances are
good that he read, heard or watched at least some of
these with real interest and made a few conscious decisions to take action or not to act. Bill may have seen a TV
or print ad for a car or home of interest, a vacation spot
he is considering, a restaurant, show, book, shirt, whis-
key or boat he'd like to buy. He saw a news item blasting
or praising his job or industry, or another industry he
likes or hates, or covering his favorite sport or culture,
or reporting a human success, tragedy or comedy, a con-
troversial subject, race conflict, sex scandal, crime of
violence or political spending and hanky panky. These
will affect Bill's vote, purchasing, daily discussions and
even his blood pressure. Certainly every single item
does not influence every person, but it does affect many
people. Taken together, the cumulative impact of 2,000
messages a day, over some weeks, motivates thousands
of thoughts, convictions and actions.

But wait. We could also add another 1,500 messages Bill got in
combining the wonderful world of work and play. Consider all
those business communications Bill received. Letters, memos,
phone calls, documents, reports, print outs, meetings, visits, chats
in the hall, at coffee or lunch or while commuting; and even the

silent but vitally important non-verbal communications, signs and body language. Now add the songs, features and fiction stories on TV and radio that have subtle information and many less subtle messages, and add news broadcasts, sports and documentaries. We all live under a virtual blizzard of communications.

Bill might say, "Those ads, news, business messages and shows may influence you, but certainly not me." Then listen to him talk about the car, vacation or restaurant he saw advertised, the "crazy new program they have at the office," the latest gyrations of Congress or the President, or the needs of his favorite ball club.

Bill has all sorts of opinions, even powerful convictions, that were not immaculately conceived in a vacuum. Communication, inter-acting with the chemistry of his own preconditioning, generated substantial motivation in thought, work and deed. Without a doubt, we can easily see that communication built motivation for Bill and for millions of others.

Communication Can Be Your Easiest Power Secret

Communication! The presentation and exchange of words, images, facts, feelings and ideas. What a power house of excitement, enlightenment, influence and motivation. Communication has been affecting people since the first "cave man" scratched on the wall. Men have been exalted, defied, rewarded, tortured and killed for the concepts they communicated, for one simple reason: messages motivate men. Ideas have consequences, perhaps today more than ever, because we now have appropriate time, health, education and the inquiring attitudes to more fully apply new ideas. Communication becomes more than ever a major, massive mover of men's minds. It is perhaps the greatest motivator on planet earth. Describe any highly motivated person you have ever heard of and you will soon say something about his or her beliefs, ideas and communication with others, especially in the world of business, employees and managers. The power of communication is yours when you understand a few basic and new tools and techniques. If you only become skilled at one or two of these, you should substantially increase your ability to motivate and manage people.

What Communication Power Means and How It Helps You

We are all communicators. We all must do it if we are to survive and prosper in todays world. But some of us are a lot more effective than others. One of the easiest ways to improve your communication skill is very simple: have a clear understanding and gut feel of just what communication means today.

Just a few years back, most people believed that the message was the total communication. But today we know better. Some of the highest paid communicators will often describe it as a three stage activity: message sent; message received; message confirmed.

Three Power Secrets

Therefore, first: send the message. Recognize that in today's environment just the word "message" has a new meaning. Some years ago it meant information or direction, spoken or written. But increasingly, today's message also means images, opinions, concepts, thought-starters, exciters, feelings, even highly charged emotional vibrations. Today we increasingly view messages as visual—as shapes, light, pictures and color. Psychologists say that 80% of everything we learn comes to us through our eyes. Some of the most important messages are purely visual or non-verbal; a boss that smiles at you, a thug that follows you on a dark street, and a sexy lady that gazes at you in a cocktail lounge are all sending you a message. It is unspoken, unwritten and non-verbal, but clear, simple and strong.

Second, be sure the message is received. There's an old conundrum that goes, "If a giant tree were to fall in the forest, but there was no person there to hear it, was there any sound?" And the answer can be either yes or no, depending on how you define sound. If it means vibrations of the air, then certainly there was sound. But if you define sound as vibrations sent through the air and received by a healthy human ear drum, then there was no sound. The message was sent but not received. When you send a message, you must do more than talk to the wind or write to ghosts. You must be reasonably sure there is someone there to hear, read and receive the message. Some managers write "memos to the file" that are never seen. They make talks or comments to people who are not listening or who are asleep or totally tuned out.

Third, be sure the message is confirmed by the recipient. Mainly, be sure that it was not only received but that it was understood. A talk or gesture or letter in English, sent to a person who is not familiar with the words or gestures of that language, may have been seen and heard, but communication never really took place because they did not understand. A typical example is a professor or consultant talking far over the heads of his students or clients. When a supervisor talks too fast—with strange words or gestures or incomplete thoughts—to his or her secretary, she saw and heard but certainly did not understand. There was no real communication.

Case history: Robert R., a new college graduate, recently conducted a training session called a "Pre-Business Workshop" for a small group of disadvantaged people in New Orleans who wanted to start a business. Bob told them about equity and debt financing, accounting methods, balance sheets, P&L statements, cash flow, break-even charts plus purchasing, marketing, inventory control and other like subjects. The group listened politely and nodded knowingly. The next day a top supervisor of these programs who had heard the workshop called Bob into his office and said, "You did a fine job with your workshop yesterday Bob, but you forgot one thing: Most of your group were grade school dropouts! You covered all the right things, but they hardly understood a word you said. You sent the message. They received the words, but they could not possibly confirm or play back even a tiny fraction."

Conclusion: You really cannot communicate until your message fits the receiving equipment; in this case, the educational level.

Management's Major Failing

World famous consultant Peter Drucker often says that "communications is modern management's major failing." We simply are not communicating properly.

If this is true, then is it any wonder that we are often failing to motivate? Or, to turn this into an advantage for you, common sense suggests that if our communications are poor but you know how to use improved methods you will correct and fill a need, a void, a failing; and you will be able to motivate where others could not.

The Harvard School of Business Journal published a new famous article called "The Fateful Process of Mr. A Talking to Mr. B." It outlined the dozens of mistakes we all make occasionally, reinforcing Drucker's position, but suggesting ways to overcome the problems and so become a better communicator.

The key points in this and similar studies are: *first*, listen and understand people and the situation; *second*, prepare a message that is clear, strong, meaningful and properly tuned to the target audience, one that gets their attention, interest, desire and action; *third*, send only messages that are confirmed and understood (this does not mean they agreed with the message, but only that they knew what it said).

For example: Recently, in a crucial televised national championship football game, the quarterback failed to properly communicate the key play in the closing minutes. The end went out for a pass and cut the wrong way. The ball was on its way out there, for what was a sure touchdown, but it fell to an empty field and the game was lost. The fans were furious, and the poorly communicating quarterback barely got out of the stadium unharmed.

Case history: Three powerful secrets for confirming communication. A major fabric manufacturer asked Chuck R., account executive for a small advertising agency, to prepare a sample ad. If accepted, this would give them the whole corporate account and favorably change the financial future for the small ad group. But the manufacturer sent only a vague, uncertain and conflicting message as to what was needed. Chuck received the message all right, but he completely misunderstood it. Weeks were spent preparing the presentation. Chuck made his pitch and missed the point by a country mile. He lost the account, and his job was put in danger—all because of improper communication and misdirected motivation.

People are not mind readers. You can't expect and assume that they are going to get your message via mental telepathy, E.S.P. or osmosis. You do this only at your own peril. You should take every reasonable precaution to make sure the message is properly designed, properly sent, well received and understood. When there is any doubt, repeat and be sure that the message was properly received.

There are several ways to confirm understanding of communication. One is a standard procedure with the military, where the recipient routinely answers, "I read you loud and clear," possibly followed by "wilco, over and out," meaning, "I will comply. I turn the communication back to you."

A second way to confirm is to simply watch what the recipient does next. If you ask for a start-up of a program but nothing happens, that tells you something. Unfortunately, this can take valuable time and give you an unreliable reading. The employee may have understood the message just fine, but ran into some other problem.

A third method to confirm is to simply ask for playback of the message. This is often the fastest, easiest, most reliable and practical. It gives maximum assurance to you that your message got through and you are truly linked to at least a part of your world.

Secrets for Avoiding
Typical Modern Extremes

Too little communication leaves the person you seek to motivate baking on the desert of despair and disillusionment, thirsting for facts, direction or some other message. This is today's most common communication problem. The second is too much communication, where the recipient is drowning in a sea of paper or verbal or non-verbal messages. We Americans tend to swing from one extreme to the other: first too little, then too much. A swamped recipient is not really receiving or understanding the message. And with no communication, he or she is not getting much motivation either. Almost any of the twelve major motivation tools covered in the book—goals, fear, respect, meetings, group planning, heart and mind, work, delegation, coaching, butt-out, leveling and award—depend largely on good communication.

Here is how to balance your communication flow and avoid either starving or swamping your recipient. First, consider a slight modification of the golden rule: not necessarily doing unto others as *you* would have them do unto *you*. You might like to be deluged, but they may hate it. Do onto others as *they* would have you do onto *them*. Or, as Marshall Field said, "Give the lady what *she* wants." Second, avoid extremes. Either one, starvation or deluge, brings problems; so seek a middle ground. Third, give it a whirl. Try out your approach to see how it takes. Watch the person for reaction. He may want still more or he may be choking on the moderate communication you fed him. Fourth, adjust the flow.

Example: Some secretaries like lots of communication, instruction and direction. Others climb the walls if you say much more than good morning. You may feel you are being servile if you adjust to fit their needs, but in reality we all adjust our input flow to almost any system so we can find the approach that best meets our objectives. This provides the most help to you, personally.

Secrets for Getting the Powerful FOWD/PA Formula to Serve You

FOWD/PA is just a simple acronym that makes it easy for you to improve your communication skill. The formula is built on several studies that were made to find out why Pete Drucker is so concerned about our poor communications.

Findings showed major errors were: inadequate and insufficient volume, poor use of sources and mediums, poor preparation, no reading of results or modification of future communication flow.

But rather than emphasize the negative, these findings were turned around into six simple positive steps, expressed as letters into a word, FOWD/PA. It means: Frequency, Oral, Written, Done carefully/Playback, Adjust.

"The frequency" was just covered, with emphasis on finding the ideal volume flow of communication.

"Oral/written" means we should not use just one method or medium but both sight and sound, including spoken statements, music, personal gestures, expressions, body language, printed words, sketches, photos, diagrams and charts. Use of several communication media multiplies the motivational effect. The reason: some people are highly oral or sound oriented, while others respond best to visuals and the written word. You probably have noticed that the most effective advertising programs use both print and broadcast.

"Done carefully" means the transmitter is well tuned to the receiver. The message fits the person's frame of reference, intellect and understanding level. Don't talk in complex terms to grade school dropouts or in baby talk to Ph.D's.

"Playback" refers to using at least one of the methods suggested for confirming or verifying that the message was actually received and that communication really did happen.

"Adjustment" means that after you have followed all the other five steps even to your own personal assurance that communication occurred, you should still keep an open mind and adjust, modify or correct what has been done. You may have communicated, alright, but perhaps your recipient got a distorted message. This last step is where even some of the best professionals fall down in their haste to get on with other things. They continue gleefully and enthusiastically sending the wrong message.

Follow the ugly, awkward sounding little "FOWD/PA" acryonym, and you will find your communication motivation system working better every week—more results from less effort, as proved by this next case.

How an Advertising Agency Executive Used "Green Sheets" and FOWD/PA to Motivate

The problem was simple: a small group of key people were mad, hurt and frustrated. Time and manpower were being wasted. So it was more than just emotions and human feelings. Money was being lost. The cause was bad communications between the client, who wanted advertisements prepared and the creative people who prepared those advertisements. The client would make a request. Writers and artists would design the ad. The account man, Dick N., would present it. Then the client would say, "That's all wrong! You missed the main point! The headline is an error. The visual a mess! The body copy forgot to mention the third and fourth sell points. And you used the wrong logo!"

One such episode of this kind got so bitter that the client threw the ad board across the room at Dick. They had "created an abortion!" But why? What went wrong? Obviously something failed in the fateful process of client "A" talking to writer "B."

The problem worsened when Dick had to return to the agency and ask the writer and artist to re-do the ad. This angered, even infuriated the swamped, over-worked creative team. The agency Vice President was also upset. "Don't you realize re-dos cost money? Those creatives don't work for nothing, you know. But we get the same 15% commission on the ad whether we do it once or re-do it a dozen times."

Solution: Dick was clearly caught between three people, the client, the writer and the boss. He decided that the problem was poor communication, possibly somewhat on his part; and the solution was to improve communications from the client, through Dick, to the creative team.

Dick met with the client and explained the problem. He suggested that together they prepare a simple, one page check list of key facts, needs, wants and direction. This would assure the client that his exact message was reaching the creatives and would save the client from wasting his time reviewing improper ads. The client liked the idea and suggested a few key points to be included.

Then Dick met with the creatives. At first they felt that such a system was too rigid, restrictive and dictatorial. "If the clients want to do that, then they should write their own ads instead of hiring us!" they said. "Why buy a dog, then bark yourself?" But Dick explained that this would only cover key items such as logos to use, ad size, medium, deadlines, visuals to avoid, problems and opportunities and goals—leaving plenty of latitude for creativity. In the end this would save them time in both initial preparation and avoidance of annoying re-dos. They agreed to give it a try.

Results: Dick added one extra feature, a sentence at the bottom saying, "If anyone wishes any changes to points here, please let me know promptly." The form was printed on green paper and filled in when each ad was ordered. Copies were sent everyone concerned in both the client and agency group.

The client liked it, since it helped him communicate more quickly, easily and thoroughly. It also helped him assemble and sharpen his own thinking.

The creatives took to it rapidly. The message was sent to them, and they received it loud, clear and accurately. Misunderstanding was minimized. They were not swamped with too much or starved with too little communication. It followed the FOWD/PA formula of Frequent, Oral, Written, Done carefully/ Playback, Adjust.

Re-dos dropped to nearly zero. All involved knew where they stood and where they were coming from. Both the client and the creatives were motivated to more efficient and pleasant productivity by using the "green sheet" of improved communication.

Ten Power Secrets for Using
the New Mechanics of Communication

In recent years, all sorts of communication research studies have been made to learn how we can further improve, sharpen and refine our methods to get still more motivation for the same effort.

Summarizing these findings gives us ten commandments or at least suggestions. Most of these are often ignored by amateurs but used widely by leading professionals. And yet these are practical, easy steps that, as you think about it, are also quite reasonable and logical.

Power secret one: understand the problem faced by your message recipient—the problem as he sees it, not as you see it. Otherwise you will be communicating to yourself, not to him.

Power secret two: recognize opportunities for your recipient and yourself. If your communication offers reduced trouble, or increased gain, more pleasure and less pain, it increases motivational effect.

Power secret three: aim communication at objectives that have been mutually agreed upon. As Machiavelli points out, people will respond strongly to a shining goal, even one that is far in the distance. Example: for ten years Americans listened to and were motivated to massive sacrifice and support in Vietman by communications about "light at the end of the tunnel."

Power secret four: learn people's strengths and likes and design your communication to fit. Discover what it is that enthuses them, turns them on—their hot button. With young women it may be the new world of freedom, independence and personal identity. With some people it may be job security or recognition or new responsibilities.

Power secret five: encourage "plan" thinking with and through your communication. Perhaps use talk structured towards the S-O-S (Situation, Objective, System) formula. For example: communicate about their problem, your mutual goals and ways to reach these. When your message uses these terms, most people start to and want to understand it, like it and be part of the plan, and they are usually motivated to action.

Power secret six: use oral, spoken approaches, eyeball to eyeball, one on one. Don't always hide behind a desk or written memo. This may be comfortable, but it is not very productive communication for you, and if done too much can be destructive.

Power secret seven: put some messages in writing. We noted earlier that over 80% of what we learn is through our eyes. Keep your writing clear, crisp, simple, easy to read and understand. Famous journalism authority, Rudolph Flesh, in his "Art of Readable Writing," says to keep written material at about the 7th grade level even for executives—not that they are necessarily uneducated, but they are busy. They greatly appreciate and respond well to simplicity in an infuriatingly complex world.

Power secret eight: hold meetings and encourage free exchange of comments, opinions, facts and ideas. This may not always greatly improve communications, but it seems to. It gives the feeling of communication, which can often be more important than the message, so far as motivating people is concerned. In this respect, the medium is the message. Just meeting together helps to build motivation.

Power secret nine: listen for playback or reaction to your communication. This confirms and verifies. It also tends to satisfy, pacify and reduce your own concern and adds assurance to you of probable motivation.

Power secret ten: adjust future messages on the basis of the information played back to you. This may mean that more communication, or less, or a different kind, is needed.

$1 Million Spent by a Giant Publisher and Agency Provides You with 40 Communication Power Secrets

In communication research on how to increase the impact of messages, studies verified the ten basics just listed and many additional practical suggestions. Summarized here are about 40 highlights of their published findings.

Begin with understanding of your subject and your recipient's reasoning, feeling and opinions.

Your key points should be based on goals, self-satisfaction or solving a problem. It should have news important to most readers or listeners. Present ideas in a short, clear, personal way.

The body of your message should talk directly to the recipient, sound sincere, ring true, make no ridiculous remarks or overstatements, give specifics and support points. Mention causes only to build believability. Give your reader or listener an excuse to do something.

Mechanically, write and, if necessary, re-write or practice your message until it is easy to understand and follow, especially in the beginning. Tell a story or relate frequently to human experience. Get your recipient understanding, agreeing and nodding "yes." Use the "problem-solution" concept. Itemize the recipient's benefits in accepting your plan. Keep your sentences fairly simple and flowing, not complex or confusing.

Your policy or philosophy should be truth told with vigor and imagination—more earnest than glib—using original, provocative ideas. Be simple without talking down, accurate without being boastful, colloquial and friendly without being phony or contrived. Use emotional appeals that seem logical. Be disarmingly honest and forthright. Emotionalize and rationalize, but in good taste.

Your words should be conversational, person to person, relaxed, natural, short, simple, specific, concrete, personal, colorful, believable. They should conjure up visions. Stay positive and in the active voice. Use verbs, but few adjectives. Avoid unnecessary or irrelevant words: exaggerations and strange, abstract, trite or bombastic words. *End by telling the recipient* what you hope he or she will do. Make a call for action.

Make your point. Prove your point. Tell them how to use your point.

Using the "O-S-P" Formula: One Strong Point

You can borrow a technique from major communication motivators, the advertising and marketing people. They use the "O-S-P" formula, meaning One Strong Point.

Here is how it works. If you select a single, powerful thought to use in your letter or talk, if you present it, develop it and show how it benefits your listeners, if you do this without cluttering up or diluting your communication with side issues or other points, no matter how brilliant, your message must have much greater motivational impact. You have pounded home your own favorite O-S-P.

Advertising, selling and readership research have frequently proved and reconfirmed the influence, response and effectiveness of the O-S-P formula. It concentrates people's attention on a single point. It looks at this O-S-P, this thought, and supports the idea from several directions. When you have completed your message, you will have made your point and your people will have received it, loud, clear and emphatically. If you can end a talk or letter so that your people have an O-S-P or "one strong point" to remember and act on, you have done more to motivate than the great majority of message senders. You will be a stronger communicator.

For example: Just take a quick look back at the last three paragraphs. Notice how we selected a single thought, the O-S-P. We defined it, developed it a bit, proved it and showed how an O-S-P can help you. We looked at just one concept. As you leave this paragraph, you have the letters O.S.P. in your mind, and you have added another practical technique to your motivational tool kit—a technique that can work for you the rest of your life.

How to Plan This Week's Secret Power: Communication

Let's make a simple, practical program you can use this week to motivate people.

First, pick your target. Perhaps it's a person or a small group.

Decide on an O.S.P., one strong point or message you want to have received by your target. Perhaps you want to register "interest in them, appreciation or encouragement and respect."

Run a small "pretest" if you can, by simply asking one of them for their opinion of the O-S-P. You may find they don't understand it at all. Conversely, they may want it expanded.

Now select your method and frequency. Will it be oral (short talks or long ones), or will it be in writing? It might be a combination or even non-verbal communication, such as simply stopping by twice a day just to wave or nod hello.

Be careful not to swamp them or starve them. Be sure your message is crisp, clear and tuned to their receiving frequency and frame of mind.

Plan some check on playback. For example, after you have delivered a message or two, watch, listen or visit with them. See if the message really is getting through. Or does it need adjusting? At this point you have completed the FOWD/PA formula. And chances are good that you have substantially improved your communication skills toward increased motivation.

Summary: Communication Is a
Powerful Secret to Serve You

It is motivating all of us, every day in hundreds of ways, for better or for worse. We not only react to these messages, but we initiate a lot of them. And we do this in many ways, but usually oral and written. Drucker says most of us fail rather badly in our communication efforts. To really communicate, we must be sure the message is sent, is received and is confirmed. This will improve the fateful process of Mr. A talking to Mr. B. Such improved communication can avoid personal disaster and create constructive motivation.

To assure better messages, avoid extremes of starving people for communications or swamping them with input. Use the FOWD/PA formula of frequency, oral, written, done carefully, with playback and adjustment. Use good mechanics of understanding the problem, recognizing opportunities, aiming at goals, learning strengths and weaknesses, encouraging plans, using both oral and written approaches, holding meetings, listening for results and adjusting future messages.

Begin with insight. Use an O.S.P., or one strong point. Employ key points that emphasize self-satisfaction. Talk to the listener in a believable way that is easy to understand, earnest, provocative, accurate, friendly and conversational. End with a call for action. Check back early and often to judge results and make changes needed. Follow these guidelines, and they will serve you well in substantially increasing your motivation of people through communication.

12

How and When to Let People Be Their Own Bosses

Here's a tough power secret to believe. You can often motivate most by doing least—even by doing nothing, by stepping away, backing off and "butting out," to let people do their own thing. There are two power secrets to doing this right: (1) proper preparation, and (2) proper timing. Both are vital. Fail at either, and the system bombs. But it's easy when you know how and follow some simple guidelines. The next few pages give these to you. We will look at: preparation and direction of people; how to be tough or easy; how to move between these and find the right balance or system; when to be autocratic, when to be democratic; and when to "butt out" and use independent group feelings, the desire to "be my own boss" and the urge for extended independence. Even though people may "mess up" a little, if these techniques are done right the price will be low compared to the results you get in motivation.

How a Government Branch Manager Used "Sliding Scale" of Power

The problem was mostly lethargy, disinterest, lack of enthusiasm, drive and team spirit in the office of some 30 people. Richard C. was appointed as District Director, and he quickly diagnosed the situation. He recognized one interesting peculiarity that shows up in many organizations: there had been a long, dreary spell of sameness, routine and monotony imposed on the group. The preceding director had been an excellent paper processor but not very notable as a motivator.

Solution: Dick decided on several fairly courageous steps. First, he was very firm in reviewing major regulations. Next, he permitted much easier, relaxed procedures in other, far less vital areas. But in most cases, Dick took a middle position of neither excessive firmness nor high permissiveness. He watched as these tactics generated interest, excitement and constructive activity. He then moved away from close supervision, noted steady improvement and encouraged extended independence. People increasingly became their own boss. They made mistakes, but not in major areas. In any case, Dick was watching and usually had anticipated the problem before it got serious. He would then step in quickly, to minimize difficulties. And he would do this with the least possible turmoil.

Results: Using good motivation techniques, Dick developed a highly turned-on team. They greatly increased service to their clients and in recognition of this won many new awards. Enthusiasm, drive, spirit and performance went up to record highs as confirmed by three separate surveys and a comprehensive internal morale audit of the district.

Power Secrets Using the "Sliding Scale"

We all know what it is to be addressed roughly, perhaps by a parent, acquaintance or teacher. Maybe we've done the same thing to a dog, a kid, a friend or even ourselves. We accuse, shout, insult, order and sometimes threaten. This hurts others, and we know it; it hurts them just as it has hurt us in the past. In a sense, we sort of "get even." Unfortunately, being too tough builds resentment, paralysis, possibly hatred and some resistance. The result can be more trouble than it was worth. Constructive progress is often reduced.

At the other extreme is being too easy, docile and permissive: the anything-goes attitude. This can and usually does produce uncertainty, distress, confusion and chaos. This is often followed by irregularities and abuses that again greatly reduce constructive progress.

When you are too tough or too easy, you lose either way.

Seasoned professionals find there is a line, or "sliding scale," between these two extremes. They get the best motivational effect by moving along this line, sometimes being pretty tough, sometimes being fairly permissive, but tending to avoid extremes and to stay in the middle ground, moving toward one end or the other only as conditions indicate.

Six Power Secrets for Firmness: When and How to Be Tough

This is a problem that has plagued leaders, managers, executives and supervisors for many years. There is no clear answer, but there are some practical guidelines.

Power secret one: if you must be firm, tough and even rough, you are better off doing it *early in the game,* not near the end. Machiavelli says people will respond favorably and forgive a leader who is overly aggressive, but just briefly and at the start. Two points of caution: you should be firm and decisive, not mean, vicious or destructive. Machiavelli showed brilliant insight into human nature, but he is useful today only if he is softened, modified, modernized and humanized. Let them know that later procedures will loosen up and become easier if this is earned.

Power secret two: you should be tough when hard decisions must be made. At that point you have very little choice. *Example:* Choosing which of two excellent candidates is to be hired is a difficult decision. It calls for hard-nosed, practical, steely-eyed action. It's no place for permissiveness or sentiment. One person goes on to fame and fortune, while the other may sink into despair. You made a tough decision, and you had no other alternative.

Power secret three: you must be firm, decisive, even unpopular and rough *when the good of the group* and its customers are at stake, or when an action must be taken for the best interests of all. *Example:* When an unlawful act has occurred or threatens, this is no time for permissiveness.

Power secret four: if you must be bold, firm and decisive, do it in *an impersonal way.* Avoid selecting some one individual (even though you may be aiming at a certain person). *For example:* One ploy is to use a little generalized misdirection, such as accusing some total, ill-defined group (or even some enemy person or group) of bad behavior, when you are really talking about someone much closer to home. This gets the point across, but avoids destructive humiliation and loss of reputation for someone. You let him save face. With many people, their reputation is their most valuable possession. For most of us, our reputation is about the only thing we take to our grave, except for a few gold inlays.

Power secret five: recognize that some people want, need and even crave much firmer direction than perhaps you do. (You might want to "do unto others not as *you* would have them do unto you, but as *they* would have you do unto them.") Also, nearly all of us want clear, definite, firm direction at certain times.

Power secret six: avoid excesses in both severity or length of time. Such over-reaction will eventually lead to resistance, and then the whole system is likely to break down or at least become ineffective.

Case history: Joe T., a management consultant supervisor, was asked by a small town council to help organize a workshop on simple bookkeeping for a group of six one-man shops. He agreed, but was very firm and clear about the way letters were to be sent out, mentioning abuses of improper mailings by other groups. Joe was firm, right from the start, for the good of all concerned. His criticism was never aimed at the current organization, the small town council, but at "another" group. He was specific without being excessive, and he got excellent results.

Five Power Secrets for Permissiveness

This is almost as dangerous as being too tough, since in large amounts it can lead to chaos. Permissiveness is particularly tempting right now for at least two reasons: it is easy to do, and in today's social climate it is greatly encouraged. But there are a few guidelines as to the best time and methods to use this.

Power secret one: lean toward the easy or permissive extreme right after you have been obliged to be tough. It helps offset bad feelings or resentment, mends fences and binds up wounds.

Power secret two: you should tend towards the easy, relaxed, less demanding posture and instructions *when there is no real need to be tough,* especially when things are going along fine. Avoid continuous use, over-use or mis-use of your authority, or it will lack impact at the time you need it most. You don't want to wear it

out or cry wolf too often. An occasional reminder and reinforcement is usually sufficient.

Power secret three: use an easy, more relaxed, less demanding
approach *when firmness or aggressiveness might actually hurt
feelings,* progress and results. *For example:* You can be easy and
still safe when a simple routine task is requested and there is no
reason to believe it won't be done promptly and properly, or when
spirit, enthusiasm and creativity are already present and functioning well. That is a poor time to get tough. You just rain on the
parade.

Power secret four: when permissiveness gets results and is
wanted, sought for, needed and appreciated, then use it. Some
people are a bit mulish and need firm words. But others are the
family pet pony or a race horse, and a kind word or a gentle tug on
the bridle is all it takes. More than that is resented and is counter-
productive.

*Power secret five: your method can be as important as your
policy.* As the old cliché goes, it's not what you do, but how you do
it. Your best bet is to be moderately rather than excessively permissive. Excesses encourage abuses. *For example:* Rice's Rule of
Reality says that power application corrupts in direct proportion to
its unaudited availability. Let them know you realize that you are
being relaxed and that you are doing this on purpose, not by acci-
dent or disinterest—and that procedures will tighten up if necessary. Be sure they recognize and appreciate your permissiveness.

Case history: Jerry L. was the supervisor of several volunteer
workers who had just been told that they must complete special
reports or leave the group; and Jerry said this in firm, uncertain
terms. Jerry also wanted to assign some routine projects. He said,
"All four of you guys have some standard projects to do. These
should be done by Tuesday, but Friday is OK, too." Jerry was
being relaxed and easy right after directions had been rough.
There was no need to be tough. That would have simply developed
bad feelings. His people appreciated Jerry's casual attitude, and all
the jobs were done and done properly by the following Tuesday.

Four Power Secrets for Using
the "Movable Spot" to Motivate

As we see that there are at least the two extremes, being
tough and being easy, and that there is a sort of line or continuous

scale between these, we now realize that it is quite possible to move or *slide along that line*. Here are a few guidelines for using this technique on the scale for maximum motivational effect.

Power secret one: staying at either extreme—being too tough or too easy all the time—is rarely the most effective or efficient system.

Power secret two: the mid-point is generally the best position for maximum results per unit of your time and effort. This is partly because people tend to see what they want to see. If you are moderate, but they want to believe that you are permissive or firm, they will often see this, and you will fill their wants.

Power secret three: but you should stay flexible. Be ready, willing and able to move along the line, not necessarily to the ends, but moving occasionally near these. Says Alexander Pope, "Virtuous and vicious, everyone must be. Few in the extremes, but all in the degree." We must all stand up for our beliefs at times and back off at other times. Move to "firm" then back to the center; move to "easy" then back to the center.

Power secret four: swings should be moderate and rare rather than violent and frequent. Studies show that people want dependability and consistency in a manager more than brilliance or skill. On the other hand, you don't want to be too predictable. Movement avoids this problem.

Case: Bill S. was supervising several three-man teams of college business students, who were helping companies. He outlined some rules that absolutely had to be followed, such as a report deadline of July 1. Other steps, such as their daily activities, were strictly up to them. But generally, they were asked to follow simple guidelines, and checks were made on this. Bill got excellent results. He had moved from firm to easy but mostly stayed approximately in the middle of the extremes.

Three Power Secrets for Being Autocratic Yet Democratic

Here is another problem that has challenged managers for centuries. It has become a special problem today, as we seek to become more humanistic, considerate, concerned and even permissive. And yet, demands of society and our economy urge greater technology, accuracy, discipline and performance. This seems to be almost a contradiction in terms; be soft and easygoing, but get greater, concrete, hard-nosed results.

The answer is simple. We have just looked at it and at least partly solved the matter almost without knowing it: the sliding scale—moving from one extreme or, better, from *near* one extreme, to the other.

But, for you to be truly successful both autocratically and democratically, you should consider and apply the three Rice's Rules of Reason:

Power secret one: to make it work and to live with one foot in each boat (autocracy and democracy) *requires high flexibility.* That means you cannot simply plot a course and forget about it. You must communicate and adapt. In short, apply intelligence and "work smarter rather than harder." It requires much less intelligence to set one pattern and stay there, like the dinosaurs. It takes more intellect to adapt to changing circumstances, as did early humans. This intellect obviously had survival value. The dinosaurs are no longer with us. And rigid managers may not be with us for very long, either.

Power secret two: understand; show some respect, concern, appreciation and liking for others. This is the foot in the democratic boat. It doesn't mean you are fully committed, but it does mean you are partly there—at least somewhat identified and interacting with the person or group.

Power secret three: on the other hand, encourage their understanding of the problem and their intellectual as well as emotional commitment to both mutual objectives and the agreed upon systems to reach those goals—in other words, results. This is something of the foot in the autocratic boat, although it does not mean you are a tyrant or despot. As a side issue or modification to this leg of the journey, don't take circumstances, or yourself, too seriously (democracy). A person who can laugh at things or himself, can be amazingly firm (autocracy) with little or no resentment from the person or group. It's usually the "airs" of superiority that they dislike most. As a manager or "supervisor," you gain by soft play on the "super" part and strong effort on the "advisory" part.

How to Employ "Independent" Group Feelings and "Butt Out"

Once you have all agreed on mutual goals, encourage them to select their own independent methods for getting there. Most people are already thinking about their tactics well before the ink is dry on their list of objectives. They usually have a desire for independence. If their particular approach is legal, reasonably efficient and does the job, why should you care how the cat gets skinned—especially since they are likely to operate with twice the motivation and spirit when doing things their way than they would with some imposed, ordered or dictated method.

Your technique might include some suggested alternate approaches. But the main point is to be certain that some sort of system starts working. Then step back and let them roll.

Give them their head, some freedom to breathe, a taste of independence. Let them know that they can use their own ideas, and, in fact, that you expect them to think for themselves, make most minor changes and meet the little difficulties as they come along. After all, you can't be hanging around their neck all the time. You certainly won't be with them every moment to figure out the small adjustments needed with each new situation.

New Products Group with Independence Generates Millions

The problem was new products; none were coming off the drawing board. An ethical drug division, a relatively small operation but a big profit maker, depended on a steady flow of new products to maintain those profits. Without new improved items, the market of prescribing physicians would swing to brands that offered the innovations. The drug company manager, Edgar B. had tried a tough, demanding, aggressive approach. This worked for a while, but then paralysis crept in.

Solution: Edgar decided to be both autocratic and democratic—to maintain a firm posture, but also to adapt to the current difficult conditions and encourage independent thinking and group initiative. He let the small group know the problem and the urgency. He got agreement on mutual goals. Then he elected to butt out. Edgar let them generate more of their own systems for getting results. He met with them only occasionally and then more to get a progress report than to give directions.

Results: At first the little group was a bit stunned. (I was the co-chairman and note taker.) Then ideas began to seep out, at first, just as a trickle and then a bubbling stream. Innovative and dynamic plans were developed. Things started to happen: a new cough syrup, a new children's aspirin, an anti-histamine, a thyroid preparation, a muscle relaxant and several others. The group worked up their own new product report system, description and introductory marketing plan, which was assembled in a special blue folder with summaries, charts and uniform tab labels. Soon the company became excited about the latest new product, "Blue Book." Enthusiasm and motivation ran high. New items were introduced into the drug stores, and sales increased by several million dollars. A combination of firm and easy direction by Edgar—autocratic and democratic—plus developing independent group feelings and their own individual, undirected initiative and butt-out action all motivated excellent programs and profitable results.

Why People Have a
Secret Desire for Power

We just saw that you can motivate by using independent group feeling, and we proved that it works when we reviewed the case of the drug company.

Most people have a secret yearning. They want to own and operate their own business, to control and direct their own destiny, to have some of their own turf or at least to decide some of their own activities. In other words, they want to be their own boss.

Your best technique for employing this drive toward reaching your mutual goals, surprisingly, is to encourage it. Re-state it and reinforce it. *For example*: You might say something like, "Why don't you run this thing? Decide what you want to do and how you want to do it!" Perhaps you can even add, "So long as you make progress, I'll support you and help you, but only when you want it. Until then, I'll stay out of your way."

Show them that they have the freedom to do their own thing. Avoid directions, nagging or "buttinski" action. Stand clear out of the way and let it happen.

How to Use "Extended Independence"

A key to really effective motivation through "direction then butt out" is to maintain vigilance. Keep watching. If you don't do this, harmful, abusive, even disasterous things can happen. Your own observation can prevent this.

And watching has another advantage: it tells you when things are going well. This is also important because then you know when to expand your method, to open freedom still more.

This is sometimes called "Extended Independence." It moves further away from the extreme of over-supervision, as you begin to see that moving towards independence got you some good results.

For example: This compares with working with a young student who responded well to a taste of freedom to act a little on his own, to use his own initiative and ideas. As your observation confirms that such freedom is well used, it can now be expanded. But continued watching is still essential. Encouragement and compliments should be added to both reinforce the enthusiasm and justify the surveillance. Aside from that, things can roll pretty well on their own, and you are free to concentrate on other projects. You have achieved "Extended Independence and true Butt-out."

Four Power Secrets for Handling Errors

Yes, of course people will make errors. Nobody's perfect, not even you or me. But they would have messed up even with less independence. Your best bet is to anticipate it and be ready for it. Don't be caught unprepared as so often happens to the novice, while the truly seasoned executives, when things go wrong, can be heard saying, "I was afraid that might happen."

Power secret one: your best bet is to be sure not to drop your monitoring procedure, but to keep it constantly sharpened. That way you will know of problems at the earliest possible moment. A few hours' headstart can make all the difference—applying the "stitch-in-time" concept.

Power secret two: Take reasonable safeguards, where you can, to prevent the problem from ever happening in the first place. Here we have the "ounce-of-prevention" idea.

Power secret three: another good step, to maximize future progress and future motivation, is to minimize whatever damage might occur from the error. One way to do this is to have a contingency or stand-by procedure to use, "just-in-case."

Power secret four: to avoid seriously reducing the motivation you have built up, and to assure that most of it continues, you should not over-react to the foul-up. Study it as calmly as you can and work out a solution just as calmly, even when you are furious. Anger is usually counter-productive to both you and your objective, unless it is directed by cool design. General Eisenhower once said, "I never get mad, except on purpose."

How a Government Clerk Was Allowed to "Mess Up," Yet Output Doubled

Situation: a complex and difficult new written reporting procedure was required of a small government department—a problem that faces most all of our organizations, especially these days.

Objectives: to learn and install this new program with minimum fuss and feathers, maximum efficiency and results.

The system used was basically simple. The supervisor Scott S. was firm in the need for all to know and understand the procedure. Several attended a course on the subject—including Scott. But then he made it well known that he would let the key control clerk Grace M. handle the thing in her own way.

Results: Grace took the project over and applied her own, individual, independent ideas. She made some minor mistakes. She messed up on a few occassions. But both Grace and Scott were ready for this and made corrections quickly, with minimum emotional stress. She even developed some methods that streamlined, simplified and increased efficiency. The goals were quickly accomplished and then exceeded. Output more than doubled. Proper instruction, flexibility between tough and easy, plus "butt out" and extended independence built highly productive motivation.

Summary: Proper Directions and Butting Out Are Great Power Secrets

We can easily see that there are extremes in attitude, posture, firmness and direction from tough to easy. Be tough early on, when hard decisions must be made for the good of your group and your clients. Do it briefly and impersonally. Be easy when you have been tough, when there is no longer the need to be firm and you can do so moderately with appreciation for your position. Avoid staying at either extreme; seek the mid-point; but stay flexible. Adjust according to conditions; show respect; and enlist both people's logic and their emotions. Then employ their wish for independence to use their own initiative. Step away, back off and butt out. Let them be their own boss to at least some degree. Give them their own turf. Expand this freedom as you have evidence that it gets good results. Yes, they will mess up. Expect it; do what you reasonably can to avoid it; and be ready for it. Keep watching. Minimize damage and trauma. This will permit you to generate substantial motivation through proper direction and extended independence or true butt-out.

13

Powerful Reward
Techniques That Move People
to Action

President Gerald Ford decided to visit a series of large
cities and hold a sort of town meeting with leading citizens. The objective was to let them hear from members
of his cabinet, each speaking for five or ten minutes on
key matters; then they would hear comments and answer questions from the citizens. Naturally, it was important for Mr. Ford and his cabinet to understand the
major local issues before arriving on the scene. This understanding would affect both their short talks and the
answers they gave when put on the spot by questions
from the audience.

By a series of purely lucky circumstances at that time, I happened to be assigned to the White House staff. A designated task
was to initiate, motivate and supervise gathering of local information into a careful briefing document for Mr. Ford and the cabinet.
His close advisors had devised a system of award recognition and
motivation of major resource authorities that was both elegantly
simple and dramatically effective—a system that has proved practical and workable in everyday business and one you can easily add
to your motivation tool kit.

His advisors wanted a one page, written report from 20
local leaders, each person covering their one specialty in 20
key subjects areas such as labor and employment, schools and
colleges, hospitals and medicine, welfare, transportation, crime,

commerce, population, disasters, politics, news media, recreation, churches, homes and construction and weather.

Unfortunately, a big problem was that this had to be prepared quickly and personally by the leading authority, not by an assistant or secretary. Also, there was almost no lead time. Authorities were notified just two days before the material was due. Most of those people were either out of town or in town and swamped with meetings, visitors and other urgent, even emergency matters. These were all principal community leaders, deeply immersed in some of the most important projects of their lives. They were hardly interested in cutting off these activities to write reports, and most were not even reachable by phone.

The advisors were told to promise them a personally written thank you letter from the President if they would push everything else aside long enough to prepare their report.

And it worked. To a man (and woman) everyone co-operated. They held up on high priority, urgent matters and delivered not just one page reports, but in most cases five or ten page reports, overnight, and in plenty of time to be condensed and edited into the Presidential briefing paper.

Obviously, the importance, prestige and impact of a request from the White House staff played a major role. But these were people who dealt regularly with senators, governors and even the President; so they were not easily impressed.

The key point is that a promise of recognition, personal recognition, written recognition, a paper they could frame and hang on the wall (as some later did) proved to be a great motivator, even of very highly placed people.

This same technique of honest compliment, expression or appreciation and awards that really get to people is used thousands of times each week, on all levels and at very low cost. You too, can easily put this practical tool to work towards your goals.

If you are a supervisor, then to your workers you are at the moment the nearest thing to a president that they see or talk with and just as important to their lives—perhaps more so.

The Power of Compliments and Awards

Compliments and awards are major power secrets. These are motivation devices that have been used and abused for many years. They are powerful tools when used right, but devastatingly humorous disasters when used wrong. Here are a series of new and better techniques for putting these devices to work for you: how to apply compliments so that they are well accepted, turn people on and do the job; how to use honesty to get into their skin and feelings; some do's and dont's for comparison charts to build acceptance and effect; some suggestions and guidelines for using certificates, awards and trophies so they fire folks forward and don't backfire. We'll look at some mistakes that I and other people, have made and some highly rewarding successes we all achieved when things were done right.

Four Power Secrets for Using Compliments

Nearly everyone likes a compliment. Most of us eat it up. Some people crave it and must have their "strokes" or their "fix" every day, almost like an addict. To enjoy a compliment is not only perfectly natural, normal and human; it is almost instinctive. It has strong survival value. Over the centuries, a word of praise meant you were important to the group, hence wanted, loved and secure. It became reassurance that you were going to keep on eating regularly. And it still means about that, right up to today. So not only are compliments desired by people, but the person giving the compliment gains power or influence or respect in at least two ways: first, the recipient now values the giver above others who don't give; and second, the recipient will almost unconsciously acknowledge this giver as someone of stature and position who can bestow honors. The recipient is *not forced* into believing that. Quite the contrary, *he wants* to believe that, since it then makes the compliment more significant and potent. In that way the recipient, himself, gains importance in his own eyes. Compliment a man, and he pays you with a crown. But there are a few things to watch out for, lest your compliment backfire and your crown turn to dung.

Power secret one: Be careful; think once, then twice before you speak. Don't appear artificial or contrived. People can smell a phony a mile away, and they not only will fail to react positively, but may deeply resent any obvious or even suspicious hint of being manipulated.

Power secret two: study the person you plan to compliment. Do your homework. Learn something about what they do, how they do it, their strengths and weaknesses. Few things look quite so ridiculous as a hearty compliment for a given trait or act (such as math accuracy) when everyone knows the recipient can't multiply six times six.

Power secret three: Pick their strength. Every person has some. Accent their leading one or at least the one that, if expanded, developed and enlarged, will help build action toward your mutual goals.

Power secret four: Don't underestimate the appetite for a compliment—but don't spread it on too thick either. If you do, you might have started on a perfectly good tack, only to have it go bad. Generally, however, people will gladly soak up many compliments.

Case Example: A long time friend of mine, Don R., was working with an able management consultant, Zeke, who literally thrived on compliments. He would rather sit and listen to praise than eat, though ideally he preferred a rich mixture of both. Don happened to be driving with Zeke on a highway trip of several hours; so he decided to run a little experiment. He proposed to see just how many compliments and how much praise Zeke could swallow before he choked and said, "Aw cut it out. You're giving me the baloney."

The interesting result was that Zeke never did say "stop." He accepted and enjoyed the flood of praise for over two hours, until Don had exhausted nearly every conceivable subject and even some rather inconceivable ones.

Practical application: Some people, perhaps most, have a large, nearly insatiable appetite for compliments and praise. For many, it makes life worth living.

Three Power Secrets for Using Honesty to Turn Folks On

For centuries, mankind has been a seeker of truth. But this interest is particularly strong among Americans who have an unusually high regard for education and facts. Witness the growth of our schools, news media and press compared to most other nations. We increasingly equate knowledge with progress, success and security. This has been especially true in recent years as educational levels have grown sharply. We have an almost dramatic indignation, revulsion and anger towards authorities who mislead, deceive or outright lie to us. (Watergate is only one case in point.)

The flip side of this becomes a practical advantage to you:

people seek, respect and respond to reasonable candor, frankness and honesty. Here are three basic rules that can help you match this system together with praise as an extra effective motivation method.

First, give compliments that they will agree with. Now you have a double-positive: praise they appreciate and truth they respect. You have said something they truly want to believe. You made their day. (Just recall the last time someone complimented you on a thing you knew to be true and you got a pretty good feeling when you thought about it later.)

Second, state the compliment flatly, plainly, almost awkwardly. Why? Few remarks gain as much credibility and believability as ones made spontaneously and obviously from the heart, rather than those contrived, smooth, slick statements from the manipulative mind.

Third, one whiff of baloney blows the whole thing. Baloney here means exaggeration, excess, error (the wrong thing being praised) or a clear effort to con someone. Most people quickly detect this, identify it and resent it. But when you are sincere, honest and factual, they almost always know it and appreciate it.

Case history. Jerry L. meets monthly with at least eight or ten volunteer workers and begins most meetings with a short, simple, accurate acknowledgment of good work that one or another accomplished. The group has not only become highly dedicated and motivated to their task but recently chipped in to get Jerry a printed, framed statement of appreciation.

Five "Extra Techniques" for More Effectiveness

You can have all sorts of lovely compliments lined up and have them well checked for truth and accuracy, but there are a few extra techniques you need to use if the effort is to generate employee's best effort, maximum effect and constructive action.

Power secret one: Show a real interest. A compliment that seems casual, offhand, incidental or sort of a second thought has much less impact than one that seems to really mean something to you and be important to you. It then becomes more important to the recipient. You get closer to him or her.

Power secret two: Smile. This is a plain, simple, outright physical demonstration of pleasure and approval. A small compliment given with a broad, friendly grin has far more impact than elaborate praise delivered with a sneer.

Power secret three: Use the person's name. Motivator Dale Carnegie says a person's name is, to him, the most beautiful sound in the English language. This clearly adds impact to the compliment and gets closer to the heart and mind.

Power secret four: Talk about things of major interest to the person. There is no sense in complimenting a trait he cares nothing about. When you discuss and praise his key interests, you are singing his song. You are simpatico. You are in his skin.

Power secret five: Sincerely show how he is really helping you. This recognizes that you are in debt to him in a small way. You and I both enjoy knowing that someone owes you something and freely admits it. When someone says he is in debt to you, your value, self-esteem, importance and security goes up. Even a Mafia boss will say to a compadre who helped him, "I owe you." And so in this same way your recipient also feels good when you acknowledge that he helped you. And you get even more into his skin, his heart and mind.

Results: Employee dedication increases towards helping you reach your mutual goals. You brought out the best in that person for your good and for his. You used an emotional award to generate increased motivation.

Power Secrets for Using Comparison Charts

Let's define comparison charts as simple little lists of people or groups showing their performance, results or score. This might also have columns that show individual's score over each month or other time period.

An advantage is that it is, or seems to be, fair and objective. Each person can see how he or she is doing, how he ranks with others, who's doing tops and poorest, how status changes from month to month, who went up this time, who down, and how they are personally trending over several months.

The most important advantage is generation of a competitive spirit, the embarrassment of a poor showing and pride in a high score or improving one.

To work best, you will be wise to consider four modifications: (1) Be sure the scores or statistics are as fair, equitable and comparable as possible. A good equalizer may be comparison of actual performance of group members in terms of a percent of their goal, if the goals are equitable. (2) When unusual conditions or circumstances occurred that were specifically beyond their control, these should be footnoted on the chart, or goals should be modified up or down. This includes both windfalls and disasters. (3) Don't let management tools become management masters, as Peter Drucker says. The comparison chart should rarely be made the only or even the major tool for judging performance. While this may be the case in sports or elections, business is not the same as either. People and management have many vital variables not always reducible or translatable to charts and statistics—attitudes, for example. If you let people know that the comparison chart is only one basis of judging their performance, the tabulation will be of greater service to you both. They will still try to score well, and you will have avoided some problems. (4) Be sure those involved know about the chart and know that each person concerned is seeing it; and, if possible, give the chart moderate but appropriate publicity.

How a Utility Soap Company's Comparison Charts Motivated Action

Problem: Business growth of the brand had been very spotty around the country. Some regions were doing beautifully. Others were making little progress.

Solution: The soap brand manager developed a simple comparison chart, dividing the total market into some 20 regions. He expressed sales or business development in terms of cases sold per thousand population ("cs. per m. pop"), thus washing out differences in large and small populations and making the figures more fair and comparable. Areas of natural disaster or weak competition were footnoted, and copies were sent to the supervisors in each region.

Results: The lowest regions were amazed to find that their performance was so low, and as a matter of self-pride plus security and professional position they took positive and strong action. Their business development levels increased rapidly. Surprisingly, those with high scores gained increased confidence and, realizing that other districts would now make major efforts, they also moved aggressively to extend their lead. The total brand position improved sharply. Comparison charts had motivated highly positive performance.

Five Power Secrets for
Using Trophy Awards for Best Results

A trophy, scroll, certificate or like award is essentially a formal compliment.

The actionable word here is formal. The award takes on impact in almost direct proportion to the amount of importance and ceremony attached to it. Suggestions:

Power secret one: Pick the right person and performance to award—one that is not only recognized but, since this should be a somewhat public affair, that you wish to encourage in others, not just in the one recipient.

Power secret two: Select the right time, usually after some specific success or before a new challenge dominates people's attention. Ideally, it might be just before such a problem becomes widely known, since the reward gives people a reputation to live up to and enthusiasm to help them in meeting the challenge.

Power secret three: Space awards out far enough apart so that a second one does not come rapidly on the heels of the first. If this happens, they become too commonplace and lose impact. People start treating them lightly. Worst of all they may treat them as a joke.

Power secret four: Be sure the award is goal related or has some direct connection with earlier agreed upon objectives. This reinforces concentration, dedication and determination to reach current and new goals. Strongly avoid granting major awards for action, even good action, that was not part of the goal. To do so weakens current focus on new objectives.

Power secret five: Present the award with unusual sincerity and dignity. Make an occassion of it. It should be happy, important, significant. There can be joking, laughter, good cheer abounding. But the award granting ceremony must also have at least a few moments of serious respect. Anything else makes the award insignificant and possibly humorous. It is almost an insult. Under such unfavorable circumstances, it is best you do not give it out at all.

Case Example: the Olympic Gold, Silver and Bronze metals, worth under $400 each, inspire four years of the hardest kind of work and self-discipline. They are given to the right person at the climactic moment every four years as a direct recognition of reaching the major goal. And while there is joy and tumult and cheering, when the solemn moment comes there is silence, attention, respect, sincerity and dignity of the highest order . . . and many a moist eye. The award has magnificent motivational magic. The same can be true, on a smaller scale, for your award granting occasion.

Don't Let Trophies
"Make One Person Happy but 50 Sad"

This is a common criticism about awards. Some managers feel that the trophy motivates only the recipient, but saddens, angers and demotivates all the rest. A few points to consider: *First, under some conditions this can be true,* especially if a strong implication is made that the losers have failed or goofed up, or that the winner didn't win by pure effort but because he or she is superior or better than the others. Avoid very extensive honoring of star players. They are already motivated and more awards to them stimulate few other people.

Second, on the other hand, a major objective of the award is to interest, encourage and challenge the others. The implication, in fact the statement, should strongly be made to the effect that "You can do this, too. Maybe next time *you* will be up here getting this trophy." If that real hope is kindled, the award effort will produce much greater motivational momentum.

Third, give out lots of second, third and honorable mention awards. This has at least two advantages. Nearly everybody gets something. Everyone becomes "a winner." God smiles on us all. And second, it makes an honest person of you by proving that they can do it, too. And maybe, sure enough, next time one of them will get the top award. The fire, flame and driving force to do better burns brighter than ever. You have much increased the motivation of your team towards greater results, towards doing the best they can.

Gas Station Owner Weeps

Gerald M. was taking part in a small award luncheon to honor several small business owners. They had done well in a management workshop seminar, and it was Gerald's job to hand out certificates of achievement. The top awards were bestowed, then the second and third level certificates, and finally a few honorable mentions. The last was to Frank Z., owner of a gas station, who had not done all that well at the workshop, but who had tried hard. When he came up to the roster to receive his certificate, Frank hesitated for a moment. Then he turned to the little group assembled. "I just want to say . . ." he choked up. His eyes were brimming. "I just want to say that I never finished school. This is the first time in my whole life I ever got a certificate of any kind. I will never forget you guys for the rest of my life, and I . . ." He could go no further. Today that $3 certificate hangs in a place of honor in his prosperous and growing service station—a business he runs with new pride, vigor and dedication. Awards motivate in remarkable ways.

Four Common Award Errors to Avoid

Obviously, awards generate motivation; but are we always doing this properly? Are we operating at the best, most effective level and method? No, certainly not, unless we consider a few ways to modify and refine these methods. Here are the things we should check:

Power secret one: Give awards only where earned. Recipients, co-workers and audience know very clearly who has done outstanding work and exactly how well. They resent being hoodwinked by your bringing in a ringer who didn't really earn anything.

Power secret two: State honors only to the level earned; nothing more, nothing less. Don't pump it up, exaggerate or guild the lily—at least not much. A little is all right, expected, even wanted. But gross exaggeration can hurt the whole thing.

Power secret three: Make it sincere, genuine, honest. Better to lose a little glamour and drama in the name of accuracy and honesty than to make it even slightly fake, false, phony or cont-rived. Even a small lie puts the whole award or honors statement in doubt. It will create a large credibility gap between you and your group. Motivation spirit is gone with the wind of distorted rehetoric.

Power secret four: Use compliments fairly often, but formal awards only at a moderate, infrequent level, not for every little thing or every month or week. A quiet, not very subtle protest against over-used awards sometimes appears in a manner that is particularly devastating because it makes sarcastic humor and mockery of awards. It is occasionally in the form of a certificate saying, "This certifies that Joe Blow has received one Genuine 'Atta-boy.' Upon receipt of 1,000 'Atta-boys,' he will be eligible to work nights, weekends, holidays and have the key to the Executive washroom, and he will be entitled to being addressed as 'Sir.' But upon utterance of just one. 'Aw, the hell with it,' he shall lose all his 1,000 'Atta-boys' and must start all over again."

If you ever see this sign around, or even suspect your team feels this way, you should thoroughly review your awards program. Look for errors, especially the possibility that you are giving out too many too often or that people feel they are being manipulated.

How a Company's Awards Generate Extra Effort

One pen company's managers are masters at the fine art of award giving for maximum lifting of employee spirits.

At one annual awards dinner, they had the various trophies beautifully displayed in a giant special case, lined with purple velvet and illuminated with a series of inside lights and outside baby spots.

The awards were given in reverse order of importance, honorable mentions being first. The award statements were finely wrought, and carefully worded, with scrupulous accuracy. Every statement was one that precisely matched commonly known facts or widely felt emotional convictions about the recipient.

Each person was individually called by name and asked to come up and stand in a spotlight next to the president. A short, human, complimentary story or comment was made. Words were plain, simple, personal, homey, folksy. They were expressed slowly and quietly, with kindness, warmth, sincerity, dignity, justice and respect. Comments spoke directly and only about the recipient's key, vital or major performance as it related to his other goal. There was clear, strong implication and understanding that others could soon do as well.

The presentations were always in good taste and grew in a gently rising level of importance, until the first prize was given, in a virtual crescendo of appreciation. There was hardly a dry eye in the house.

Results: Morale and motivation among employees soared to high levels of spirit, activity and constructive team work that was evident for many months, even growing as the season approached for the next awards dinner.

Summary: Compliments and Awards Are Major Secrets for Building Power

Most of us like compliments and respond well to them. They give us a reputation to live up to. When you use this approach, however, move with care and thought. Don't be contrived or artificial. Recognize real strengths. Make the compliment strong and meaningful but not excessive. Make statements that your recipient knows to be true. Keep it plain, simple, acceptable, believable and credible. Get into the recipient's skin with real interest, a smile, his or her name, things of interest. If you use comparison charts, use fair comparisons, acknowledge unusual situations and don't over-use or over-idolize such charts. In giving certificates or awards, pick the right person and right goal-related action to be recognized at an appropriate time. Make a dignified ceremony of it. Avoid angering those who did not get a top award by giving many second and third level certificates, or building a strong and realistic hope of winning next time. Give awards only as earned and in some reasonable proportion to the performance; awards should not be overdone in words, value or frequency.

14

A Surprising Secret:
How Honesty and Candor Can Build
Your Managerial Power

Frank R. had a common, everyday problem. He supervised a small group of unenthusiastic, almost indifferent clerks. They weren't exactly hostile or angry or even unpleasant—just not really very interested in doing the job. Throughout the day, they thought mainly about their breaks, their friends, their lunch, their date that night and their weekend camping or boating or their upcoming flight to Chicago. They arrived late, left early and took long lunches. Work production was declining in volume and quality.

Frank gave this some thought, then decided to simply be candid about the whole thing.

He talked privately with each person. He outlined the problem: not only were work results low, but this was hurting *their personal goals* and worst of all, making *their work* a dull drag and a bore and making life a "bummer." He asked for *their ideas* on improving matters and reaching goals. Then, as a group, they got together with Frank and suggested a few changes in the system. They recommended some shifts in delegation, new authority and responsibilities plus a motivational program of performance charts and awards. All these were the clerks' ideas, not Frank's.

He agreed and put these into effect. A couple proved impractical, but by then the little group had some additional thoughts. Their interest went up; their enthusiasm became contagious; simple awards were given; and the unit became so well known for performance that managers were sent in from out of town to see how Frank did it—when in fact he really didn't do much of anything except "level" with his group.

How Openess Can Be a Remarkable Secret Power

Here is a new system for your motivation kit that most managers never think about: simple candor, leveling with people—old-fashioned honesty. But (and this is an important "but"), it must be seasoned with some discretion, restraint and common sense. It is based on a very simple but unusually ignored principle (for some reason educated people too often avoid simple truths): Motivation is not trickery, even though it might seem so at times. People increasingly respond well to candor, and so this becomes an unused power source for you. We will look at ways to employ this to build a self-motivating system for your people. Many highly successful health and body building programs are based on the idea that most strength comes from within; you can build your muscle by exercising against your own weight as with jogging, chinning, push-ups and sit-ups. The organization can build its own strength, spirit, and motivation by recognizing its own weighty problems and rigorously reacting to them. But this can only happen if you apply some straight talk, open thinking and level or candid relations. Let's take a look at how this can be done.

What "Leveling" Means As a Secret Power Source

When some managers try to motivate, they often get obsessed and confused by techniques and details. They get all tangled up in their own underwear of hidden devices. In reality they are making things difficult for themselves when, if they would apply the "K.I.S.S." formula (keep it simple, stupid), they would get much further with less effort.

Begin by looking at motivation as just a pure and simple technique for getting from point A to point B. Motivation is merely a method, a system, an approach to getting the job done. A way of reaching a goal.

Second, recognize that motivation is not, need not be and should not be closed, secret, hidden or contrived trickery. For one thing, we only kid ourselves if we think our employees or team members don't at least partly recognize our motivation efforts. They aren't totally ignorant. If they were, we would never have hired them. There is a slogan among advertising people: "The customer isn't stupid; she's your wife."

Case history: The "savvy" employee. Don B. had several key people on his team, and he decided to increase their motivation (especially that of Al H.) by secretly and slyly applying some basic techniques. About that same time, Don also got active in the membership committee for a local service club. Who should pop up as head of the committee but Al H.! And Al proceeded to not only apply the same motivation techniques Don was using, but to add a few more that Don was just learning about. Don had deceived himself into thinking that motivation was a closed, hidden system and his employees were ignorant of his efforts. Quite the contrary, they were very knowledgeable.

Third, people resent being manipulated, conned or deceived. They don't like a snow job or "tricky" stuff. Worse than being resentful, they will resist—sometimes in ways you don't see and will never know about until it's too late and you have been badly hurt.

Four Power Secrets of Why Leveling Works

People will respond to candor four favorable ways, and this can become a powerhouse of often ignored, untapped, unemployed motivation to reach your mutual goal.

Power secret one: They appreciate openness, partly because it is so rare and refreshing—like a cool, clean breeze. So many people are heatedly trying to push them, pull them, con them and sell them with broadcast and print ads, politics, scare stories and pleas to give more, do more, care more and work more.

Power secret two: Candor creates "believability," particularly when the news is not all good, and especially when you tell both sides or admit some point you might otherwise be expected to hide. They might not like it, but most people would rather hear the honest bad than the lying good.

Power secret three: Problems don't often shock people. They expect them. People live with problems every day. A human is partly a problem solving animal.

Power secret four: You prove you are like them—fallible, not perfect. A touch of humanism makes the whole world one. People identify with you and you with them. Suddenly, its "us" working together against "our" problems. We are all in the same boat pulling on those oars together.

Candor is too often avoided by the pseudo-sophisticate, who feels it is childish, naive and simplistic. This is not really so. Done properly, it is often *the most* sophisticated, since it rarely calls for total openness and candor, because people don't really want to or need to know all the who-shot-John details. This can bog things down in confusion and interfere with activities.

There is such a thing as immoderate or excessive honesty, especially when it gets too boring, irrelevant and detailed. (Ask some people what time it is, and they will build you a watch factory!)

So candor represents openness but not the whole load of hay. It is frankness without offense, facts without tedium, problems without devastation. Net: leveling is appreciated, believable, normal and unifying. But to be done right it must be tempered with reason, proportion, restraint and common sense.

A case in space: During a recent manned space mission, the command pilot said, "Mission control in Houston, we seem to have a problem." He described it, and the team promptly developed a solution. They appreciated his candor; they believed him; and they responded favorably.

Power Secrets for Using Leveling to Stimulate Motivation

If leveling is not trickery but "sensible openness," how can we use this—with what mechanics? Here are a few suggestions:

First, use techniques clearly and frankly—right out there in front of God and everybody. For example: If you are going to use respect to motivate a person, you just might come out flat-footed and say something like, "If we respect each other, we'll both feel a lot more motivated and steamed up. I respect you for your thoroughness and great attitude." Or you might say, "I have confidence that you'll do your part, and I hope you respect me in the same way. So let's get on with the job." Notice you didn't hide anything. You admitted that respect was the motivating force for you both. You showed your cards and explained what you were doing and why. You can use this technique effectively in meeting problems, goals or plans to build motivation. Say it and let it all hang out. You defuse and disarm most criticism by frankly facing and admitting your approach.

Second, don't let a few scoffs throw you. Some people are likely to laugh or make a joke about being motivated or manipulated. Let it go with little comment, or laugh right along with them. "You're right, we are motivating ourselves. And why *not* make the job more fun with a little spirit?" Or maybe, "Let's be at least half smart. Beefing just adds to our load. Makes everything twice as tough. Winners believe in themselves." Pick your phrase to match the person and the situation.

Third, hang in there. Don't expect instant results. When you level with people, don't expect them to jump up and down saying, "Boy oh boy! An honest person at last!" Frankly, you *are* a bit strange, unusual and unexpected. Give them a little time to think it over and digest the shock. In a few days they will begin to understand that you actually are leveling with them. (Some take a few weeks.) And they will start responding to you.

How to Get People's "Monkey" Involved in Self-Motivation

One of the great advantages of leveling is that when you admit the truth you toss the ball to others and let them play with the problem. It helps to get the monkey off your back and on theirs. And most of these riders have spurs that create self-motivation.

Case example: Chris J. is manager of a small department in a food manufacturing firm. Chris's group is made up mostly of records processing clerks. He likes to tell the story of how when he came to work in the morning at least one or two of the clerks would stop him before he even got halfway to his office and they would complain or ask him to do something. Then one day he got to his desk, stopped, thought a moment, turned around and went back to each clerk. He admitted there was a problem and asked both their advice and their help to solve the problem. He took each monkey off his own back, leveled with his helpers and put at least part of the monkey back where it usually belonged. Then he went back to work with only half the monkey business he once had. And those who so fervently wanted service were self-motivated to perform at least some of this themselves, in their own self-interest.

An easy technique as you prepare to rid yourself of a monkey is to: first, listen carefully and recognize the request or complaint; show you understand; second, show respect—so *much respect* that it is clear you value their opinion; then, third, candidly and forthrightly ask for that very same person's opinion as to how the problem might be solved and what part each of you might play. Obviously, that third part is where it all fits into place. In fact, you had set it up to happen just that way.

Three Power Secrets for Applying a "Leveling" System This Week

If you want to put "leveling" to work for you to motivate others, it can all boil down to this: simple, sensible candor plus the highly useful S-O-S formula (situation, objective, system).

Power secret one: Level with the person about the "situation." This is usually the most important part, because it does at least two things: (1) By admitting to the facts, in a reasonable, candid and open way, you show that you are trying to be honest with them. It shows that you have a problem, you are plagued with a difficulty and you admit it; and that makes you human. "Your" problem became "our" problem, for "us" to solve. (2) And perhaps most important, you can emphasize, dramatize and emotionalize the problem into recognition of it as a really serious matter that must have action for the good of all.

Power secret two: Level with them about your "objectives." Remember, these are mutual goals—targets that you both agree are worth reaching. Sometimes they have forgotten or never actually realized or verbalized these objectives. You might say, "Obviously, John, we have got to get more stores in this town using our services." (A goal.) Or, "We must get these reports done by Friday." (Another goal.)

Power secret three: Level about the "system." This is the strategy to solve the first step, "situation," and reach the second step, "goals." Usually, this is pretty easy. It just requires you to re-state the procedure that you have both already agreed to follow and probably are at least partly doing. But now you emphasize it more. You clarify the system. And you do this in an honest, open, level and candid manner. "Frankly, John, if we are going to get our service in more stores, there is no sense in kidding ourselves. We simply have to make more calls and better, more effective calls." (Candor about the method.) You didn't really say anything shockingly new, but you did level with John about the strategy system.

Power Secrets for Using a Group Plan and Involvement

This is a little less simple but still pretty easy. Instead of working with one person, you may have two or three, or maybe a few more, but not a large group.

The key difference now is that with group leveling and involvement you simply get the several people directly concerned in their own team program to reach their own goal—same as elsewhere in this book. But in this case there is one, basic exception: now you level with them with openness, honesty and candor, encouraging them to their own personal, individual devices.

Here's how you can do it: You might say something like, "Hey guys, we can all see we have a problem. The parts arriving out here on the plant floor are always in boxes of five, yet we need them in units of six." You just stated the key factor of the "situation," without color or emotion or drama, just as a fact—a level fact, an honest fact. They know the problem; you simply clarified the focus.

"We want to get this done right with the least effort." (Goal stated honestly, candidly and openly.) "So what do you think is the best way to solve this?" (System.) "How about putting in a group suggestion that these items be packed in units of six? (System again.)

You have been open, honest and candid about the situation, objective and system you should all consider. You used the S-O-S formula, but you presented it coolly with everyone directly involved. This is leveling with *the entire plan*. In that sense, it is total leveling.

To carry leveling motivation even a step further on the scale of sophistication, you might apply the sensible candor and S-O-S formula directly to the actual program of stimulating action. In short, be frank, open and candid about motivation itself.

For example, you might say something like: "Let's lay all our cards on the table. Let's look at our 'situation' and the problem of motivating ourselves. We sure aren't too well turned on. We're not moving much. We have a mutual 'goal' of some action and getting the job done. Nobody doubts that. Now, what 'system' or strategy should we use to stimulate and activate ourselves? We respect each other. Maybe we should combine that respect with planning for our little group plus some nice juicy awards for ourselves. That should motivate us way over our goal! It is sure worth a try, isn't it?"

This is high "leveling" indeed. You have not only been candid and open about your S-O-S program, but you have been open about the very need for and selection of motivational tools to move forward.

How Salesmen Set Their Own Motivators and Tripled Sales

The sales manager said to Diane G., "Diane, you have been doing such a good job at record keeping and correspondence with customers and our sales staff that I'm going to put you in charge of selling canned pop through our brokers. They'll do all the selling to stores and others. You mainly keep records and correspond with the group, but meet with them and work out a simple sales plan."

Diane had been in the business for several years and knew the product and prices quite well. She also knew that the broker salesmen and women were not too gung-ho on the cola. Naturally, they would rather sell colas of the leading competitors.

So she met with them and leveled. "I know we aren't the leading brand, but maybe we can use the best ideas we have as a group to really build some great sales volume. What do you think?"

They reviewed the problem. But they also noted some opportunities. They asked, "What kind of quotas shall we set?" She replied, "What goals do you want?" They did some calculating, some arguing, some dreaming, some laughing, but finally picked some cold, hard objectives. They were ambitious goals, *but their* goals. They also set up their own performance charts, sales leader club and awards dinner program. This sparked new marketing ideas, and sales began building. Over the months, volume far exceeded each month of the preceding year. Total volume ended up more than triple that year. Diane felt her success was largely caused by her candor and honesty with the broker sales people about their problem, their goal, their systems and their own personal motivation.

Examples of Candor As a Power Secret in 14 Major Motivators

We have looked at some 14 prime movers in this book: (1) opportunities, (2) goals, (3) fear, (4) respect, (5) meetings, (6) group plans, (7) work, (8) heart and mind, (9) delegation, (10) coaching, (11) communication, (12) butt-out, (13) awards and (14) leveling. *Clearly, we can apply* the candor of number 14 to each and every one of the others. But there is a good, right and favorable time to do this. And a wrong time.

The right time is when you already have a generally favorable positive or receptive attitude reflected or showing in the person or people in your group. They have at least some insight into the situation, objective and system—plus a willingness to accept some motivation. They may have already thought about motivation and may even be using some methods. Obviously, these people are likely to understand and appreciate candor and openness in the other 13 prime movers or builders of their own motivation.

The "Go-Getters" Club

Bobby T., a route supervisor at a bottling plant, had a small group of truck drivers serving the north side of town. But sales and enthusiasm were both pretty low. Bobby would meet with his drivers nearly every morning at the coffee shop, and they would complain about "how lousy business is this year."

They all agreed that something was needed to boost their spirits. They feared that if things kept on like this the company would probably drop some drivers and combine routes.

So, they talked about setting some informal goals, just among themselves. Each driver had some ideas for these and suggested ways to reach the target. Bobby recommended that they pick just three simple devices each week and mainly use these. The devices could be something such as more calls, better displays and at least one new sign up in each store. Then, at the end of the month, they were to pick the three that seemed to work best and just use those all the next month. They applied their thought and spirit to the program and agreed to Bobby's suggestion.

Records would be kept and the best producer would get a small bronze "Go-Getter" pin (about the size of your thumb nail) that one of the men had won in a sports event and now donated to the team's program.

Results: Most drivers pitched in. Spirit and sales went up fairly well the first few weeks. When the "Go-Getters" pin was awarded at the end of the month, there was considerable comment and joking about "who would win it next month."

The interesting thing was that after a few months more award buttons were purchased and soon about half the drivers had a "Go-Getters" pin. A "Go-Getters" club was formed. They sat together at coffee in the mornings, began socializing together for beers in the evening and were regarded as an elite group. After all, they were the most successful young drivers. Morale and performance were high among the "Go-Getters," and others were determined to get into the "club."

The supervisor had done very little aside from some coaching. And the cost was about $10 for a few little bronze pins.

The supervisor had applied nearly all the major motivators; opportunities, goals, fear, respect, meetings, group plans, work, heart and mind, delegation, coaching, communication and butt-out. And to all of these, the supervisor had applied leveling, honesty and candor because the circumstances were favorable for this. There was already a concerned, positive attitude with some understanding of the situation, objective and system. They wanted to motivate themselves, and they did it through applying leveling directly to all the other prime movers.

Summary: Surprising As It Seems, Candor Is a Key Power Secret

"Leveling" is even a bit shocking to some managers. But in practice, it is refreshing relief from being all tangled up in the underwear of techniques. Just tell it like it is, and K.I.S.S. "Keep it simple, stupid." Motivation is not a trick, but a way to get from A to B. Most people know a little about motivation, although if you've read this far you probably know lots more. People like openness because they at least partly understand the process of solving problems, and they tend to believe it when you outline troubles. Don't hide techniques; instead just state them frankly. Don't let a few scoffers throw you, but hang in there. Get people's monkey (complaint) off your back and partly returned to theirs as a motivator. Use the S-O-S method of situation-objective-system, plus simple, sensible candor as an easy approach. You don't need to be a "tricky" person. Actually, that turns out to be just too much work; and it loses you leverage, credence, power and brownie points—for nothing. Leveling with your group to build their own action program is a lot easier, with more results. It works even better when they admit that they need motivation and you encourage them to "hype" themselves. Leveling is a major motivator (#14) that can be applied to each of the others; opportunities, goals, fear, respect, meetings, group plans, work, heart and mind, delegation, coaching, communication, butt-out and awards. Of course, one of these may not be right for you. But then you can't expect to do better than the Lord, and even he was wrong one time out of twelve.

15

A Three-Point Formula
for Management Power

Dave Riesman got the social scientists pretty well
steamed up when he came out with a new theory some
years back. In his classic book, *The Lonely Crowd*, he
said that the world is mainly made up of people who are
mostly motivated or directed by either of three factors:
(1) "tradition," or (2) their "inner" beliefs, or (3) "other"
people. While this is no longer a novel idea, what is new
is use of this as a tool to help you motivate. So the purpose of this chapter is not to explain Riesman's theory
but to show how it can be applied to generate constructive action. This can be a rather fun project. Unfortunately, people rarely fit into nice, neat little pigeon
holes. Most have the nasty but interesting habit of sliding around between categories. This means you should
be observant, flexible and adaptable if you are going to
make The "Lonely Crowd" formula serve you very well.
We will look at some practical programs and procedures
to serve you in applying the simple, basic formula and
then in making some realistic little adjustments to shifting contemporary human nature.

The "Three Point Formula" of Secret Power

Riesman's theory that many of the people of the world are
directed either by "tradition" or "inner" drives or "other" people

is easy to visualize if we look at three typical types of individuals.

Example: "*Tradition directed*" people are best illustrated by Asian, African and South American societies. Here nearly everyone follows patterns of his or her parents, just as their parents did, and those before them. Home, religion, work and personal relations are nearly identical to those of long ago. Tradition not only directs but orders and dictates. Those who deviate are exposed to severe criticism.

This "social dictatorship" is changing, but, for obvious reasons, the shift is not rapid. And don't laugh. Even the Europeans, British Islanders and Americans have semi-sacred tradition that still dictates to us. Examples: Freedom of speech and religion; reverence for education; newspapers; sports; dogs; autos; shirts and ties; screen doors; traditional foods and feasts such as beef, turkey, cold cereal, burgers, Coca-cola and beer; Christmas, New Year, July 4th; shaking hands; saying good morning. We are at least partly *tradition* directed.

Example: "*Inner directed*" *people* are best illustrated by the American pioneers and immigrants: your grandparents or their ancestors. They came to an open land, a blank slate. They set up a lot of their own rules and life styles. The kids grew up with far fewer traditions than were found in "the old country." Pioneers had that independence of thinking, that personal self-confidence we sometimes call "rugged individualism." They directed themselves from their own *inner* opinions, beliefs, drives and feelings.

Example: the "*other directed*" *people* are typical members of modern, contemporary society, who are greatly influenced by the wants, needs and opinion of others—which is most of us. This includes people who are merely "aware and concerned," and it goes all the way up to the extreme of those who do and think only as others seem to be doing. Conform: comply; go with the flow; keep up with the Joneses, the Jacks and the Jills. Wear jeans if they do. Wear only frayed and faded jeans, if they do, etc. These people are hardly tradition directed or inner directed, but they are largely influenced *by others*.

How to Use
"Tradition Direction" to Motivate

Now the fun begins, particularly if you employ tradition to help bring out the best in people. Here are a few suggestions for obtaining most results with least effort on your part:

Power secret one: Identify long standing traditions within your company, group or industry. For *example:* On some production lines, such as in the food canning procedure, the filler head supervisor traditionally controls the line speed. In most businesses, salesmen traditionally make presentations to prospective customers. Clerks prepare and file written correspondence. Managers plan and measure results.

Power secret two: To motivate, re-emphasize those very expectations as "our tradition" and "the way we do things around here." *For example:* Communicate, explain, demonstrate and make it clear that everyone expects practical performance and compliance and breach of tradition is disruptive, damaging and destructive to both morale and "our mutual objectives."

Power secret three: Explain that "following tradition" has assured peace, tranquility, security and accomplishment in the past. Complying with tradition makes people feel good, comfortable and acceptable. Further, it shows respect for forefathers, for today's social structure and for yourself. Also, "Anything that has endured for all those years can't be all bad," especially considering all the new things that have been tried and failed. Traditional methods are proven methods. They work. One need not be bound by tradition, but one can be inspired by it.

Appeals to tradition and use of customary methods still motivate many people. Tradition may have been dying since the Renaissance and Columbus, but it is not totally dead. *For example*, most of us still eat three meals a day and wear at least some clothing even in the summer. Neither of these practices is completely necessary. But both are powerful traditions, and we follow them.

Case history: A pen company motivates salesmen through tradition. One company's managers tell many stories about their founder and his great tradition of quality production. This product reputation became so well known that during World War II our allies and *even our enemies* used the company's pens as medals of honor. Salesmen knew this, appreciate it and are proud to always make sales calls with the pen's distinctive clip well visible.

Five Power Secrets for Using "Inner Direction" to Motivate

First learn a person's individual inner goals or interests. This is one of the most important steps you can take in motivating because it gives you a highly useful, powerful and versatile handle.

Second, build these goals up. Congratulate their personal beliefs, their individual drive, their independent thinking, their sense of their own identity wherever you reasonably can and whenever these at least partly match the group goals and systems. Associate them directly or indirectly with "the pioneers and those who built this nation." Mention the individuals, the great need for people who march to a different drummer—their own—as the "leaders and doers" of today and of the future. This is absolutely correct and honest in many respects.

Third, mildly question and pity those who are "blind, automatic slaves to tradition or to 'popular' wisdom and fickle fashion—with no personal thought, initiative or individual creativity." Again, this is an absolutely accurate and reasonable statement.

Fourth, demonstrate a little individuality of your own—perhaps new and better ways to accomplish current tasks by working smarter not harder.

Fifth, provide maximum authority and responsibility to a person showing interest in thinking and acting for himself. This directly stimulates the motivation of inner direction.

Inner directed motivation has declined sharply since the pioneers. The great depression of the 1930's, World War II in the 1940's and the emphasis on "grey-flannel-suit" conformity as a requirement for success in the 1950's and 1960's were in many ways discouragers of individualism and independent thinking. And yet, much of our contemporary news and fiction in print and on TV acknowledges "the courage of the individual." Kojak, Columbo, Clint Eastwood, John Wayne, Billy Graham, Bette Davis, Muhammed Ali, the Lone Ranger, Mario Andretti, Hank Aaron,

Billie Jean King, and Elvis Presley are just a few symbols of this. The individual thinker is usually pictured as a hero, but one who pays a big price. Inner direction still lives, and it is admired but recognized as a bit exciting, challenging and maybe a little dangerous.

Case History: How a Company Motivated with "Inner Direction"

Bill Petersen was a good Nebraska blacksmith and metal worker who invented a tool like a pliers that locked onto the work but released at a touch. He got a few local men to help him set up ways to make these in quantity, giving each person considerable authority and responsibility over his own individual work. Tradition was ignored. Personal innovation became the name of the game. The little group developed hundreds of ingenious techniques in both production and sales. Today, the company is one of the leading trademarks among hand tools, sold in nearly every country throughout the world.

How to Use "Other Direction" to Motivate

This should be fairly easy, since there has been a 40 year trend towards direction of our lives by others, rather than by our independent feelings or by our traditions. The last 20 years have seen a veritable boom in such peer group influence. Concomitant with this, we have seen a decline in the traditional figures of authority: father, teacher, doctor, preacher, president, policeman.

In fact, this trend has approached nearly epidemic proportions among some people where almost any authority is criticized and vilified, just for being an "authority" . . . a dirty word to certain groups. The trend even extended to the iconoclastic pattern of finding dirt or allegations to "de-deify" traditional heros such as Washington, Lincoln, Roosevelt, Lindberg, Kennedy, Henry Ford and John D. Rockefeller.

The king is rotten. The peer is king. You go with the flow. Detest the establishment. Eat, dress, live, sleep, speak, sing, act and think as everyone else does. We eat bitter foods (almost no one really likes tonic water). We wear uncomfortable clothing, shoes,

have permanents and hair transplants, ride in cramped cars and go
to dull meetings, all mainly to gain social acceptance.

Even then, with all this effort, our social state shifts
steadily—as illustrated by changes in the pecking order, status
symbols, the position on Lenin's Tomb, at the conference table, or
on the memo route list.

And here comes your motivational handle. When you can
show a person, especially an "other directed" person, or one who
leans that way, that "others" take a certain action and that current
heads of the pecking order believe in this action, you have probably
made a sale. You have convinced the person to take that action or
at least seriously consider it.

Technique: provide substantial, strong and frequent evidence
that "everyone else does things this way, especially the successful
ones." Give people their daily strokes of appreciation, thus reinforcing greatly wanted recognition, acceptance and approval from
"other" sources. Also, this reinforcement of approval from others
moves the total orientation and system further away from tradition and inner self-direction.

Examples and cases of effective "other" direction are all
around us, every day—both voluntary and less-than-voluntary
cases. We elect to do things that are fashionable in clothing, opinions and behavior (such as vested suits, adoring Elvis Presley or
going to college). We less voluntarily follow the "other" direction of
supervisors or bosses who ask for overtime, trips, more work and
better work.

How to Adapt to
Today's Changing World

Now things get a little tricky, because people are so change-
able, even a little slippery and uncertain. This also gets to be a bit
more fun because, like a kid playing with an electric train, instead
of going around in a nice neat simple oval, suddenly we have some
figure eights, cross-overs and switches. People act one way for
awhile, then another.

The beauty of it all is this: if you understand and can use the
basics, you can use the switch tracks almost as well as the simple
ones, especially if you're a little flexible.

A slight return to "tradition direction" away from "other direction" has become noticeable in the last few years.

Examples: There is an interest in old movies, old fashions, old traditional furniture and decor, such as bentwood rockers and house plants. Almost 50% of all home owners today plant gardens—a hugh increase over a few years ago. There is a growing respect for those declining numbers who work mainly with their hands, such as mechanics, laborers, artists and farmers. Even a small number return to old fashioned natural foods (like granola) and old dress such as pierced earrings, lipstick, men's vested suits, workshoes and bib overalls. While these are all rather minor and superficial, enough added examples can easily be found to say we have a small growth in the traditional direction.

You can employ such trends and appeals by simply identifying the action needed as "customary or tradition things that we have always needed and always do."

A shift towards "inner direction" is even more pronounced. Here we see many of our predominantly "other directed" citizens starting to talk about "doing their own thing"—and actually doing it. Some of them show an almost unheard of disregard for what others think, and they march to their own drummer of individual tastes and interests. In short, some have become an island of independence in the great warm bath water sea of mass conformity and "other direction."

Example: we see this in a far less slavish devotion to either tradition or social dictate in career job choice or the way many dress. A woman may wear grubby jeans one day, a dress the next, pants suit the next. Men dress casually one day, more formally the next. We eat a Cornflakes breakfast one day and a champagne brunch another; live in a groomed suburban home one day and a pup tent or pick-up truck another; attend Shakespeare or a display of King Tut's art objects on one day and an "X" rated movie the next. Perhaps this is simply bouncing back and forth between "tradition" and "other direction" or just enjoying the best of both worlds. But the key point is that they are personally, individually and independently decided upon. To that degree they are inner directed.

And in just that way you can help motivate people to bring out their best performance—by appealing to their desire to reach personal but mutual goals, and encouraging that individuality and independence of thinking in career or job selection and decision as to ways for doing the job. Emphasize the excitement and self-respect of individual, personal thinking and opinions. "Use your best judgment, and pick your own way to skin the cat . . . as long as we get the cat skinned."

Power Secrets for Using All Three Points of "Lonely Crowd" Formula

Obviously, there is some vitality to the idea of "tradition, inner, and other direction." And just as clearly, there is some slipping, sliding around and shifting going on between these.

To put this situation to work for you in motivating people, one of your best bets is simply to apply all three appeals at once. That way you almost can't lose. Here are some practical guidelines to do this:

Build on "tradition" by first thinking about what parts of job are truly long established and customary. Second, identify, state, explain and dramatize the value of these well tried and proven steps. Show how they fit in with a successful operation. "It's worked beautifully for years." Third, recognize, compliment and honor those who successfully apply these traditional methods. "John, you used the system, and your results are excellent."

But encourage "inner" direction or individual initiative and freedom of thought at the same time as you are building traditions: "Our custom of always greeting the customer with a smile has worked well for us over many years, but what you say next is a matter of your own, best *inner* judgment. Here is where you can apply your own personal initiative towards reaching our mutual goals." (Tradition plus inner direction.)

But also apply "other" peer power or the opinions and influence of the person's co-workers. "I notice when your top salesmen greet the customer they immediately tie some product benefit to the prospect by saying something like 'you might be pleased to know that the new model equipment is now guaranteed for twice as long,' or, 'we have a special this week of 20% off on these shirts.' "

You have now applied all three elements in the "Lonely Crowd" formula to work for you and your team. And you did it in just a few sentences. It may seem to be a small thing, but in those simple steps you have applied the motivating forces that have influenced billions of people for thousands of years: "Tradition, inner, and other direction," or proven custom, personal initiative and the opinions of other people.

How a Leading Furniture Maker Applies the "Lonely Crowd" Formula

What is now a leading manufacturer of the "upper end" (expensive) furniture, grew from a tiny six-man operation, some years back, into a top position in the market largely through effective motivation of their people.

For years they consciously and unconsciously used all three points of the "Lonely Crowd" formula: tradition directed, inner directed, other directed. Here's how:

"Tradition direction" was built into their long standing belief in above average quality, established by the founder of the company. Selection of both the managers and the non-management employees was partly on their interest in fine workmanship. Results: a staff heavily laced with lovers of traditional excellence.

"Inner direction" was encouraged among both designers and the on-line craftsmen plus the buyers of fine woods, fixtures and finishes. They were told, "use your own ideas, think, try, experiment, seek excellence. Be new, different, better. You are free, independent, a person unto yourself, to do anything you wish as long as you reach our mutual goal of product quality." Result: it worked. Hundreds of new methods, refinements, and improvements poured out, over recent years. The brand began to grow and became a major element in the market.

"Other direction" was emphasized through market research. These opinion studies reflected back to the company the wants and needs of customers, dealers and prospects. The team learned to mix some of their production thinking with their sales thinking or manufacturing to satisfy the customer in the market. *Result:* employees, designers and craftsmen followed much of the direction coming from "others" outside the company, and the sales-profit picture improved dramatically.

The managers proved that people (employees and customers) can be successfully and profitably motivated by tradition, inner and other direction. Perhaps more important, this company shows us that you can use all three of these powerful motivators at one time to gain maximum effect towards reaching your goals.

Summary: The Lonely Crowd, a Dramatic New Power Secret

The "Lonely Crowd" formula is that most people are motivated by tradition, inner or other direction. Tradition is typified by Asian culture, inner direction by our pioneers and other direction by our conformist society. To motivate by "tradition," identify customs and emphasize their values. To motivate with "inner" direction, learn individual goals and encourage independent thinking; question blind, slavish following of tradition; demonstrate your own individuality; grant authority and responsibility aimed at common goals: yours and theirs. To motivate with "other" direction, learn opinions of others and show how following these and filling their wants and needs benefits your team member. Recognize that the individual and society change and shift back and forth between tradition, inner, and other direction. After 30 years of growing direction from "others," there is currently a slight shift to "tradition" direction and an even greater shift towards "inner" direction of doing your own thing. You can employ these shifts to bring out people's best efforts by showing the values and respect of "tradition" . . . and the excitement and self-satisfaction of individual "inner" thinking. The furniture case shows that you can profitably apply all three at once to give you maximum constructive motivation.

16

How to Get Action from Small Groups of People

Typical small retailer: "Oh man! This is the pits! I just can't do it all myself!" said Gordon G., a small Chicago retail business owner. "I must work over 60 hours a week. If only I could somehow motivate my two clerks to just half the initiative, steam and drive I must use. Boy would I have it made! This high turnover and lousy employee spirit is literally killing me." Here is the lament of nearly all the nation's eight million small business managers, plus two million farms and the estimated five million small departments of large companies, if we can believe a study covering thousands of firms over the last five years. And Gordon is right. If only he could motivate his little team, things would switch from low morale, low attendance, low action and few long term employees to just the opposite: high morale, high attendance, high performance and long term employees—trained, skilled, expert and dedicated employees who would lift a great load from his shoulders. Many small businesses and small departments have been able to make just such a switch; and not too strangely, they are nearly always the most successful of their kind. And everyone gains— employees, managers, customers and owners. Let's take a look at how they do it.

Successful motivation of just a few key people in a small business unit is usually THE pivotal point between success and failure. That last sentence is worth re-reading twice because it is *a powerful secret* that has been documented by hundreds of private studies in recent years. And it stands the test of common sense. A motivated manager with just two "turned-on" assistants has 300% the drive of another unit with the same staff that, except for himself, are totally turned off. The motivated group really has much more than three times the steam and ability, since employees that are not motivated can actually slow down and damage an operation, doing far more harm than good. In the next few pages, we will look at over a dozen practical steps that have proven to be effective motivators in three types of small units: (1) first in small businesses, (2) then in small departments of large firms, and finally (3) in small service organizations. Some of these techniques are the same or similar in these cases, but each type of unit needs its own, unique combination of employee motivators.

How Ten Million Small Businesses Struggle to Motivate

If you are working in a small business, you are in a group that represents over 90% of all business units and half the U.S. employment and gross national product. Yet, you are not heard from very much. You are, in a real sense, the great, silent majority. And you are also probably well aware that the life in a small business is a struggle. This effort has goals in at least three areas; customers, employees and company control.

First, the small business tries to motivate customers to be aware of the business and buy from it. This is a true challenge to your motivational skills—and a critical one. The whole ball game may be decided right here at this point.

Second, you want to motivate employees to become interested, active, dedicated and constructive. This is another key point, since few small firms ever succeed purely on the spirit and effort of just one person, all alone. To the extent you can motivate just one more person, you double your steam, energy, power and output.

A third goal is to gain control of the operation, the supplies, the system, the services, stock, records and the interaction between customers and employees.

Power Secrets for Using Attitudes,
Action and Motivation to Win the Game

Case: Kelly R. had worked as a young man for a small bread and cake bakery. He noticed that people also asked for pretzels, which was not too surprising in this Pennsylvania Dutch neighborhood. But the bakery had a tough time making pretzels on their particular equipment; so they passed up most of these sales. Kelly decided to go into business for himself. He converted his large brick garage into a two story bakery, developed some Rube Goldberg machinery to extrude twelve inch dough snakes, bent them into pretzels, baked them and sold them in big blue tin cans to local beer halls from his little Ford pickup. Soon, Kelly had a route man and a baker helper. His wife kept the books. But it wasn't all big cigars and motor cars. Kelly (my grandfather) went bankrupt three times before he got it going right. He discovered how to stimulate and motivate his small staff. That was the turning point. He lived for many years as a prosperous, small, independent, pretzel baker, supplying thousands of retail outlets around Pennsylvania Dutch country.

Five power secrets to small business motivation used by Kelly R. and most other successful small businesses were: personal spirit, know how, the S-O-S formula, M.B.O. and A.I.D.A. Let's look at those as applied to a little company of under 50 people.

Power secret one: Personal spirit. Here is where the manager himself is psyched up. He believes in the goal and his chances of reaching it. If you have this spirit, this attitude, this belief that long, hard effort over some years of time will get results, your enthusiasm is not only contagious but will prove essential. It will overcome almost any problem and strongly motivate most employees.

Power secret two: Your "know how" or expertise stimulates others. It builds, expands, enlarges and multiplies you from one man or woman to a team, to a small army. To motivate people with know how, get this knowledge yourself and then show it, test it and prove it with your team. You will not only impress them and win their respect, but pass along your knowledge, creating expertise where none existed before. This step, all by itself, can be a strong personal incentive to constructive employee action.

Power secret three: The S.O.S. (situation-objective-system) approach to small business motivation is used, consciously or unconsciously, by every successful small company. Know your situation and the facts facing you as to potential customers, wants, competition and your abilities to compete in supplying these wants. Set your objectives for the next few months or years in sales, profits, reputation and customer contacts. Then develop your system or method to supply the goods and services to customers or clients. Finally, let your co-workers know this plan. If you make them a part of it, playing a role in its development, they will suddenly also become a part of the execution. You have generated valuable employee motivation.

Case: You might even put your plan in writing, like a major department store chain did many years ago as a tiny, ten-man fledgling business. They still post a version of it in the entrance to most of the larger department stores. It outlines the *S*ituation (customers are valuable), the *O*bjectives (they will be served), and the *S*ystem (by supplying products of guaranteed quality). Their written and posted S.O.S. plan still motivates thousands of employees and millions of customers.

Power secret four: M.B.O. or management by objectives. Once they have fixed on their goal, successful small units manage nearly all their resources—their time, money, effort, skill and employees—to be sure that everything is aimed at doing the task and reaching the objective. This singlemindedness and pin-point focus motivates you, your team and your customers.

Power secret five: Small firms sharpen their motivation with the A.I.D.A. formula: Attention, Interest, Desire, Action. Once their M.B.O. effort has the team moving, the successful small unit manager speeds it up. He or she stimulates: their *attention* with provocative and beneficial suggestions; their *interest* by expanding on these; their *desire* by showing that their problems can be solved and pleasure gained from buying or accepting a product, service or plan. Then, finally, he inspires *action* by emphasizing the penalty for procrastination and the benefit of prompt performance.

The Pivotal Power Secret: Motivating Just a Few

A small number of motivated people can produce amazing results.

An old song says, "Start me with ten who are stout hearted men and I'll soon give you ten thousand more." Ralph Nader, Patrick Henry and Jimmy Carter, the Mayo Clinic and Jesus Christ started massive movements with a dozen or so motivated followers. So it is with the successful small business manager. He or she uses at least four motivation tools: respect, plans, work and recognition.

Respect for both his or her employees and his customers (the latter are often his true boss) fills a basic human need and generates an employee team spirit, an appreciation for the manager and a desire to act, move, perform and accomplish results.

Group plan. The better manager lets employees become a part of their own program development. They contribute to the situation; they help set objectives; and they schedule portions of the system. So "the" plan becomes "their" plan, creating a close, personal feeling that generates constructive action.

Case: One small New York deli operator, a member of a racial minority, has his employees so turned on with their own program that he and his family are able to take off for a month to Miami every January. He returns to find the business rolling along just fine, the shop ship-shape and the profits every bit as good as the day he left.

Meaningful work, or work that helps each person reach their own individual objectives, is usually provided to employees by the successful small unit manager. He or she is sure to see that they have goals for income, progress, promotion, learning or self-satisfaction—and that the job is a means toward obtaining this result. The work is important, meaningful and all by itself motivates good employee action.

Compliments and awards are used with skill and care by the better small business owners. They recognize real contribution, and they express it strong and clear. This is the frosting on the cake. It doesn't work well if there is no cake to begin with. But when there is good performance, recognition motivates continued forward action.

How Departments Can Be Motivated

Let's switch away from the little businesses and look at the large firm that is usually a collection of medium or small departments. In most of these, the manager has a unique and special problem: his people are frequently average or above average in intellect and education. In short, they are pretty "savvy." They are often sophisticated and self-oriented. Proper motivation of good people is not a matter of manipulating or pushing a few buttons. Here are some guidelines:

Power secret one: Study and listen to each individual; learn a little about his or her strengths and weaknesses. If you encourage people to use their capabilities and either improve their weaknesses or not depend on those undeveloped skills, you will stimulate greater motivation.

Power secret two: Understand their objectives that also match the department's goals, such as recognition and reputation for a pleasant, willing attitude and good performance, which could lead to personal employee improvement. This sometimes takes a little digging, patience, understanding and drawing out of the individual. People rarely wear a sign saying, "I want a promotion," but many, perhaps most, have this goal.

Power secret three: Provide a challenge, work, a way to get to their goal. With good people who have ability and can use this in a constructive way to reach their objectives you will usually have a system that motivates strongly productive action.

Case: Ardell J. was a clerk for small ethical drug company in Kankakee, Illinois. She had a pretty routine typing job, but considerable talent at drawing colorful charts and graphs. Ardell's goals were to be recognized, appreciated and eventually promoted. Her supervisor understood this and gave her more and more of these assignments. Ardell was delighted, steamed up and turned on—so much so that for years she often took work home, producing beautiful charts that were later printed in special reports. Ardell got her recognition and her promotion. And so did her boss, who knew how to motivate people and bring out their best for their own good and the good of the company.

Fourteen Power Secrets
for Small Departments

Here are guidelines for direct, practical application of the motivators described earlier in other chapters, as they might be used especially in a small division of a large organization:

1. *Look at your situation;* your department's problems and opportunities, strengths and weaknesses. Decide which problems

to attack and strengths to use, and which to let alone. If you focus your employee's interest on these, you will encourage initial team action.

2. *Establish mutual goals* or targets that both you and your department really want to achieve. This will help kindle an important fire of enthusiasm inside each person.

3. *Use fear*, but mainly as it applies to individual self-respect, self-interest and self-regard. For example: build the feeling that, "I will like myself better if I succeed, and I only fear failure in my own eyes." Otherwise, strongly avoid fear of humiliation and fear of firing as a motivator, since both are increasingly nonproductive and inefficient.

4. *Show genuine respect* for each individual's constructive and real abilities, interests and input. They will usually appreciate this and respond favorably.

5. *Hold department meetings* that have a clearly stated purpose, designed to review problems and to set targets, a schedule and a plan of action.

6. *Use personal plans and time management* by considering the situation, objective, system, the options that might be used and then prioritizing them, applying management by objectives to steer each act towards a goal, investing time effectively.

7. *Provide meaningful work* for the department team—that is, assigned activities that help people reach their personal goals . . . work that they are able to do and allowed to do.

8. *Stimulate each person's heart and mind* by encouraging and really listening to *ideas*, while also building *spirit* with the A.I.D.A. formula of Attention, Interest, Desire, Action. A particularly effective way to do this is to use emotional appeals that are also logical.

9. *Delegate projects* by getting other individuals involved, because each person wants to *be* somebody with identity and authority. Don't be afraid to ask for people's assistance. That's what they are there for.

10. *Coach by working together* to understand and solve the problem. Use the highly effective Ex-Dem-Pra system, or Explanation, Demonstrate and Practical work aimed at goals and achieving specific results. Closely observe the progress and stand ready to help.

11. *Communicate* with your department by being sure that messages are sent, received and confirmed. Employ the FOWD/PA formula of communicating: Frequently, Oral, Written, Done

carefully with Playback and Adjustment. Use O.S.P., or One Strong Point, in a believable, simple, friendly message of benefits and a clear, crisp call for action.

12. *Be tough, easy and then butt out.* Be firm (briefly and impersonally) when hard rules are needed for the good of the department, and easy when it is appreciated and gets results. Stay flexible, watchful and willing to assist. Otherwise, back off. Let individuals have their own turf and be at least partly their own boss.

13. *Employ emotional awards.* These should be carefully considered, accurate, strong and believable compliments. Give awards at the right time, to the right person for activity that was a truly significant step toward mutual goals.

14. *"Level" with people* by applying open but reasonable candor, since this saves much time. Employees increasingly resent deception but respond to and are motivated by even-handedness.

A practical approach for you as a small department manager: simply pick and try two or three of the motivators. *For example:* You might study the situation, set mutual goals and make awards for results. To apply all 14 of these techniques at once would be a bit much. It would be overdone, overwhelming and take on a phony, contrived appearance that would be counter-productive.

Case: One small production department head in Detroit got good results with study, objectives and performance recognition. She then shifted to increased respect for her team members, organized better plans meetings, communicated candid facts and coached meaningful work. This increased spirit and accomplishments still further. Later she emphasized greater interest in heart and mind, ideas and emotion, personal fear of failure, time management and tough rules but growing permisiveness—and this achieved even more results. In short, she applied these techniques in groups, steps or batches and got excellent, growing responses.

Another case: The clerks and advisors on a small Presidential White House staff received rigid orders, clear definition of the situation, objectives, systems and time schedules. Yet they were given high delegation, respect and freedom (butt out) to perform. And they did just that in a highly productive, spirited and quality manner.

In a third case: An appliance company accounting department manager found that several of these steps, such as plans meetings and time management, were welcome, although these had almost no effect on team motivation. But when goals on accuracy and volume, plus personal respect, delegation and independent freedom were emphasized, then the team spirit and performance greatly improved. The manager had wisely tried several motivators until he found a combination that employees liked and responded to.

How Millions of Small SERVICE Unit Managers Can Motivate Effectively

Times are changing rapidly. Services are becoming a major part of our activities, economy, employment, need, wants and personal expenses.

At one time, 98% of our population consisted of farmers. This is now about 2%. Meanwhile, manufacturing grew to prominence during the first half of this century. And now services are on a trend upwards towards primary prominence. Some futurists say production will soon go the way of the farm and services will employ nearly everyone. While manufacturing emphasized machines, services are mainly people.

Obviously, your ability to manage and motivate people *is a major need, perhaps THE major need* for now and the next few decades. People power is the heart of service in our economy and society, both today and tomorrow.

What are these services and who performs them? As compared to farmers and manufacturers who basically produce or process a product, service people generally perform some human act or personal assistance. Some major categories: Educators (the largest single U.S. profession), local and Federal government employees (over ten million), the huge field of medical professionals (doctors, technicians, nurses and aides), church people, social workers, people in communication, entertainment, insurance, repair, science, transportation, law, museums, engineering, art, consulting, music, sports, homemakers, parents, and grandparents. Almost none produce a product. All provide services.

The service unit motivation problem begins with the human equation. The workers often feel themselves underpaid, unstimulated, uninspired, unrecognized and unappreciated. This results in low spirit, disinterest, resentment and even hostility to supervision, building resistance that grows into anger and resignation. Net: low morale, low performance and high (expensive) turnover of personnel. *Bad morale generates inefficiency*—at a rapid and prodigious rate.

Case: One Midwest city bus line reports a 25% driver turnover every year. They consider themselves typical. The company is deluged with complaints from the drivers and from customer reaction to drivers, equipment, routes and other elements of the service. They have reached a point where the managers and supervisors have themselves become irritated, angry, hypersensitive, demoralized and nearly paranoid about customer-employee gripes and even small, routine problems. Lack of motivation in this service unit has generated near disaster. A college in the Southwest reports that they have a normal turnover of instructors for their quadrant of the country: 65% a year. Advertising agencies, hospitals, cab companies, entertainment and repair groups frequently see 25% to 50% turnover of personnel each year. Very few people ever stay four years. A large number leave in six months or less. Many other kinds of service units report 50% to 100% average turnover per year. While a few employees stay for years, some leave every month or two, driving the average way up.

The Solution: Ten Ways
to Better Service Unit Motivation

Apply a unique and selected combination of the method just suggested for the little business and small department. The best elements are usually one or a combination of these ten steps.

1. *Get insight* into the situation, problems, and opportunities. Ask lots of questions. Then listen and really hear the answers. Service unit people want to be understood.

2. *Establish mutual goals*, wanted, needed and agreed upon by company and employees. This is particularly important with service units.

3. *Respect* each individual for any of their constructive capabilities and action that they aim at actual achievement.

4. *Hold S-O-S plans meetings* to agree on your Situation, common Objectives and team Systems to reach your service unit goals.

5. *Challenge both heart and mind* of each person. Whenever possible, use that golden rule of motivation: an emotional appeal that is also logical.

6. *Delegate work* that is meaningful or useful in helping them reach their own private objectives. This is particularly effective with service people because their work *is* the product.

7. *Communicate in a level, candid way.* Send, receive and confirm your one strong idea. Be open, non-deceptive, believable, simple and friendly, but make a clear call for action.

8. *Assign priorities to projects and urge good time management.* In a service unit, people's time is your prime resource; so manage it with great care by steering each and every single action and moment towards the goal.

9. *Butt out* and avoid breathing down service people's necks. Properly selected and trained, they will usually respond well to relative freedom.

10. *Recognize and award* truly constructive steps and actual results or goal achievement. Above all, avoid penalizing a person for progressive performance.

Case: At Northwestern University the downtown business instructors in our small department felt cut off from the main campus in Evanston. Spirit was low in the "service unit." But our downtown Dean recognized the problem and respected his instructors. He called us into a plans meeting, where he candidly communicated our situation. We set goals and helped plan the program for the next year. The logical need for improvements was supported by emotional drives and desires. The programs were divided up. Priorities were set, and then he backed off to let instructors do their thing. Top performers got letters of commendation—and the group became highly motivated.

Summary

Power secrets in small units. Here the successful motivation of just a few key people is usually *the* pivotal point between success and failure. The small business must struggle hard to motivate customers and employees and maintain control. Key steps are spirit, know how, the S-O-S (situation-objective-system), M.B.O. (management by objectives), the A.I.D.A. (attention, interest, desire, action formula, plus respect), a group plan, meaningful work and awards.

Power secrets in departments of large firms can motivate by study of conditions, goals, fear of personal failure, meetings plans for time management, worthwhile projects, heart and mind, delegation coaching, tough, then easy rules, butt out, leveling and recognition.

Power secrets in service units, groups which may soon dominate our economy: Best motivation methods here are insight, mutual objectives, respect, S-O-S, plans that fire emotions and ideas, assignment of work that helps reach goals, communication in a candid manner, assigning priorities, good use of time, avoidance of over-supervision and proper, appropriate awards.

17

The Biggest "Power Deflators" and How to Avoid Them

Any chance for dynamic, constructive motivation can be almost instantly destroyed by managers using any one of a dozen "super-demotivators." And these harmful methods are sometimes employed even by skilled managers, who are tempted into bad practices by the pressure of business or heat of the moment. Or, sometimes, they are just used accidentally, carelessly or thoughtlessly. I have made some of these errors, and so do most managers; and it nearly always causes more trouble than it solves.

Naturally, we want to think positively. But sometimes we can "work smarter" by being forewarned of common problems. Being aware, you become forearmed, and you can guard and protect yourself. We will also look at quick, practical, positive steps you can take to correct these errors should you accidentally make them.

Case: One general manager of a small Dallas cosmetics firm believed in the silent treatment: no communication about the company's situation or objectives for the several three man departments, not even suggestions for them to follow. There were no visits, no speeches, no memos, no reaction to suggestions, no phone calls, no calls returned—no nothing. He would go into his office in the morning and close the door, and no one would see or hear from him until he briskly went out the door for lunch: then he was back behind the door all afternoon. Result: very little team motivation. Why should they have much? They didn't know the company problems or opportunities or what to aim for. How can one shoot for something if one has no target?

Power Deflator #1

So, the #1 demotivator is silence and isolation, minimum or zero communication. *To avoid this:* be sure you listen, really hear and encourage discussion, exchange of ideas and information. Develop mutual goals and plans.

Power Deflator #2

#2 The constant "put-down," the never ending criticism and complaint of employee performance, regardless of quantity or quality of results is a sure power deflator.

Case: one bright department supervisor on Michigan Avenue in Chicago hired two creative, energetic young market research analysts, a man and a woman, both out of school just a few years before. They plowed into their jobs and produced a large volume of quality work that bosses on up the line found highly impressive. But the supervisor never expressed praise or satisfaction. Instead, he constantly criticized, demanded more and better work, nit picked on minor details, and if he couldn't find anything wrong, he changed the ground rules or made something up and "generated" some element to complain about. (He had been accustomed to dealing mostly with below average people.) Result: in less than a year, both analysts resigned and took better jobs. The supervisor then tried to do it all himself and he suffered a serious heart attack.

Power secret solution: To avoid the "constant put-down" demotivator, make complaints more as impersonal suggestions, ideas or recommendations. And then more than balance these with recognition and appreciation for good work.

Power Deflator #3

#3 Next is the "BIG ME, little you" syndrome, with threats of humiliation. This is an extension or modification of the put-down, except that here the manager spends much of his time pumping himself up and makes noises that sound like the total put-down: dismissal.

Case: A very wealthy egocentric president of several small companies in a Southern town had a habit of hiring able department managers for one of his companies. He would meet with them and deluge the group with his own far out plans. Anyone who tried to debate, question or even discuss modifications was threatened with dismissal. Result: The department managers were totally frustrated and routinely left the company, which today teeters on the brink of financial collapse.

Power secret solution: Sure, pump yourself up a bit if you feel this will give your people a little inspiration as something to admire and imitate. But keep this to an absolute minimum. Listen and respect your people, and *pump them up too.* Avoid the threats. These have few positives and lots of negatives.

Power Deflator #4

#4 Poor mechanics: twist the thumb screws; ignore their gripes; and just wave the green. Here the manager simply piles on the work, then piles on more, then demands a faster pace, unpaid overtime, shorter and closer deadlines. He pays no attention to protest and simply says, "Hell, I'm paying you plenty." He depends entirely too much on people's work ethic and need for money.

Case: One production supervisor thought he would make a name for himself by driving and overloading his people in the packaging department. The volume demands got so heavy that some items were leaving improperly packaged, breakage occured, troubles and pressure mounted and the employees actually slowed down, since they figured "what's the use?"

Power secret solution: Set reasonable goals; even stretch a notch or two. But be realistic, get mutual agreement and listen to complaints. Don't overreact to these, but weigh their merit and avoid depending on money alone to motivate. Everyone gets paid, but not everyone is motivated. Many employees get the same pay as others, yet do twice as much productive work.

Power Deflator #5

#5 Tricky stuff, like false promises, phony praise and outright manipulation, is a first rate demotivator. It also includes sly,

sneaky checking, spying and watching or other acts and words that plainly say, "I don't trust you."

Power secret solution: To avoid these demotivators, work fairly openly and candidly and be as level and straightforward as reasonably possible. Don't blatantly manipulate. Either be highly discreet or be frank and participative with mutual group motivation. If you want to watch without creating employee resentment, a good technique is to simply ask their opinion about what they are doing, their likes, dislikes, problems, opportunities, goals and methods. Keep tuned for the specific items you need to know, like results.

Power Deflator #6

#6 "Here we go merrily round in circles," pitting one group against another and a third against the first and chasing their tails with seemingly pointless projects—in other words, meaningless work that may help with someone's goals, but not their own. These are frustratingly effective demotivators. People sometimes develop a quiet anger that bubbles to the surface as equally quiet, passive but effective resistance, and sometimes, open hostility. The offender, of course, can be fired, but to what purpose if the next person does the same thing? Humans are humans and that does not change simply because the cast of characters is revised.

Power secret solution: Modify the system, not the team structure. Avoid pitting one group against another, but encourage mutual co-operation for mutual gain. And make sure projects requested are tied directly to individual goals so the work is truly and clearly meaningful to those doing it.

Case: Two sales districts of a Kansas City wholesale shoe company served about the same size territory in area and in purchasing potential with staffs of about equal number and ability. But the Southern manager used the ring around the rosie system, while the Northern manager generated mutual co-operation and meaningful projects. He secured more than twice the results, enthusiasm and motivation for the same effort. And they had more fun with much less internal conflict and frustration.

Power Deflator #7

#7 Using the "fear stick and the dollar carrot" is a technique that is always with us, always has been, and always will be. But

the key point for smart executives to remember is that these techniques are often overdone, time worn, threadbare, declining in impact, even revealed as blatantly manipulative devices. There are other ways that get better results per hour and dollar invested, with much less manager effort.

Power secret solution: Develop understanding of the problems, resources and opportunities. Encourage mutually accepted goals and unified group plans and show respect for individual ability. Provide meaningful work, delegate, communicate, use people's emotion and logic to solve mutual problems. Give priority to action steps, and reward constructive results.

Power Deflator #8

#8 The "purely academic" approach: forget feelings and let money do the motivating.

Case: A business college professor I knew during my teaching days told his class, "Economics and business are purely mechanical. Pay people, and they jump through hoops. Don't pay them and they don't jump. It's as simple as that. Economics have nothing to do with feelings. Feelings have nothing to do with economics. We teach economics here. If you want to discuss emotion, go to church."

This instructor would experience spirited and heated disagreement among people in the very heart of free business economic activity—the stock market, the board room and department headquarters—where in candid moments leaders passionately declare and lament that many, perhaps most, major economic decisions are largely emotional. Anyone who doubts this need only insult or emotionally offend a boss, co-worker or subordinate during a decision making meeting and then watch what happens.

Power secret solution: Avoid thinking of people as machines or robots. They are not and never will be. And they are less so, every day. We are moving more and more into the humanistic era of personal challenge and personal response. For better or worse, emotions are here to stay and getting more important every day. *Master emotional methods and you master modern motivation.*

Power Deflator #9

#9 "Manipulate and sweet talk the oafs; they'll never know what's going on." Promise them prizes like possibilities of pay

raises and promotions. That will get results every time, right? Well, this is only partly right. Unless you can deliver each time, the team member becomes disillusioned, resentful and sometimes even a bit bitter. People at all levels deeply dislike being manipulated. They are offended, hurt and insulted at being considered stupid enough to be deceived and hoodwinked.

Power secret solution: Try not to ever fall into the trap of believing that the only way you can motivate is through big, unrealistic promises, dangled like shiny beads and trinkets before the saucer-eyed natives. Those days are gone forever. Such action is regrettable residue and waste matter from the "money-does-it-all," fear-stick and dollar-carrot approach. Rather than insult your team with transparently phony promises, use the exact opposite approach. Compliment them with a show of confidence and candor about the situation—a display of your conviction that they can understand the problems and handle them. Then build team insight into "our" goal, and plan for meaningful work that gets recognition and rewards. This develops spirit that: (a) properly done gets twice the results of the purely dollar motivated team, (b) makes the whole thing more fun for everyone and (c) ends up getting the money as well (that's the beauty of it), with a lot less strife and effort.

Power Deflator #10

#10 *"Performance or merit review charts do it all,"* say some supervisors. They are mislead into believing that marks on a chart are the only thing it takes to achieve good motivation. They forget that there is a human side to enterprise.

Case: One hospital supervisor kept a chart on the wall of her office listing her ten subordinates and showing scores for various items, such as attendance and report accuracy. Otherwise, she said nothing. She just let her fingers do the talking. This worked for a while. But then several employees had problems beyond their control that hurt their "scores." A good worker transferred out. Then one day the chart was discovered to have been defaced, and a week later it was torn down. The team was clearly demotivated.

Power secret solution: There is nothing seriously wrong with performance charts if properly applied. Here are a few guidelines: *First,* use it as just one advisory or assisting tool for yourself.

Don't expect it to do the whole job, or it will come back to haunt you. *Second*, do it in private. Don't wash dirty linen in public. It is humiliating and demotivating. *Third*, apply it with moderation, extra courtesy and respect. Don't make a federal case out of it. Figures and marks on paper can hurt and are lasting, so use with a little care, restraint and even gentleness. *Fourth*, the performance chart will work twice as well if you approach it as a joint effort with "a problem we will solve together" (coaching) rather than "you against him" or "him against others." And *fifth*, let it lead to a mutual plan or program. "What shall we do as our next step? How can I help?"

Power Deflator #11

#11 *"Smother 'em with double talk and the Emperor's clothing."* "If you can't blind 'em with brillance, baffle 'em with baloney." Drown 'em in a deluge of words, rules, regulations, directions and demands. Then add some jibberish, jargon, jabberwocky and gobbledegook. If they don't comprehend the mindless prattle and psycho-babble then, like the Emperor's tailors in the folk tale, just announce that those who don't understand simply must be "unqualified" for their job.

Those are the beliefs of some supervisors, who are often quite bright in many ways but have a blind spot on ability to see the world through other's eyes, like those of employees or clients. So they employ the jargon and veiled threat demotivators.

Power secret solution: Communicate by sending clear messages tuned to your receiver. Make sure they got the message and understood it. Keep it clear, simple and reasonably honest. Avoid put downs or hidden threats. Forget the Emperor's clothing bit. Remember, in the end it was really a "rip-off" of the top supervisor.

Power Deflator #12

#12 *"No, I never flew a plane, but here's how you do it."* How would you like to learn from that guy or worse yet, fly with him? He is telling you that he never did it, but it doesn't make any difference. He is an authority or expert that will lead and guide you out of the darkness of ignorance and into the promised land. Does this turn you on? Probably not very much. Why should it? In fact, it may turn you off pretty fast. Yet many supervisors attempt to motivate their team in just this way.

Power secret solution: To build your status, prestige and authoritarian position or at least avoid embarrassment: *first*, get some experience in the subject you are teaching, if only for a few weeks, days or hours—enough so that you know the problems and procedures or at least the terminology and the flavor. *Second*, if you can't do this, then get someone in the act with you who does know. Pick his brain or use him as the authority on this one subject or project. *Third*, if neither of these first two steps is practical, level with your group and candidly admit that you are not an expert on the *one point*, but "together we will work it out." *Fourth*, above all, don't try to bluff it out totally and pretend to possess complete expertise that you don't have. They will spot it in a minute, and this will damage your reputation in other areas where it may be well deserved.

Case: A complex new computer report was required from a small department. The manager did not really understand it very well, yet was expected to supervise its preparation. She wisely spent some time with another supervisor who had done the report, and she got to know the "lingo." Then she helped one of her group get added training in preparation, and she labeled this person as the expert in this one activity. Finally, she admitted to her group that she was not too good at this but, "together we will work it out and do it well." And that's exactly what they did.

Power Deflator #13

#13 *"Selection and training, does it all;* just let 'em alone after that," say some supervisors. And there is a lot of truth and merit to their position—except for the last part about letting them alone, totally. Ignoring people is a quiet, indirect insult that most find to be a steadily growing offense. If you depend *entirely* on good selection and training, this can be equally disillusioning. In that case, all West Pointers and Harvard MBA's, honor students or secretaries who passed their civil service exam wih a "98%" should be left completely to their own devices. True, these people may require far less supervision, but they all need direction, goals and motivation, just like everyone else.

Power secret solution: With very carefully selected and trained employees—the above average group—you can create effective motivation for them to bring out their best by using four key guidelines: *first*, apply motivation methods *lightly*. These people usually need only a gentle touch, not a sledgehammer or a hot poker. *Second, move fairly rapidly* along the S-O-S, Situation-Objective-Systems, path. Labor it and you lose them. *Third*, encourage maximum personal and *individual involvement*. Good people are usually self-starters. *Fourth*, understand, consider and use the Riesman's concept of *inner-direction*, the idea that some people (particularly those above average) march to their own drummer. Just be sure to get them marching in step with mutually agreed upon goals.

Power Deflator #14

#14 "Punch 'em in the gut."

Case: One Alabama State Government Agency Director is fond of saying, "The way to get people motivated is to punch 'em in the gut and kick 'em in the crotch. That gets their attention every time." He sure is right about the last part. That kind of supervisor is hard to ignore. Of course, he's speaking figuratively albeit colorfully, and he gets away with it. Strangely enough he is feared, followed, even respected by a portion of his employees, especially those who are below average. And the approach may succeed until some other person has the same conviction, which could cause serious sparks of disagreement. Or a less pugilistic individual may simply file a grievance or civil suit, causing some unpleasant ripples. But worse than that, such an offensive policy is a super demotivator, a super turn-off to the average or above average person, and often the most valuable members of the team.

Power secret solution: Avoid the negative, combative approach if you're trying to motivate average, and especially above average, people. The rock 'em sock 'em routine will always be with us, but is losing its punch and can even boomerang rather unpleasantly as employees steadily become more educated and better tuned to human insights and understanding. Instead, look for the positive, stimulating, exciting, and dramatic—the mutual problem, mutual goal aspects, participation in method planning, personal delegation and leveling with the individual. The aggressive, negative threat is rapidly going out of style and becoming less effective.

A Summary of Secrets for Avoiding Major Power Deflators

You will greatly increase your motivation ability if you simply avoid most of the super demotivators. To sidestep the "silent treatment" deflator, listen and really hear, discuss and communicate. You won't get tempted into "constant put-downs" if you criticize impersonally and accentuate positive, honest appreciation. Managers can avoid the "BIG ME, little-you" syndrome by spending much less time pumping up their own reputation and more effort building the status of their employees.

Try to stay away from excessive or impossible "overloads" by setting reachable and realistic goals. Dodge the tricky stuff by being as open and candid as reasonably fits conditions. Don't get caught in the "merry-go-round" of apparently pointless projects; tie assignments a bit more closely to your team's personal goals. Use "the fear stick and dollar carrot" with great restraint and in balance with other approaches. Avoid the "pure academic," unfeeling, mechanistic approach by using a little common sense and consideration for people as humans, not machines. Don't let yourself be tempted to try "manipulating the oafs" with impossible promises, but instead, stay realistic, respect their intelligence and try to build some united team effort.

Avoid overdoing merit review charts by balancing them with other approaches, staying private and approaching it as a joint effort toward mutual plans. Rather than "smothering people with jargon," the wise manager keeps communication clear and simple and doesn't use it for a concealing smoke screen. Avoid directing activities you don't understand by getting at least a brief feel for them. Don't depend totally on good selection and training of above average people, but also lightly apply mutually beneficial motivation methods aimed at personal development and inner direction toward objectives. Rather than using the negative "punch 'em in the gut" routine, build positive development of mutually agreeable respect, goals and methods and candid delegation. Avoid these super demotivators and you will double your motiviational effectiveness.

18

"I'll Work for Nothing"—
Proof That Power Secrets Work

"That's right. They will work for nothing . . . and on top of that, they'll work harder than if you paid them!" said a key manager.

"That's unbelievable," replied a slightly younger, but still middle-aged executive who reported to the manager. "That just doesn't match up with everything I've been taught in graduate business college and seen in the last 20 years of management. I am 'Mr. Economics Man,' and I know that people work for money and only for money, and that's that. Without money you just kid yourself. Your position or theory is just hot air, images and ridiculous wishful thinking. You'll have to show me some pretty strong evidence if you ever expect to prove anything different."

But Mr. Key Manager said, "That's just because you don't know how. You are the victim of some economics professor who never managed a business in his life! You are in an old fashioned Adam Smith rut, wearing a pair of blinders that give you tunnel vision. I'll provide you with plenty of evidence if you want it." And he did. He not only proved his position, but he more than proved it, with thousands of quality people—many average but most above average—over several years and from border to border and coast to coast. The doubting executive who came to scoff remained to praise—and to eat crow, which wasn't all that tasty, as I recall, since I was the doubter. Mr. Key Manager's position required some reappraisal of my old beliefs, some re-ordering of concepts, priorities and methods. But best of all, it opened doors to getting much more done with less strain, less pain, less expense and more fun for all concerned, including the employees *and* the manager.

How Power Secrets Can Work for You Every Day

Let's look at this "ridiculous" idea, examine the evidence, check where it is wrong, but also where it has some merit, and see how you can put it to use serving you. Money still remains *an* element, but *only one* element. The key manager's concept, idea and position not only proves to be true in many cases, but to be more true with each passing season, as money loses some of its importance and other things become more vital. In a sense this chapter closes the loop by bringing us back and connecting us up with the first chapter, where we saw the motivation gap of greater employee independence, yet less employer power, where money is not as important as other things.

We will take a look at the economics professor's position as it actually *supports* Mr. Key Manager. Then, we will see where money alone fails with average people, executives, plant workers, young people and old, salesmen, supposedly greedy folks and a dozen large worker groups, and how you can use this situation to help you motivate constructive action that helps everyone.

The Power Secret of "Extra Units"

Who wants a SECOND grand piano after you already have the first one? Or a second dishwasher, turkey dinner, raincoat or pool table, or a fourth car? In other words, once most people have purchased a good supply of something, they don't really want much more of it. They have little motivation to earn more money for such a purchase. In fact, if you add one more such unit, this may actually be a nuisance or have negative value, like two grand pianos jammed into the living room. Economists call this the V.M.P.P., or *V*alue of the *M*arginal (one more, or extra) *P*hysical *P*roduct. V.M.P.P. is often low and sometimes a minus.

This applies to our everyday life because most employees very quickly reach a point where they essentially have the basic necessities plus some luxuries; so there is no great incentive to earn a lot more.

A Power Secret Formula: "FCSR+"

When employees reach and exceed income to fill their needs, this is expressed as the "FCSR+" formula, or *F*ood, *C*lothing, *S*helter, *R*ecreation plus extras." At this point, money alone fails to be a strong motivator. The green stuff still has some value, of course, to assure that its benefits continue, and to get better *quality* "FCSR+," and of course, while a person's *needs* are finite or have limits, *wants* and desires are infinite and unlimited. And then there are some rare folks who, perhaps because of a deprived youth (now a very rare thing), simply can't get enough money even after they have far more than they need. But want of luxuries for today's employees is rarely as motivating as the first, early basic needs or absolute necessities of life. Newly-weds or couples in their 20's with new children (a declining group) will sometimes work a little harder for the dollar than will younger people or people in their 30's, 40's or 50's.

Three Steps to Motivation Without Money

Your best bet is to begin with people's general objectives and private goals. *First*, try to identify these aspirations, secreted away as they often are in the employee's mind or even totally undefined, unstated, unclear and uncertain. Nearly everyone has hopes and dreams. And the more income they have, the fewer of these dreams are piles of money, and the more are the hopes for status, respect, fulfillment, fun, learning, satisfaction, accomplishment, recognition and awards. *Second*, sharpen, accent, develop, clarify and build these goals in both the employees' own mind and in yours. Now, *third*, show how mutually agreed upon steps or systems will help reach these goals, financial and otherwise. This is particularly useful with foremen and managers. Even there, don't depend too much on money.

How Much Extra Work Will Most Executives
Do for Another $1,000?

Now, a thousand bucks is a nice hunk of cash. However, salary doesn't arrive as a hunk, but dribbles in as little bits over 12 or 26 pay periods, minus all sorts of deductions, perhaps as high as 30%. That ends up as roughly an extra $13 a week. Big deal. To expect this to generate much executive motivation, a manager would be rather naive, excessively hopeful and unrealistic—perhaps a bit out of touch with today's world. With the vast bulk of executives earning at least twenty times this in total salary, they can well look at this same extra $1,000 or 5% every year or so almost *automatically*, with little or no extra effort whatsoever.

Case: A midwestern retail store executive, earning well over $20,000 a year, was offered a promotion to a major Eastern headquarters city with a $4,000 raise. If money motivates very much, this guy should have worked up a hot sweat running for the plane. But he didn't. By the time he calculated the higher cost of living in the new city, plus the cost of moving (even with a paid move, there are dozens of uncompensated costs, of course), plus the extra duties, the added salary wasn't much above the 5% to 10% he could expect in a normal pay raise. Did he have motivation? Of course not. He declined the generous offer.

Power Secrets Beyond Money

The retail headquarters missed the boat. They could have motivated favorable action by getting him to the city, introducing him to his new leaders, his new staff (status) discussing goals and objectives and involving him in portions of planning his new operations, plus encouraging his specific innovative inputs to make "the" new program "his" new program. But maybe we are just talking about managers. What about everyday, first level employees?

Plant workers: Will they double their hours for fourfold pay? Not really. Oh, some say they will, and a few actually do it. But this is rare.

Case: A large African oil company advertised very high pay for overtime work in Saudi-Arabian desert oil fields and got hardly any takers. Then they cut the hours per week to normal time and increased the pay to more than four times the regular per hour rates and still got very few takers. A Polaroid personnel manager was quoted by the national newspaper wire services as saying that "people used to apply in droves for the company's distant, high paying assignments." But today the only ones motivated to accept are, in his words, "a rare breed." Mayflower, Allied Van Lines and others once pointed proudly to the fact that about 20% of U.S. families moved each year. But not anymore. The decline has been bad news to movers. Today's offers of more money makes for mighty modest motivation. Too many people have reached the "FCSR+" level. A hungry pet will do tricks for a morsel. But when his tummy is full, he will simply look at you and yawn. Less than one third of our work force belongs to that famous money demanding group, the labor union—and the percentage is steadily declining. Obviously, there are lots of full tummies.

Case: An actual test of factory workers in the Southeast was run, offering them more money per hour, in the hope that this would stimulate them to put in a few extra hours each week. Instead, when their total weekly pay had reached their old level they simply took time off. They preferred time to follow their own pursuits, rather than the extra (or marginal) money. The added pay actually acted as a demotivator, since they now worked fewer hours. Managers reluctantly concluded that, were they to raise hourly wages still higher, the employees would put in even less time on the job. The "FCSR+" level had been reached, and money had very low motivational impact—perhaps almost a *negative* value.

Three Secrets for Gaining Power

First, don't depend entirely on money alone—some, of course, enough to reach or approach the "FCSR+" level. Much more than that could be the waste of a valuable resource (cash) because each added or marginal dollar has less and less impact. In other words, the law of diminishing returns has taken hold. *Second*, make the job mean something, mean more than it once did. And most important, *third*, make the person *be* somebody more vital, more key, more essential, more responsible, more authoritarian, more respected, more influential and more involved. Encourage people to consider "our" problem, setting "our" goals and executing steps that "we" do together.

The "Quality" Power Secret

Even young employees seek more quality of life; old folks do too. Of all the people we would think would be driven, aggressive, ambitious and grasping for the buck, we would think it would be the young people, since they usually have the lowest (entrance) wages, yet have the most urgent need for the basic necessities of life.

And yet, if we listen to their songs, read their popular writers, work with them in college and on the job, live with them in their homes, listen to their comments about the news broadcasts, their friends, their world, TV shows, newspapers, and movies—even in surroundings that emphasize money's importance—the almighty buck is not very mighty. Surveys show that, above all else, people of all ages seek a job that is "meaningful," not a job that is highly paid.

There are probably many reasons for this, including: (1) A small and shrinking percentage of all teenagers and young adults has ever had to really *worry* about money. It was always there. In the same way few middle aged people have ever worried about water. Turn the tap and there it is. (2) *The turbulent 60's* saw extremist youths who were reacting (and over-reacting) to a shift in values among most young people—a shift away from materialism and "the plastic society" towards caring and being concerned, involved and valuing themselves and other human beings. (3) *We also see a GROWTH in what many call the "quality* of life"—desire for fun, pleasure and psychological enjoyment rather than "things" alone. True, many people want a good stereo and camera, but they also like inexpensive wine, guitars, blue jeans and candlelight. Young men and women go out to eat fast food and stay in to cook gourmet food; make shirts and moccasins; ride ten-speeds; hike; play tennis; share small apartments; go to art shows and vintage movie seminars and take night courses in pottery, painting, music, sociology, gardening or writing far more often than courses in finance, economics and banking.

When we combine these three trends—the low initial concern with money, plus shifting values towards humanism, plus emphasis on low cost food, clothing, shelter and recreation ("The quality of life")—we should not be too surprised to find money losing much of its importance, and other interests gaining.

Case: "We Americans live in a near saturation of things," said a secretary whose husband is a middle income electronics technician. "We bought a deluxe CB for the car, and we almost never use it. I go through stores and purely on impulse blow $20 or $30 for my nephews on plastic toys they don't even play with for 30 minutes. We have a boat, new home and two nice cars, and we take a cruise each winter—but that's getting boring. At Christmas and on Ralph's birthday I simply don't quite know what to buy him for a present; he has everything plus a lot of stuff he doesn't want, which we stick in the closet awhile before we toss it. But I guess we're just average people. All our friends have about the same problems. I read recently where even the school kids throw away nearly a billion dollars worth of school lunch food every year."

Can you imagine trying to motivate this gal with an extra $13 a week? Money isn't meaningless, because she must pay bills every month, but a few added dollars have little importance to her.

Case: Nearly 10,000 former managers work for free in a program called SCORE (Service Corp. of Retired Executives). Many of these people earned $50,000 a year and even twice this. They can and do earn several hundred dollars a day as consultants; yet they get their biggest kick by spending most of their time as unpaid advisors to small retail stores on Main Street, small manufacturers, printers, bars, restaurants, and service firms. Their number is growing every year and has been for 13 years, It should soon exceed 10,000. Literally hundreds of them have recently told me, "I'm working harder than I have for many years when I was well paid, and frankly, it makes my life worth living."

Case: Housewives and others help (for free) in dozens of programs for the church, schools, colleges, community centers and city government in such projects as nurses aides (Candy Stripers), Meals on Wheels, Red Cross, Daily Visitors (to invalids) and readers to the sick or blind. Are these just rich women with nothing to do but roll bandages? Not really.

Case: Over 20,000 graduate BUSINESS students and Ph.D's work free. And there is a neat switch. These people are raised, steeped and saturated in the economic "Get-the-buck" philosophy of Marshall and Adam Smith. Yet here they are *giving away* literally millions of their personal man hours to help small, community organizations in a program called S.B.I., or Small Business Institute.

True, they are paid a little for out-of-pocket car expenses, lunches and report printing. However, they are hardly motivated by these few bucks, but instead, more by the desire to reach personal goals, learn things, apply their skills, be involved in program planning, be respected by society and *"be"* somebody. Or are these simply wide-eyed idealists?

Case: Employed, middle-aged executives work for free in many programs such as "A.C.E.," Active Corp of Executives. Thousands of these men and women donate part of their time, their lives and professional skills to help counsel and train many of the nations ten million small business owners who, not incidentally, employ almost 50% of the nation's wage earners. Here we see professional, employed executives giving their time to help secure jobs for half of our workers.

Case: Multi-millionaire Leo Burnett took Christmas morning off. He was a little, quiet, chubby, unpretty, rumpled sort of guy. The first time I met him, his vest was opened, and the ashes from his dangling cigarette were spilling down across his tie as he shuffled past a receptionist. I did not know who he was at the time, and (horrors) I honestly thought he was janitor for the building. But he had an incredible ability to move people and make money for clients. He had started in a grubby little office but built his advertising agency into a giant. Over the years of working with Leo, our group came to know that he had many millions of dollars in personal wealth. One more million clearly meant very little to him. He was hardly motivated by money, but instead by what he frankly said was "the fun of the game." He loved it so much that he worked nights, holidays and weekends. It was a standard gag around the shop that Leo always and religiously took Christmas morning off. But is this just a disease of a few, rich work-aholics? Not so.

Case: Truck drivers ignored money but responded to motivators. We looked at the activities of route truck drivers elsewhere in this book. These men had faced a serious problem of poor sales, low spirit and little action. Then they developed their own programs. A key point, not mentioned earlier, is that their commission per case sold had been adjusted *both* upwards and downwards without much noticeable effect. It was not until they personally worked out their own plan of action that major improvement occurred. They organized an awards program, establishing a "Go-Getters Club" for outstanding performance. Members got to wear a small, round button-shaped bronze pin.

This developed an emotional stimulus and new social structure which generated such remarkable results that bottlers for many miles around tried to hire these men, thinking they were something special. But they were not special. They were average (most had never finished high school, some were "trouble makers," and a few even had prison records). The only thing special about them was the fact that they had not relied on money as their major motivator. Instead, they had used self-respect, mutual goals, participative plans, self-coaching and awards to develop motivation. And this resulted in an outstanding performance of action, morale and sales production.

Case: "I'll work for nothing," said the National Sales Manager. Bernard D. was a middle aged, Harvard Business College graduate, with a Masters degree in management, who had been given responsibility for the expansion of sales for a major food company. His salary was very average with little prospect of much increase in the near future. Bernie worked closely with his supervisor, and they became good business friends (not social friends). His previous supervisor had tried to motivate everyone purely with fear and money—the stick and the carrot. He had fired several managers. The action, morale and volume of results in the sales department were all pretty grim. But the new supervisor decided to use a different approach. He and Bernie analyzed the problems, set mutually agreeable goals and discussed programs with the salesmen.

Ideas and enthusiasm were encouraged, welcomed and praised. New programs were explained and demonstrated by Bernie and his supervisor; then portions were delegated. Sales people were allowed to fine-tune things in their own way, and high performances got awards. Sales doubled *and then re-doubled.*

Motivation, spirit, results, self-respect and community acknowledgment grew dramatically. They were even written up in the newspaper. A union tried to organize the sales force, and then a competitor tried to hire them. Both efforts were flatly and vigorously rejected by the employees themselves. Bernie enjoyed high prestige, spirit, dedication and enthusiasm. Both he and the sales group publicly stated that they had never had jobs they liked nearly as well. "If you'd find some way to take care of my family," Bernie told his boss, "I would *work for you for nothing.*" His tone of voice and later actions showed that he meant this statement with all possible sincerity.

A Final Power Secret

Millions actually do work for free at least part of their lives. For openers, most wealthy people get automatic income from their investments, but spend much of their working week serving, unpaid, on boards of charities, fund raising organizations, museums, colleges, parks, commissions and dozens more. Many people with lower incomes serve as hospital, sanitarium, handicapped and invalid aide volunteers.

Literally hundreds of thousands help in the prevention and treatment of alcoholism, anemia, arthritis, autism, birth defects, blindness, cancer, cerebral palsy, deafness, cystic fibrosis, epilepsy, heart disease, lung disorders, multiple sclerosis, mental health, muscular dystrophy, and hundreds of other illnesses.

Elks, Rotary, Lions, Shriners, Goodfellows, Kiwanis and many other similar service clubs give away millions of hours to help solve their community's problems.

Millions of other people work for no compensation, or very little (below minimum wage per hour) in Red Cross work, blood banks, Boy Scouts, Girl Scouts, U.S.O., playgrounds, organ donations, YWCA, YMCA, Salvation Army, eye banks, flood disasters, kidney transplants, National Guard, day nurseries, Traveler's Aid and other programs.

Middle sized and smaller town, state and county government administrators that serve 66% of our nation's population often work for little or no pay on sewer, water, electricity, gas, street, license and dozens of other commissions. Several authorities estimate that over 20% of our work force, or nearly 20 million people, work in some form of small local government.

Scientists often work nights, weekends and holiday overtime without pay. It's the same for most teachers, clerics, Big Brothers, Big Sisters, artists, musicians and entertainers, the P.T.A., drama groups, athletic teams, mothers, fathers, grandparents and hundreds of other groups—easily 10% of our 90 million employed people. The U.S. Bureau of Census says that, "37 million people in our country do some kind of volunteer activity." And a recent Gallup poll found that an astounding 89% of urban residents said they would be willing to do such work.

Our nation's famous "put-the-wagons-in-a-circle" syndrome, still seems to be a strong old American custom. It continues to live in the idea of serving for free to help our friends, neighbors and communities. In recent years, countries in Europe have sent droves of representatives over to view this phenomenon, but they admit real difficulty in understanding it and leave shaking their heads in wonder at those "crazy Yankees."

Personally, as a depression child, I have not been totally converted by this altruism and am still largely a member of the get-the-buck-school. Yet, the powerful trend towards work and motivation for *things other than money* is much too large and lumpy to sweep under the rug. Only a myopic, tunnel-visioned person could totally ignore it. It's better that we recognize this dynamic trend and put it to good use for everyone concerned.

Summary: We Proved That
Power Secrets Do Produce Progress

Now we have come full circle, back to the comments in the first chapter. There we noted that there is a growing "motivation gap": increasing employee independence, yet less influence of money from employers. We are not "putting money down," just putting it into its place and proper perspective. It can't do everything and never could—less so all the time. Other motivators can be just as effective and often far more so. This is particularly helpful if you have limited funds and must find other ways to motivate. Under the right conditions, most people will work at least part time for free, especially after they pass the "FCSR+" level (Food, Clothing, Shelter, Recreation plus extras). Then, objectives such as quality of life become important. Employees want to candidly know the situation, reach mutually agreeable goals, plan constructive systems, use heart and mind, be delegated, coached and allowed to perform and get recognition for excellence. These will often massively motivate people either without using money at all or where money alone has failed to do the job.

Index

A

Advertising, 118
A.I.D.A. formula, 14, 117, 211–212
  examples, advertising, 118
Attitude:
  being one's own boss, 29
  cases:
    disinterest, 23, 26
    unions & small business, 29
  employee, 25
  hidden, 29
  opinions, 29
  power source, 28
Authority, 127, 128
Awards (*see* Rewards, Praise)

B

"BE" somebody, 127, 128
  case, Hush Puppies, 128
Big-effort/little results:
  case, 143
Body language:
  LLAD, 27
Boss, be their own:
  butting out, 164
  cases:
    government clerk, 174
    management consultant, 167
  firmness, 166
  independence, 170

Boss, be their own *(cont.)*
  "movable spot," 168
    case, college students, 169
  permissiveness, 167
  "sliding scale," 164, 165
  summary, 174
Brainstorming,
  case, steakhouse, 116
Burnett, Leo, 111, 114, 239

C

Candor, 196 (*see also* Leveling and Honesty)
  common sense, 28
  handling it, 27
Challenges, 114
  case, builder, 114
  case, fork lift operator, 114.
Chinese proverb, 77
Coaching:
  better performance, 147
  cases:
    aluminum company, 148
    car dealership, 143
    pen brand, 138
  coach's secret, 144
  coach's surprise, 145
  definition, 139
  ex-dem-pra, 140
    examples, 141, 142, 143
  fear of "strangeness," 140
  goal, 140

Coaching (cont.)
  over-coaching, 147
  summary, 149
Communication:
  balance, 155
  cases:
    fabric manufacturer, 154
    FOWD/PA, 157
    publisher, 160
  confirmation, 155
  definition, 151
  examples:
    deluge daily, 150
    football, 154
  extremes, 155
  Flesch, Rudolph, 160
  FOWD/PA, 14, 156
  green sheets, 14, 157
  mechanics, 159
  message, 152
  "O-S-P" formula, 161
  plan this week, 162
  summary, 163
  writing, 160
Comparison charts:
  case, utility soap, 182
Compliments, 177–180
  case, Zeke's compliments, 179

D

Deflators of power (see Power)
Delegation:
  cases:
    hamburger chain, 125
    sales crisis, 135
    SCORE success, 134
    successes, 121
    what to delegate, 122
  direct request, 134
  five W's, 121
  goal, 132
  how to delegate, 125
  power, 124
  situation, 132
  summary, 137
  task force, 136
  volunteers, 132
  what to delegate, 122
  when to delegate, 123
  where to delegate, 124

Delegation (cont.)
  whom to designate, 123
  why delegate, 124
Democratic yet autocratic, 169
Departments, small:
  cases (three), 216
  power secrets, 214
Directed (see Inner directed and Other directed)
Dreams, 34
Drucker, Peter, 153

E

Emotion and intellect (see Heart and mind)
Emotions, deliberate use, 74
Employee:
  approval, 58
  attitudes, 25
  confidence, 50
  disinterest, 24
  independence, 24
  job options (four), 47
  name usage, 61
  negative attitude, 24
  rage, 46
  resignation, 46
  respect (hunger for), 56
  sensitivity, 60
  thoughts, 27
  withdrawal, 46
Employer:
  complexity, 24
  restrictions, 24
  rules and regulations, 24
Errors:
  handling, 173
"Exchange positioning," 28
"Ex-Dem-Pra" formula, 14
  case, pen brand, 139
Extra work, 235
  case, midwest retailer, 235

F

"FCSR+" formula, 234
Fear:
  adaptation, 49
  cases:
    advertising agency, 44

Fear *(cont.)*
   cases *(cont.)*
      black (minority), 44
      blue suit Friday, 46
      bugging, 51
   declining motivator, 45, 47, 50, 51
   eliminating fear, 52, 53, 54
   elimination (by rules), 55
   firing, 46, 47, 50, 51
   humiliation, 45
   motivator, 43
   older workers, 48
   optimism, 50
   prostitute's slogan, 43
   reduction builds power, 53
   summary, 55
   youth, 49
Females, percentage employed, 47
Firing:
   case, bottling plant, 54, 55
   employer penalty, 50, 51
   income reduction, 48
   threat (reduced) 48
   un-American, 48
Five W's:
   case, steakhouse, 115
   guidance and control, 115
   questions to ask, 115
Flesch, Rudolph:
   "Art of Readable Writing," 160
Ford, President Gerald, 176
FOWD/PA formula, 14, 156

G

Goals:
   case, milk company, 40
   employees' goals, 74
   example, starving man, 39
   key, 41
   motivation target, 35
   personal, 38, 39
   power increases, 38
   power secrets, 39
   realistic, 40
   servant for life, 42
   situation relation, 26
   summary, 41
Great motivation gap, 12, 24, 33
   case, American Management Associa-
      tions, 24

Green sheets, 14, 157
Group heart and mind, 116
   objective, 117
Group participation, 86
Gung-ho team, 118
   case, heart, mind and A.I.D.A., 119

H

Harvard graduate, 15
Harvard School of Business, 154
Heart and mind:
   brainstorming, 113
   cases:
      "Big Mouth," 113
      Burnett, Leo, 111
      Dichter, Earnest, 111
      foot products (award), 109
      late supplies, 110
      sales team success, 113
      TV commercials, 111
   creativity, 112
   emotion, hope, fear, etc., 110
   emotion, intellect, 109
   ideas (four steps), 112
   intellect, calculation, analysis, 110
   summary, 120
Honesty, 179 *(see also* Candor and Leveling)
   cases:
      indifferent clerks, 188
      savvy employee, 190
   example, cards on table, 195
   group plan, 194
   leveling, 189
   openness, 189
   summary, 197
   why it works, 190
"Hot buttons," 26, 28
   case, 26
   "on" switch, 26, 28
Human relations:
   machine vs. human, 30
   understanding, 25
Hunch, 29, 30

I

I'll work for nothing *(see* Work for nothing)
Independence, 170
   case, new products, 171

Independence *(cont.)*
    extended, 172
Inner directed, 200 *(see also* Other directed)
    case, Nebraska blacksmith, 203
    use, 202
Inquiry as motivator, 90
Interest, 180

J

Job:
    cases:
        consultant, 48
        restaurant (options), 50
        retailer (options), 49
    essential, 47

K

Kipling, 47
K.I.S.S. formula, 189

L

Lakein, Alan, 147
Leveling, 189 *(see also* Honesty and Candor)
    cases:
        "Go-Getters," 197
        monkey off your back, 192
        salesmen, 195
    people's "monkey," 192
    secrets for using, 191
    S-O-S formula, 193
    why it works, 190
LLAD formula, 12, 26, 27, 33
    body language, 27
    cases:
        advertising, 27
        Burnett, Leo, 27
        walk-ins, 27
    situation, 26
Lonely crowd, 15, 199 *(see also* Inner directed and Other directed)
"Lonely crowd" formula:
    case, furniture manufacturer, 207
    summary, 208
    use, 206
Loyalty (from people), 128

M

Management failure, 153
M.B.O., 13, 211–212
Meetings:
    agenda, 69
    attendees, 70
    cases:
        results, 79
        soap manufacturer, 67
        soft drinks, $30 million, 78
    discussion, 72
    follow-up:
        assignments, 68
        confirmation, 70
    goal setting, 66, 67, 69, 72
    graphics (visuals), 72
    mechanics, 71
    motivators, 66
    power secrets (seven), 69
    pre-meeting summary, 67, 68
    preparation (by attendees), 70
    re-cap, 77
    results to expect, 68, 69
    speakers, 71
    starting, 66
    summary, closing (re-cap), 68
    summary of secrets, 80
    supplies, 71
Misunderstanding, 25
Money:
    power, 23
    wages, 24
Motivation:
    case, money is "zero," 30
    art, 30
    beliefs, 31
    Biblical quote, 29
    Chicago, 24, 25
    dictator, 30
    emotions, 30
    feelings, 30
    hopes and dreams, 30, 31
        case, popular spray cleaner, 31
    modern methods, 25
    money injection, 29
    money needs, 30
    non-cash interests, 30, 31
    praise, 25
    problems, 23
    retailer (department store), 25
    science, 30

Motivation *(cont.)*
    S-O-S formula, 32
    tools, 24
    without money, 234

N

Name (as motivator), 181
New York Stock Exchange, 29

O

Objectives (also see "S-O-S" formula)
    case, pest exterminator, 36
    example, your employees, 37
    four uses, 37
    M.B.O., 36
    Management, 13, 211, 212
    motivation, 35, 38
Open mindedness, 110
Openness, 189
Options:
    group, 86
    poor ideas, 86
    power secret, 85
O-S-P system, 14, 161
Other directed, 200 *(see also* Inner directed
    and Lonely crowd)

P

People:
    complexity, 24
Personal commitment, 90
Planning:
    case:
        cleaner, 86
        soap, 82
    example, 89
    group size, 81
    "you planned," 88
Plans:
    action program, 79
    cases:
        consultant, 95
        meeting, 78
        pharmaceutical, 94
        soap group, 89
    problem review, 83
    S-O-S, 32
    summary, 96

Power:
    advantages with employees, 25
    attitudes, 28
    definition, 9
    deflators:
        academics, 225
        "big me," 222
        case, Dallas cosmetics, 221
        circles, 224
        double-talk, 227
        fear stick, 224
        inexperience, 227
        manipulate, 225
        mechanics, 223
        performance charts, 226
        punch in gut, 229
        put-down, 222
        "selection does it," 228
        silence, 222
        summary, 230
        tricky stuff, 223
    key figures, 9
    money, 23
    money to create, 10
    motivation gap, 24
    procurement problems, 23
    secret desire, 172
    your position, 26
Praise, 25 *(see also* Rewards)
Pride formula, 129
    case, "head knocker," 129
    respect, 63
Prioritizing, 87
Problem:
    case, baked goods, 73
    image, 73
    plans, 83
    situation, 72
Programs:
    check list, 75
    meetings, 75
Prophesy, self-fulfilling, 63

Q

Quality of life, 237

R

Re-cap (of meeting), 77
Reputation, 60, 63

Respect:
  authority, 61
  business stress, 55
  case, pen maker, 57
  confidence, 62, 63
  control increase, 62
  death, 59
  delegation, 133
  desire, 56
  display, 60
  examples:
    Archie Bunker, 58
    TV business, 58
  friendship, 61
  genuine, 59
  humiliation, 85
  job performance, 62
  listening, 62
  magnifies power, 84
  non-verbal, 61
  power builder, 60
  powerful motivator, 56, 57
  pride, 63
  "respect gap," 59
  self-fulfilling prophecy, 63
  sensitivity, 60
Responsibility, 133
Rewards (see also Praise and Trophies)
  cases:
    gas station, 185
    Olympics, 184
    pen company, 186
    President Ford, 176
  compliments, 177–179, 180
  demotivators, 184
  errors, 185
  honesty, 179
  summary, 187
  trophies, 183
Riesman, David, 199

S

Sabotage, 45
Schedules as motivators, 76
Secrets:
  definition, 9
Self-starters, 126
  case, secretary, 127
Service unit:
  cases:
    city bus, 218

Service unit (cont.)
  cases (cont.)
    Northwestern University, 219
  motivation, 218
  times and trends, 217
Shame the employee, 133
Sincerity as motivator, 181
Situation, 23, 32
  challenges, 29
  common ground, 25
  forewarned, 25
  goal relation, 26
  LLAD, 26
  problem, 72
  research (homework), 26
  "revovling door" employment, 30
  summary, 33
  troubles of employees, 26
Small groups:
  attitudes, 211
  case, retailer load, 209
  department motivation, 213
  pivotal point, 209, 212
    examples, 213
  small businesses, 210
  summary, 219
Smile, 180
S-O-S formula, 12, 32, 211, 212 (see also Objectives)
  application, 88
  book organization, 32
  cases:
    motivation situation, 33
    your own travel, 33
  delegation, 134
  employee use, 33
  first step, 34
  motivation, 32
  objectives, 32
  plans meetings, 81
Suggestions in meetings, 74
System:
  fear, 42, 43

T

Territorial imperative:
  cases:
    "VP packages," 130
    "VP sanitation," 131
Time:
  Lakein, Alan, 91

Time *(cont.)*
    management tips, 92, 93
    M.B.O., 91
    pay-off per hour, 25
    personal planning, 93
    saving, 25
    summary, 96
"Tradition" directed *(see also* Directed,
    Inner Directed and Lonely crowd)
    case, pen company, 201
    use, 201
Trophies, 183 *(see also* Rewards)
    case, Olympics, 184

U

Unions, 29

V

Value marginal unit, 233
Villain as motivator, 73

W

White House, 176–177
Who does what, 76
Willingness, 110
Work:
    assigning, 104
    attractive jobs, 103
    can be done, 102
    cases:
        fire at government office, 97
        "Ian's challenge," 106
        interfere with goals, 101
        unpleasant work, 101
        warehouse clerk, 107
    challenge, 108, 114

Work *(cont.)*
    challenging people, 105
    complaints, 104
    conclusion (pleasant work), 102
    difficult jobs, 103
    dole, 105
    examples:
        clerk and production, 100
        company goal, 99
    goal emphasis, 98
    goal oriented, 99
    hate of work, 97, 100
    hopes and dreams, 98
    kinds, 97
    let them do it, 103
    meaningful, 98
    Pavlov's dogs, 104
    pointless, 100
    reasons, 100
    summary, 107
    techniques, 100
    Tom Sawyer, 104
Work for nothing:
    cases:
        A.C.E., 239
        Burnett, Leo, 239
        business students, 238
        housewives, 238
        nat'l sales mgr., 240
        saturation, 238
        S.C.O.R.E., 238
        "They'll work," 232
        truck drivers, 239
    extra units, 233
    millions do it, 241
    quality of life, 237
    secrets beyond money, 235
    secrets for power, 236
    summary: power works, 242
World changes, 204